F. (Felix M.) Philpin de Rivieres

Holy Places

Their Sanctity and Authenticity

F. (Felix M.) Philpin de Rivieres

Holy Places
Their Sanctity and Authenticity

ISBN/EAN: 9783742833624

Manufactured in Europe, USA, Canada, Australia, Japa

Cover: Foto ©Thomas Meinert / pixelio.de

Manufactured and distributed by brebook publishing software
(www.brebook.com)

F. (Felix M.) Philpin de Rivieres

Holy Places

HOLY PLACES:

THEIR SANCTITY AND AUTHENTICITY.

BY

F. PHILPIN DE RIVIÈRES,

PRIEST OF THE ORATORY OF ST. PHILIP NERI.

With Maps.

LONDON:

R. WASHBOURNE, 18 PATERNOSTER ROW.

1874.

PREFACE.

Holy Places, not in Palestine only, but throughout
the world, together with the questions connected with
them, are the subject of the present work. To every
pious Catholic it speaks of his parish church, the
churchyard in which his fathers rest, the road-side
cross; to the nun, of her cloister or the convent
chapel; to the pilgrim, of the sanctuaries which the
Holy Spirit makes centres of mysterious attraction;
to the statesman or philosopher, of the rights which
God has reserved to Himself on earth; to the politician, of the social dangers attending their sacrilegious
contempt. For one and all, it is a study of facts, an
inquiry into their causes in history.

The author has touched but slightly on details of
controversy, and prefers to point out true principles
and right deductions.

Although Palestine is not the only subject of this

work, many pages of it are nevertheless devoted to the land consecrated by the footsteps of the Man-God.

The author has not travelled farther than Rome, except in books; but he had the privilege of familiar conversation successively with two pilgrim priests, the Abbé Brullon, of the diocese of Langres, and the Rev. Father Hutchison, of the London Oratory, both "amabiles et decori," truly amiable, and graced with the virtues and talents which are the ornament of the priesthood—both taken from the Church and from their friends in the prime of life, and almost at the moment of their return from Rome and Jerusalem. The author's attention was thus more and more fixed on our great sanctuaries, and afterwards, when consulted by the excellent Canon Dalfi,* and their common friend, Mr. Girard, of Grenoble, on the subject of the movement amongst scientific men in England with regard to Biblical topography, he had just put himself in communication with the Society for the Exploration of Palestine, through its obliging secretary, W. Besant, Esq., and so was in a position to reply to their ques-

---

* Now Monsignor Dalfi, Curé of Sta. Maria di Casanova-Carmagnola, cameriere d'onore to His Holiness, honorary canon of the Holy Sepulchre, and author of the learned and pious " Viaggio Biblico in Oriente," written expressly for the younger clergy. (Turin, 4 vols., 8vo.)

tions. He was thus led to a course of studies resulting in several articles in *La Terre Sainte*, a bi-monthly periodical edited by the able and zealous Mr. Girard above-mentioned. These articles in turn formed the basis of the present volume.

The author cannot here omit to pay the tribute of his gratitude to those by whose help he has been enabled to render his work somehow presentable to the British public.

Lastly, he cannot help hoping that a day will come when English opinion and French arms may happily affect the social and political issue of the conflicts which now seem to threaten all sanctuaries, but which will result in a more solemn consecration of the earth.

LONDON, Nov. 18, 1873.

Feast of the Dedication of the Basilicas of the Apostles SS. Peter and Paul.

TABLE OF CONTENTS.

PAGE

PREFACE.   V

INTRODUCTORY CHAPTER—

1. General Connection between the Questions of Sanctity and Authenticity 1

2. The Opportuneness of the Question from its Double Point of View 2

PART I.

LOCAL SANCTIFICATION AND ITS PERMANENCE.

CHAPTER   PAGE

I. EXISTENCE OF HOLY PLACES. 20

    1. Sense of Mankind on this Point . . . 20

    2. Mysterious Absence of God in Nature . . 21

    3. Mysterious Return 24

II. FITNESS OF CERTAIN PLACES FOR SANCTIFICATION 26

III. THE ESSENTIAL SOURCE OF SANCTIFICATION . . 29

IV. CHANNELS OF SANCTIFICATION 31

    1. Angels and Saints 31

    2. The Grave 34

    3. The Church and the Priesthood . . . 36

V. AUTHORITY AND LIBERTY 39

VI. IDEAL DEVELOPMENT OF SANCTIFICATION . . 43

    1. Exorcism. Religious Labour . . . 43

    2. Transient Consecrations 44

    3. Permanent Reservations 46

    4. The Monument 50

    5. The House of God 51

CHAPTER   PAGE

      6. The Metropolitan Church 52
      7. The Holy City, the Religious Capital . . 53
    VII. Is the Development of Holy Places a Thing
           to be Feared ? 55
   VIII. Historical Sketch of the Holy Places before
           Jesus Christ 63
      1. From the Patriarchs to the Schism of Israel . 63
      2. After the Schism, Decline, Fall, or Slavery . 73
      3. Mysterious Reaction 76
     IX. The Holy Places in the Time of Christ . . 81
      1. Two Objections 81
      2. Did the Word become Biblified, Systematised,
         or Incarnate ? 85
      3. The True Idea of the Incarnation : its Local
         Consequences 86
      X. Some Reasons for the Choice of the Places
           Sanctified by Christ 89
      1. Influence of Places on Life; Natural and Mysti-
         cal Harmonies. 89
      2. Transition between the two Testaments. Teach-
         ing of the Divine Saviour . . . 95
     XI. Holy Possessions under the New Law . . 105
      1. Mystery of Detachment 105
      2. Nevertheless, Sanctity may and ought to possess
         the Earth, under the Law of Grace . . 106
     XII. The Wonderful Variety of the Holy Places . 113
    XIII. Permanence and Inviolability 117
    XIV. Teaching of the Ritual in the Consecration
           of Sanctuaries 121
      1. Plans and Preparations 121
      2. The First Stone 122
      3. The Consecration 125
      4. Other Dispositions 135
     XV. Conflicts of the Church for her Sanctuaries 137
    XVI. Constancy of the Church Illustrated . . 141
      1. Palestine 141
      2. Italy 146
   XVII. The Latest Enemies 151

PART II.

THE QUESTION OF AUTHENTICITY.

CHAPTER   PAGE

I. SUPERNATURAL AUTHENTICITY 153

II. ON THE VALUE OF EXTRAORDINARY SUPERNATURAL
    EVIDENCE 156
    1. One solitary evident Fact may be sufficient to
        establish Authenticity 156
    2. Multiplication of Supernatural Testimonies . 158

III. ON THE VALUE OF MORE ORDINARY SUPERNATURAL
    EVIDENCE 161
    1. Outpourings of Graces bestowed on Holy Places 161
    2. On the Value of a Popular Movement towards
        Holy Places 162
    3. Scholars and Saints 164
    4. Clairvoyance 165
    5. Ecclesiastical Authority 167
    6. The Authority of the Holy See 168

IV. TEST FURNISHED BY THE DEMONS 172
    1. Their Formal Testimony 172
    2. Silent Witness of the Demons 176

V. ON NATURAL AUTHENTICITY 177
    1. Archæological Proofs, properly so called . . 178
    2. Inscriptions 178
    3. Written Data 179
    4. Traditions 180
    5. Accessory Proofs 181

VI. ON THE COMPARATIVE VALUE OF THESE DIFFERENT
    TESTIMONIES 185

VII. HOW TO SIMPLIFY THE QUESTION? . . . 195

VIII. PROTESTANTS AND FREE-THINKERS AND THE QUES-
    TION OF THE HOLY LAND 203

IX. SUMMARY OF THE ATTACKS 214

X. THE MAIN POINT OF HISTORY WITH REGARD TO
    THE TOPOGRAPHY OF PALESTINE . . . 217

XI. WAS PRIMITIVE CHRISTIANITY HOSTILE TO THE
    LOCAL MEMORIES? 219

XII. ORAL EVIDENCES OF THE FIRST CENTURIES . . 223

CHAPTER   PAGE

First Channel.—The Bishops and Clergy . . 223
Second Channel.—The Faithful in Judea and else-
where : the neighbouring Christians . . . 227
Third Channel.—The Jews 230
Fourth Channel.—Heretics 231
Fifth Channel.—The Pagans 231
XIII. WRITTEN TESTIMONIES 232
1. The Evangelists 233
2. The Historian Josephus 234
3. Hegesippus and St. Justin 235
4. Origen 236
5. Eusebius—The "Topicon" 238
XIV. TESTIMONY OF FACTS 241
First Fact.—Pagan Profanations 241
Second Fact.—Restoration under Constantine . 244
1. Preparation 244
2. Publicity of the Enterprise 246
3. Was this Restoration important ? . . . 248
4. What are we to think of the silence of Eusebius as to some Churches ? 250
Third Fact.—The finding of the Holy Cross : does
it injure the cause of the Holy Places? . . 252
XV. ARCHÆOLOGICAL EVIDENCES 257
First Evidence.—Character of the Ruins of Palestine, and particularly at Jerusalem . . . 257
Second Evidence.—Natural Landmarks . . . 263
1. The Platform of the Temple 264
2. Calvary. The Holy Sepulchre . . . 272
3. Sion 280
4. The Pools and Aqueducts 286
Third Evidence.—The Objects discovered in the
Excavations 287
XVI. ARCHITECTURAL EVIDENCE 291
1. General Idea of Styles of Architecture in Palestine 291
2. Remains of Constantine's Basilicas . . . 297
XVII. NAZARETH AND LORETO 303
CONCLUSION 319

ILLUSTRATIONS.

                                                        PAGE
APPROXIMATE PLAN OF THE ROCK SITE OF JERUSALEM . 259

PLAN OF JERUSALEM, WITH TRADITIONAL SITES   .   . 274

FERGUSSON'S TOPOGRAPHY OF THE BIBLE 277

NOTE.

THE following sentence must be added in page 268, line 7 :—
" The Golden Gate, or the foundations observed on the north side of the Dome of the Rock, can hardly be quoted in contradiction."

HOLY PLACES:

THEIR SANCTITY AND AUTHENTICITY.

PREFATORY CHAPTER.

1. GENERAL CONNECTION BETWEEN THE QUESTIONS OF SANCTITY AND AUTHENTICITY.

THE idea of a Holy Place is that it belongs to God in a
more special way than others, either from being set
apart by the Supreme Ruler for His own service, or
from being dedicated by men to His Divine Majesty.

There must be marks by which it may be known
that a place is really thus set apart. A Holy Place
should be able to prove its claim and show its credentials. There must be an authority to decide whether
it has really been the object of a compact between
God and men.

The question, then, of authenticity is closely connected with that of sanctity. A Holy Place is only
considered as such in so far as the truth and the continuance of its consecration are believed in. It is
authentic, if it is able to tell us the original fact on

which the choice and acceptance of God and men are
founded; if it has a history whose course we can trace
in the past.

As there are two parties interested in the matter, so
there are two classes of facts capable of bearing witness to this sanctity and authenticity of places—the
Divine, Heavenly, supernatural facts, which prove that
the shadow of the Most High has visited and rested
on a spot of our earth; and the human and material
facts, such as monuments, titles, traditions, emblems,
religious ceremonies, or customs. Consequently these
privileged Places may have a double history and a
double authenticity; the one founded on proofs known
and appreciated by faith, the other on proofs of good
sense or reason, acknowledged by science.

Sometimes these two kinds of authenticity are perfectly distinct; sometimes, they blend and intermingle,
and any attempt to separate them would involve the
inquirer in inextricable puzzles. Hence the necessity
for the theologian of making a right use of the light
of human science; for the philosopher, the man of
learning, and the politician, of knowing the supernatural side of the question, and the connection between the two classes of authenticity.

2. THE OPPORTUNENESS OF THE QUESTION FROM ITS DOUBLE POINT OF VIEW.

In times of religious peace, when the matter in question is a parish church, or a place of pilgrimage protected by universal respect and a long tradition of

love, it might be possible, up to a certain point, to leave the question of sanctity and authenticity untouched; but in times of conflict, Holy Places present to the enemies of religion a vulnerable and easily assailable side. The man of letters argues, denies their sanctity, raises even the question of principle; the politician and the financier draw up clever schemes; the man of rapine looks on them as his prey, plots his deeds of violence, and calculates the spoil. Christians must be prepared to defend the rights, the religion, and the interests of all.

Mankind has always ascribed importance to places set apart for worship. There is a universal feeling that the earth must be blessed and sanctified, and that this work should begin from consecrated centres, that worship, to have its full force, must not remain floating in the air, but strike deep root in the soil. The Catholic Church, in defending what she regards as the inheritance of her children, whether patrimony, dowry, conquest, or lawful salary, and in undertaking this defence in the Name of God Himself, only follows the tradition of the human race. As the sacrilegious contempt of this tradition has always been considered a heinous crime, and a mark of impiety and malediction, so we are justly prepossessed in favour of a nation or a generation by the magnificence of their religious edifices and endowments.

It is true that the splendour of sacred buildings and the number of religious services also depend on the reign of peace, or the wealth of nations and individuals. The Church has passed through times of persecution, when the glories of her worship have necessarily disappeared from the face of the earth; but, even then, she remained faithful to her principles. When she could not worship in magnificent basilicas, she could cherish memories and ruins. She guarded with jealous care her title-deeds, such as they were, her tombs and her catacombs. Whatever may have been said of her detachment in primitive times, she had her sanctuaries and her places on which love had set its seal—a love all the stronger and deeper, because it was bound up with the history of the Man-God.

She was the successor of that people whose local affections were more tenacious than those of any other, whose cradle had been haunted by dreams of a Divinely-promised land, afterwards its glorious possession, and the recovery of which, in spite of a world-wide dispersion, is still its dearest aspiration. From this people, whose latest literary *chef d'œuvre* is called "Judaic Antiquities," she could not but inherit and carry to perfection all pure and holy affections.

Long before the world had given a name to archæology, and allotted it a place among the sciences, she had her learned archæologists; for the present I need only mention St. Jerome. So jealously did she preserve the memorials of the past, that we owe to her in large part the preservation of the archives and monuments of pagan antiquity. She overthrew its temples and idols so far as was necessary for the destruction of their prestige, and to ensure the triumph of Christ. When this was done, she stopped short in the work of destruction, and either turned the temples of the devil into churches, or left them standing as trophies of her victory, and as a warning to men, that they might see into what monstrous errors they would fall without the grace and light of the Incarnate Word.

The Middle Ages were a period of prosperity for the Faith, and consequently the golden age of the Holy Places.

The nobles of Christendom were rich enough to flock to the ruins of Jerusalem, destroyed by the Saracens, and to found a kingdom beneath the shadow of the Holy Sepulchre ; and this without interruption to the building of great monasteries and wonderful cathedrals, which were rising on every side, or to the noble donations which were laying the foundations of the ecclesiastical principalities and completing the patrimony of St. Peter.

No man, unwarped by interest or fanaticism, will hesitate to condemn the sixteenth century for its robbery and destruction of churches, monasteries, and every kind of ecclesiastical property. If it has any merit, it certainly is not on the score of its declared enmity to every sacred memory and tradition. On the other hand, it was only partially given over to iniquity, and iniquity, as usual, lied to itself.

It was the boast of the Renaissance, that in falling in love with Greek and Roman antiquity, it was emerging from the darkness of barbarism. Every one talked of Demosthenes and Cicero, of Phidias and Praxiteles; but, like all exaggerated fashions, this pagan infatuation of Christian nations cooled down in the end; and when once the literature and antiquity of Greece and Italy were well known, their exclusive prestige was lost. The facility of distant voyages, the discovery of a new world open to commerce and to conquest, destroyed the artificial horizon which had hitherto shut men in. New races, new civilisations began to excite interest; and when the heat of the philosophical animosities of the eighteenth century had died out in indifference, historians, poets, amateurs, artists, travellers, turned with renewed spirit to the study of Christian ages, and gave it once more a place among the sciences. Italy and Palestine were the principal scenes of this reaction.

It was impossible for the learned explorers of Egypt and Asia to pass over Palestine at a leap. Baalbec, Palmyra, Damascus were powerful inducements. Besides, in Greece, in Italy, everywhere on the old Continent, archæology was in vogue; were all the principles and habits of science to be forgotten on touching Biblical ground? Protestants were not the last to point out the wonders of Arabia-Petræa, the beauties of Lebanon, the strange peculiarities of the Dead Sea. While traversing, Bible in hand, the land of Abraham, Isaac, and Jacob, the soil which the feet of the Holy Family had trodden, and which Jesus had watered with His Blood, they were compelled, whether they would or no, to follow in the footsteps of the Catholic monk. However much they might dislike our traditions, they found themselves confronted with them in such numbers, and in such battle array, that it would have been folly to deny everything; so the Protestant author duly mentioned them, always taking care to find the monk wrong about some point of detail, and to call him idle and ignorant. Whereupon the said author was registered as the discoverer of our ancient traditions, or at any rate as having verified and rectified them by the light of science.

Moreover, though Protestants and Free-thinkers might agree to undervalue the practices and the learning of the Pères de Terre-Sainte,* they were unable to do so with such unanimity as to avoid refuting each other; and Catholics might safely leave it to them to answer their own rash assertions and violent criticisms.

Those amongst them who defended the Bible were unable to accept the impieties of Volney, whilst in their turn they had amongst them as many shades of opinion as can be imagined between the Pope and Volney himself.

In the East, on the other hand, Catholics were not always represented by the poor Franciscan, whom the "milord," judging by his coarse brown habit, rated a little lower than the Arabs and other savages of Palestine. They also had their noble travellers, their men of learning, their authors. It is scarcely possible to imagine the effect produced at the beginning of the

---

* A title in use for the Franciscans.

century by the "Itinéraire de Paris à Jérusalem."
France, just released from the clutch of the Reign of
Terror, hardly dared to breathe under the iron hand of
Bonaparte; and here was a young author, bearing a
noble name, already famous for his romantic descriptions of the free forests of America, recalling to the
sons of the knights of old, by the magic of faith and
genius, the land of pilgrimages and crusades, and striking dumb with admiration a generation of philosophers
and Jansenists.

Châteaubriand was not the first nor the last of these
illustrious pilgrims. In our own day the impulse towards historical and archæological science has increased
considerably. Catholics and Protestants, Free-thinkers
and believers of all sorts, have made it their study.
Ruins and antiquities are all but neutral ground, where
they meet on friendly terms. The English nobleman
takes a pleasure in doing the honours of the old abbey
whose ruins adorn his park, and is delighted at finding
in Palestine the arch of the Crusaders between a memorial of Abraham and a bit of wall of the time of
Herod. He treasures in his library our old illuminated
manuscripts, and new editions of the travels of old
pilgrims, re-edited by English societies or amateurs;
and these ancient voyages, together with modern explorations, form a considerable collection.

It was natural that all this scientific movement
should take form and organisation. Seven years ago
there were archæological societies, learned associations
for a multitude of objects and departments compara-

tively unimportant to the history of the world, when the most prominent students and amateurs of Biblical archæology in Great Britain, with a few distinguished foreigners, held a meeting, and drew up the plan of a Society for the Exploration of Jerusalem and Palestine. Anglicanism was the predominating element, and tho Archbishop of York presided; still tho only profession of faith required was archæological enthusiasm, and the Comto do Vogué, with the other few Catholics invited, sat side by sido with a select company of Jews, Free-thinkers, Freemasons, and Protestants of every shade.

It was decided that local committees should bo formed for the extension of the Society, and the collection of funds and subscriptions; whilst expeditions, provided with everything necessary, should set out for Palestine, study the archæology of tho country, make excavations, and, in short, carry out a complete survey of the Biblical lands with all the resources afforded by geology, ethnography, and other modern sciences.

Public opinion being thus prepared, the scheme, under the patronage of the Queen, was at once supported by persons distinguished for rank, science, or, what is not to be despised in a work of this kind, for wealth. The Jews connected with the Bank, and most of the Lodges of Great Britain, subscribed largely; and America, scarcely recovered from the effects of civil war, eagerly offered her contingent of subscriptions and antiquarians.

Orientalists, engineers, and experienced travellers

answered readily to the call. The work is now going on vigorously with committees, directors, agents, &c.; and on the part of all concerned, the zeal and desire to know and make known the truth is beyond a doubt. It would be unjust not to give the heads and members of the Association credit for their evident desire to act fairly, and to accept science, from whatever source it comes, with impartiality. It would be absurd to predict that all these treasures of perseverance, good-will, learning, and sacrifices of every kind will only turn out to be a new edition of the mountain producing the mouse. It would be rash and untrue to deny that this work, undertaken in an age of reconciliation, and with a religious object, may enter into the secret designs of Providence, or that, in fact, it has been already rewarded with successful results.

Up to this time no excavations, no certain discoveries have, I will not say destroyed, but so much as seriously endangered our principal traditions concerning the Holy Places. And this result, although entirely negative, should be enough to make us approve of the work already executed, and augur well of what is to come. But there is more than this; the labours and sacrifices of the Society have been rewarded by a number of facts and positive results, by which Christian archæology is henceforth permanently enriched.

As an instance, we may mention the explorations round the Temple, and the analysis of the seven strata of that *débris* of centuries, on which, one after another, so many towns have risen since the time when the first aqueducts and other excavations were made in the rock.

Neither should we forget to mention the formation in London of a Museum of the Holy Land. It is but in its infancy, but already it contains valuable treasures; among others, some interesting relics of Christianity in the Roman period.

We ought also to make honourable mention of the "Quarterly Statement," a report, issued every three months, of the Exploration Fund. This periodical is not a bare account of the receipts and payments of the Society; it is the organ of the Committee and of its meetings, the history of the labours and discoveries of the Commission, in short, of whatever may interest the lovers of the Holy Land. It has been, and will be, the source of more than one important publication.

But, on the other hand, we must not deceive ourselves. It will be very difficult for the active portion of the Association to set itself free from the antecedents and ideas out of which it has sprung. Its attitude is professedly that of being superior to *any sectarian spirit;* and as the word "sectarian" is applied by it to the living Body as well as to the separated members, it thus adopts as its fundamental rule that masonic indifference which is the secret enemy of all ideas of dogma, of worship, of obligatory moral law, and of tradition.*

* In speaking of Freemasonry in England, we do not forget that the conduct of Protestants who enrol themselves in

Whatever they may be, Protestants, Freemasons, or mere antiquarians, their principles are not ours, and hence it would be strange if they invariably arrived at our conclusions.

Moreover, we are thoroughly alive to the almost universal tendencies of travellers and scientific men, who do not own the authority of the Church. Few amongst them are exempt from the mania of fanatical negation, or from the corresponding mania of audacious assertion. The most absurd proofs pass muster when the object is to overthrow a received tradition.

The antiquarian, who would not venture in the face of the world to place the ancient Lutetia in the Ile de la Grande Jatte, Montmartre at Ste. Geneviève, or the Sainte-Chapelle at Belleville, will commit himself, without the least difficulty, to propositions quite as wild about the sacred sites of Jerusalem. And it must be confessed that the result of these bold theories is very encouraging to their author. He gains far more credit by them than he would do by serious labours. He is complimented as the hardy pioneer of future discoveries; a score of academies open their doors to him, to forget him in turn on the appearance of the next novelty.

---

masonic lodges is not to be compared to that of Catholics, who cannot do so without braving the warnings and threats of the Church; nevertheless, they are not altogether excusable in blindly taking an oath, which would be useless if it were not dangerous, and which may be required for the service of secret superiors, and of projects which will not bear the light.

Tendencies like these cannot fail to be very injurious in so important an exploration as that of Palestine; they are sure to lead to the neglect of many valuable indications, to mislead investigation by turning it from its natural course, and to throw the explorers into hopeless entanglements. Vast sums will be expended on researches, whose indirect results may now and then be of some value, but on whose final aim Catholic Faith has pronounced her verdict beforehand.

With unprecedented material resources, under the most favourable political conditions, with a tolerance most unusual on the part of the Mussulmans, the able, courageous, and learned men forming the Commission will gain but very poor results, compared with those attained by others, in spite of isolation, poverty, and difficulties of every sort.

Another—in appearance, purely human—circumstance has drawn the attention of the world to the point of junction between Asia and Africa, and, consequently, to that land of promise once blessed with the dew of Heaven and the fatness of the earth. After flowing with milk and honey, and being enriched with the commerce of all the great ancient empires, that land became the object of a malediction without parallel. Of the neighbours whom she had known in the days of her prosperity as the rich Idumæa, the powerful Assyria, the wealthy Asia Minor, and the fertile Egypt, nothing remained but the sands of the desert, the Bedouins, and the Mussulman tax gatherers.

But another change seems to be at hand; in the most desolate, the most unstable, marshy, and sandy part of this circle of desolation, modern enterprise has opened the Suez Canal. It would seem as though the curse were removed, as though life had returned; and it is at the gates of Palestine that the great communication between the Atlantic and Indian Oceans, with the Mediterranean as a connecting link, has been established. Thus a route is opened, in one direction to the entire basin of India, China, and Australia, and in the other, to the whole of North America, and by the way, to the British Isles, France, and Italy—the Italy of Rome and of Catholicism, modern liberalism notwithstanding.

It is but a step from Palestine to the general question of Holy Places; and, moreover, the subject of the banks of the Jordan is one of those which fate, or rather Providence, has pre-destined to interest the whole of the world.

For some time all this was supposed to concern only a few Christians oppressed by the Turks, some relics sequestrated by the Sultan, some disputes between Greek, Latin, or other monks. Now people are beginning to suspect that the future, the real progress and welfare of nations, have something to do with these questions of monks, relics, and sanctuaries.

The questions of local Sanctification and Authenticity are in fact important wherever any disciple of the apostles has planted the Cross; they are mixed up with everything—history and tradition, dogma and morals, politics and science, arts and piety, archæology and previsions of the future, time and eternity. They are, therefore, important wherever there are men who would banish God from the earth, and no longer have Him for the Supreme Guardian of the rights of all men; wherever, again, there are men who perceive that the surest basis of property, both for societies and individuals, is to keep close to the thought of the true God, dwelling amongst us to save us from our follies, and to teach us how to possess the earth without shutting ourselves out from Heaven.

For the last forty years, our diplomatists and statesmen, guided merely by political and social instincts, have come to see that the questions of Rome and Jerusalem are always cropping up in one form or another, and that they underlie our great problems. This remark may be generalised by saying that the struggle for or against consecrated places has lasted as long as the Church herself, and that now this struggle is the greater because of the empire of Catholicity in the world. There were in the last century, and there are still, a good many believers who saw no use in a Divine Supremacy exercised on earth; they would fain deny to Christ the right of reserving to Himself a single spot or privilege on earth. Well, revolutionists have taken pains to show them that where these rights are denied, there is no other basis left for property or authority but conflict and violence. They themselves understand this clearly; they make no secret of it. Wherever they have got the upper hand, they have

robbed, confiscated, destroyed ; in a word, employed
every means, legal or illegal, as best suited them, to
extirpate sanctity wherever they have found it. Rome
being the metropolis of sanctity, they raised the cry of
" Rome or death !" and if the men who were their instruments had obeyed them to the last, there would be
at this moment neither temple nor priest in Rome,
save such as Jupiter and Venus might claim as their
own. Their example would be followed by the
world.

The band of writers who act as vanguard and stand-
ard-bearers to this army, leave us ignorant neither of
their plan, their means, nor their object. Their books
and journals are nothing but a commentary, more or
less modernised and improved, on an old text much
more ancient than the art of printing. They say, as
others like them said in the days of Solomon, " Since
our time is as the passing of a shadow . . . come,
therefore, and let us enjoy the good things of the present ; . . . let us fill ourselves with costly wine ; . . .
let us crown ourselves with roses before they be
withered ; let not an individual, not a flowery meadow,
not a corner of the earth escape our riot. Down with
the man who says he has no money, and who wants
to preach morality ! Down with sentimental talk of
widows and gray hairs ! *Our* morality, *our* justice is
a good appetite and a strong hand. Away with weakness and pity ! Away with the scrupulous fanatic
who will not do like the rest, and who looks reproof
at every one ! He would weary us with his lectures

on pretence of being a child of God. Well—we shall see whether God, his Father, will be able to protect him, and to save him from our snares" (Wisdom ii. 5—8).

I will put the question to all Christians: Is this a time to ignore Consecrated Places, their rights, their titles, their utility to every one—above all, to the victims of the world—*now*, when the theory of the enjoyment of this world, everywhere, in spite of everything, *without excepting a meadow, or a corner of the earth*, is enunciated with fresh energy and made into a formula with all the pride of science?—*now*, when a sect, or rather a whole world of sects, is regularly organised for the robbery of the asylums and sanctuaries of virgins, of the poor, and of all the miserable, and when this is done no longer in spite of their holy or charitable destination, but on the very ground of it? —*now*, when men have recourse to sacrilege for the sake of sacrilege, and use petroleum to make a bonfire of what angels venerate?—*now*, when this work has grown into a taste, when there are rejoicings over the dawn of success, when it is said: "We have stored our forage in your churches, stabled our horses in your convents, kennelled our dogs in your schools: we have paid our courtesans with your monstrances: we have drunk the savings of your priests and your widows . . . and what are we the worse for it? Where are the thunderbolts with which you threatened us? No one trembles at those of God or of the Church; and science mocks at your bugbears!"

2

No, this is no time to neglect the question of Holy Places, nor to let it be said that our most ancient possessions, our dearest memories, and our most venerable traditions are only founded on superstitious fables, and have their origin in trickery and imposture.

The duty of a Catholic is to follow the advance of science, to be ready to turn every discovery to advantage, and at the same time to be on his guard against accepting hastily everything which professes to be the verdict of science.

It is well not to ignore archæology and its kindred subjects, but, before all, it is necessary to take up the vantage ground of higher principles in order to judge the contradictions and arrogance of our opponents. We must be prepared to build up a solid foundation for all that we maintain, and to turn everything to the service of truth, holy love, and the greater glory of God.

Men of science outside the pale of Catholicism should beware of being carried away by excitement and anti-Roman prejudice. It is possible that contempt of our traditions, indifference to our sacred relics, antipathy to our memorials may carry them farther than they wish. If they reverence the Bible, if they have religious memories and places of worship themselves, it is their interest not to loosen the foundation of all belief, not to cast discredit on the Book *par excellence,* and not to encourage robbery and profanation by sneers.

As lovers of science, they ought to shrink from dwarfing the science they profess, and from opening a gulf in their minds and their whole moral being between the things of Heaven and those of earth.

PART I.

LOCAL SANCTIFICATION, AND ITS PERMANENCE.

CHAPTER I.

EXISTENCE OF HOLY PLACES.

1. *Sense of Mankind on this Point.*

WE know all that a proud philosophy can advance as to the right of indifference appertaining to the Supreme Being; so that He is in no way bound to concern Himself with any particular spot on our ant-hill of an earth. We know, better than philosophy can teach us, that "the earth is the Lord's, and the fulness thereof," and that He may be, and ought to be, worshipped everywhere; but does it follow that this indifference is His law, and that it has not pleased Him to depart from it? That is the real question. There is a feeling deeply implanted in us, and confirmed by experience, which forces us to acknowledge that all places are not equally suited for prayer, or equally marked by Divine consecration. This is a fact recognised by all generations of the earth, the causes of which lie deep down in our nature and destiny.

If we consult revelation, it teaches us that the Author of all things has not used His right of indifference, but rather that of choosing places suited to His relations with men. It teaches us that the Fall has laid waste, overthrown, sullied a part of nature, and thereby made it more than ever necessary to purify, separate, and sanctify the world, bit by bit, in order to restore it as a whole to the Lord.

There is sacred geography and profane geography—nay, there is a satanic geography. One place seems to open and draw down Heaven: another is as if given up to evil—it is an opening into hell, a conductor of infernal electricity: some places appear to be neutral, while others are like great points of junction where all the powers of Heaven, earth, and hell come into conflict.

2. *Mysterious Absence of God in Nature.*

We acknowledge, teach, and adore the Omnipresence of God; but, at the same time, we must admit the fact of a strange and mysterious absence of this God, without Whom nothing can exist. From the first, He made, as it were, a void in Himself, in order to call the creature there, beginning what St. Paul calls His " annihilation." He was as though absent from the angelic world at the time of its probation, in order to leave freedom to those high Intelligences who would have

been overpowered by the full consciousness of His
light. A Presence full of glory was the reward of the
faithful angels, while those who claimed a right to
take advantage of their Sovereign's absence were ter-
ribly punished by that very absence made eternal :
life, plenitude, sanctity, all the attributes of beatitude
are for them as though they were not.

So for matter, which neither knows nor feels God,
He is as though He were not.   It is the office of man
to be its priest, that is, the intermediary, whose part
it is to elevate and offer it to God, and, at the same
time, to draw down sanctity and benediction upon the
earth.

From him, too, during his probation, God hid Himself, but it was impossible for this absence to be in any
way absolute ; it was only a veiled Presence, and man
ought to have known this ; he ought to have called
God back to him, and he did not do so ; he took pleasure in the absence of Sanctity.   Now, when man does
not give God His place in nature, when he uses it for
purposes of vanity and falsehood, he gives it over to
the spirit of darkness, it becomes possessed by that
spirit, and in its turn takes possession of man, intoxi-
cates and blinds him ; it is, in spite of itself, *nolens
volens*, an instrument of evil : it becomes sullied and
impure, an alien from God, and, above all, from His
attribute of sanctity.   And such is the world we
live in.

Scripture teaches us that God re-appeared after the
Fall, and His re-appearance bespoke a whole world of

mercies; but, nevertheless, it was but momentary, and left the culprit to himself in a new cycle of probation. If God had not promised a Redeemer, men would have been almost led to think that He was taking leave of a world unworthy of Him. Let man make what he can of the earth which has been given him! Let him struggle among its thorns and briars! Let him multiply, and fill, and possess it all alone! He has chosen to attach himself to senseless dust—then let him return to it, and remain in it! It shall no longer be God Who possesses the earth, filling it with His life and beatitude, but the children of men, filling it with the noise of their follies. They have so thoroughly taken the Giver at His word, that at length He has no place, whether in things, in understandings, or in hearts. When man is thus abandoned to his decay, visible things hide rather than reveal to him the Divine attributes. Nature is everything, it eclipses Providence; physical laws usurp the place of the Ruler—blind forces, the variety of the elements, and the invariability of results are enthroned instead of the fertile and eternal Omnipotence—visible order and beauty are spontaneously reproduced, what need of going on to a First Cause? Man is surrounded by relative immensities, what need has he of an absolute immensity? Is not the infinite which he sees before him more within his grasp than the Infinite Himself?

Thus, beneath the dust of the visible images of God, God Himself has disappeared. Forgetfulness, ignorance, and sophistry have killed the Divine life in humanity, and, by the same blow, in the material world also. Idolatry, which is the deification of matter, deism, which is the deification of nature, and other ideas differing in degree of grossness have usurped the place of the simple and adorable truth. The thought of God, as He is, is blotted from the earth.

3. *Mysterious Return.*

Here a new mystery meets us. Beneath this Divine annihilation, we see the germ and development of a new Presence, perfectly distinct from absolute Omnipresence. It is a Presence of grace. As yet it is veiled, but the veil is transparent, and allows us to see beneath it infinite beauty and condescension. The world of absence in which God had wrapped Himself will now bring out more strongly the faintest light of His visits. As the Lord had withdrawn Himself, as He had abandoned, left desolate, so now He is about to draw near, to re-possess, illuminate, console, and fill.

The creature, which acknowledged its God, turns again to the breast which nourished it, and drinks deep draughts of life, joy, and light; it casts off its darkness and its stains, and abjures the folly which tends to separate it from the source of all good. It finds again its true place in creation, and longs to see the Sovereign Love once more everywhere supreme. Its aspiration is that in itself and in all things God may be All in all.

This marvellous return is not effected all at once. It is especially by men, and with their consent, that

God is pleased to bring it about. I might almost say that it is from them that He wishes to obtain it. Man, that priest of creation, who has become the priest of forgetfulness and error, must re-assume his office, and become once more the organ of nature's legitimate aspirations. By a renewal of grace, the visible things which had misled him will become the means of leading him back into the right path, and of keeping him in it. The Divine attributes will break themselves up so as to be within his reach and compass; they shall spring forth at his touch as the fire flashes from the flint. All sanctity must have and find its proper places: evil alone has no right to that which it occupies. Saint must follow saint, place must be joined on to place; and the chief place, the centre of every place, must be ultimately the *Holy of holies.*

Sanctity! . . . how is it possible for this indefinable attribute to quit its home, its necessary element, and impregnate a spot—earth, stones, or other materials? How can it be infused into them, diluted so as to mingle with them, be exhaled from them? How is it possible for God to seem more Himself in these "weak and needy elements" than elsewhere? How is it possible for Him to emanate from them, like a perfume, a flame, a vapour unlike anything in the world, so that sooner or later, men shall exclaim, "Deus! ecce Deus?"

No doubt we may answer that this is so because He has so willed it, and that with Him will and power is the same thing. Nevertheless, if we consider His ways, we shall perhaps see some reasons for His passing or His dwelling; we may be able to catch a glimpse of the motives and the harmonies of each; we shall enter into His Mind, and be better prepared to admire and adore Him, as He would have us, in the Places of His predilection.

CHAPTER II.

FITNESS OF CERTAIN PLACES FOR SANCTIFICATION.

THE Divine selection may be seen in a local fitness, which is felt by every one, although it is difficult to define precisely, and its limits are so vague and delicate that they cannot easily be perceived. But still it is founded on nature, and universally acknowledged, whenever passion does not come in to destroy the feeling. There are Places predestinated, marked out by Providence, suitable for holy things; something not to be defined bars them from common uses; in them nature speaks to the heart and to our noblest faculties; in them she has deeper mysteries; the idea of a temple—of contemplation rises in the mind; we look for an Altar, for a Presence; we question the very echoes of the spot.

Symbolism is like a seed hidden in nature; and this truth is the foundation of all that "religiosity" of which certain deistical dreamers have raved so much. Following them, the romantic school diligently worked the same mine; they had caught a glimpse of a world of religious harmonies in the physical order, and would gladly have persuaded us that the magnificence of night, the gloom of the forest, the mystery of caverns, the awfulness of storms, were enough to lift the soul to God, and to form the whole of religion. On some points they went farther than we do; for we should not venture to assert, with one of their patriarchs, that "there is nothing in existence more religious than the wind breathing through the reeds."

We have very little faith in the dogmas and the prayers of the romanticists, and still less in those of the deists; but, without suspecting it, they get their comprehension of nature in a straight line from Catholicism and its traditions. But as of old, the spectacle of mountains, and vast plains, and bold promontories was not enough to preserve man in the primitive times from the most monstrous idolatry; so, with the majority of deists and romanticists, modern religiosity has issued only in a sensual and superficial mysticism, a more refined idolatry than the earlier one.

However, we take note of their admissions and their tendencies, keeping our opinion all the same, that the person best able to distinguish a Divine voice amidst fields and forests is, generally, neither the dreamy sentimentalist, nor the proud thinker, but rather the man who knows also how to pray in an humble chapel. He knows how to appreciate the symbols and harmonies of nature as others do, and he knows, besides, other kinds of fitness.

There are, in fact, moral, social, material fitnesses, a fitness of expiation and of piety, a fitness of condescension to the poor and to little ones, fitness of the war with vice and infidelity. There is one standard of suitableness for the way-side Cross, another for the pilgrimage or the cathedral.

A well-known couplet on the localities suited to certain Religious Orders, comes to the point :

> "Bernardus valles, montes Benedictus amabat,
> Oppida Franciscus—magnas Ignatius urbes."

There are, moreover, fitnesses of contrast, founded on a discord, and which, consequently, are of a higher order. Neither God nor the Church ever violates a fitness of a lower order except for the sake of establishing higher harmonies. It was thus that a spot strewn with dishonoured human remains, a place of shame and punishment at the gates of Jerusalem, was all the more fitted to become the holiest spot of the universe, from the hour when the most heinous of crimes was consummated there. Thus have foul underground dungeons, Mamertine and Tullian prisons, been marked for worship; so temples of Venus, caves of abomination, have been regarded as trophies worthy of the Queen of Virgins. It was not possible for the Cloaca Maxima to become the Church of St. Sebastian, but still the place where the saint's body was thrown by order of Diocletian is enshrined in memory and in poetry while still remaining what it has been since the days of the Tarquins.

CHAPTER III.

THE ESSENTIAL SOURCE OF SANCTIFICATION.

NATURAL fitness, of itself, will never sanctify a place. No ; it is not within the power of disgraced nature to unriddle herself, enlighten herself, make herself Divine.

Even the help of man is not enough to tear away the veil, and to discover the hidden God. There must be an initiation from above, a supernatural sign.

As Solomon teaches, the eternal wisdom prevents the children of men, shows herself to them without their seeking, and takes them captive by the ecstatic joys of her apparitions.

So, "at sundry times, and in divers manners, God spoke to our fathers"—(Heb. i. 1)—in apparitions, multiplying prodigies as signs of His intervention, and foreshadowing the Incarnation by the human forms with which He clothed the angels whom He made His representatives.

Miracles—the whole supernatural order—have been denied for the sake of denying God and His revelation; but what other manifestation of the Supreme Ruler could be more in accordance, on the one hand, with His Greatness and Majesty, and, on the other, with our nature ? Whatever may be said on the subject, a miracle will always be the most glorious sign of Divinity which will command the love and the belief of all who are not determined to deny everything.

One of the effects of apparitions and prodigies is to associate an ineffaceable remembrance with the places where they are vouchsafed.

" I will go," said Moses, "and see this great sight, why the bush is not burnt. . . . And the Lord called to him out of the midst of the bush, and said, Moses, Moses, ... come not nigh hither, put off the shoes from thy feet, for the place whereon thou standest is holy ground." Thus, amidst the glories of nature, the still grander memories of apparitions, visions, and voices, such as the world had never known, struck deep root. Every step of the Lord was marked by benedictions—here, a miraculous victory ; there, a deliverance, an instantaneous cure, a solemn promise.

It is not, then, surprising that grateful men should have chosen these favoured places in which to offer up their thanksgivings and sacrifices ; and as gratitude and prayer bring new graces and prodigies in their train, an increase of sanctification has been the result. A network of traditions, monuments, symbols, images, and holy ceremonies has been formed around the consecrated spot. Hearts, minds, memory, imagination, and senses, all have been subjugated—none has dreamed of disputing God's presence on the earth, which He has marked with His seal.

God may make use of angels and men as the instruments of His consecrations ; but, even then, He is Himself the hidden sanctifying principle. His instruments do their work by His mercy, by His spirit; it is He who makes the saints, who guides them in their choice, and consecrates by their means. That is not the work of "him who willeth and runneth" at random through the world; the whole depends on " God, who sheweth mercy" (Rom. ix. 16).

It is not for us to compare Divine sanctifications, but we are naturally inclined to set a higher value on those which seem to come more directly from the Fountain-head, and which bear about them, as it were, the fresh stamp of Sovereign power and love.

It is only when our nature has been utterly perverted by a bitter and determined war with grace, that we go so far as to treat the idea of a Divine intervention with contempt, or even detestation.

CHAPTER IV.

CHANNELS OF SANCTIFICATION.

1. *Angels and Saints.*

WHAT are the Places marked by the Finger of God, from the beginning of time ? Who will point out to us the bright and shining track of the footsteps of His eternity ? Gladly should we all recognise them; but to forget is in the nature of man—especially of fallen man ; and for the primitive nomadic races, a remedy was scarcely possible. Happily, God stoops to our weakness. He does as the sower does, scatters the seed lavishly, so that, in spite of accidents, enough may still remain, and, if need be, employs His servants to multiply the sowing.

The highest of these servants and channels of sanctity are the angels; but although their part in the exorcism of matter, and its subjection to God, might form a most interesting subject for meditation, we will only consider them here as agents of the supernatural, in very close union with its Source, and pass at once to visible agents.

The Great Founder of all sanctity having prepared all things, either by Himself, or by His ministering Spirits, man may come in his turn, and sow some seeds of that precious plant.

In the original order, the principal trust was committed to Adam; his presence was to sanctify the earth. Wherever the just man turned his steps, God would have been in his heart, His praise on his lips, His law before his eyes. Blessing, gladness, and fertility were to follow him.

God yearns for the heart of man; it is there that He has chosen His dearest dwelling-place—it is preeminently the "Holy Place." And it is, above all, from the heart of man that blessing and praise are meant to overflow the material world, so as to purify, consecrate, and restore it to its Maker.

Consider Eliezer, the aged servant of Abraham. At the faintest shadow of a Divine favour, he falls prostrate in the dust, no matter where—amidst the confusion of a caravan, or among the young maidens at the well. For him there is no necessity that nature should disappear from his sight. Nature is a temple where he feels and sees himself surrounded by God's benefits, and he is absorbed in adoration.

As the saint carries God in his soul everywhere, so God follows him in his journeyings and his repose, and casts on every side an eye of love for his sake. Jacob, fleeing from his brother, falls asleep; while he sleeps, the things of the invisible world are manifested to him. He sees a ladder, the foot of which rests on the earth where he lies, while its top reaches Heaven. God is there. As the angels go up and down the steps, He blesses Jacob, He blesses the land around him, and promises it to his posterity. In this favoured spot, the Patriarch sees but one thing—God, Heaven, and the angels who have been manifested there. The soil is no longer common ground; it is a "terrible place —the house of God, and the gate of Heaven."

Wherever a saint is, waking or sleeping; wherever he is able to adore, to pray, to suffer, to give thanks, God finds a spot whereon to plant the mystical ladder. Not that the vision will be the same everywhere; but wherever he has felt the most fervent love, and received the greatest abundance of Divine favours, there is the blessed spot which he will be inclined to choose, and to offer for consecration from Heaven, and God, in His turn, will accept every offering that is made there with the requisite conditions.

The saint bears about everywhere the sweet odour of his virtues. His friends, who are also the friends of God, love and cherish his memory, with which are bound up the places that he has made centres of prayer, charity, and holy traditions. There his family, his countrymen, naturally feel more confident. " There," they say, " his prayers seemed omnipotent ; there, while with him, we felt nearer to Heaven; there we shall love to unite ourselves to that God Who, were there no other miracle, made the whole of His pure life a miracle."

Nay, it may be that the saint is able to say, as Jacob did to the inhabitants of Luza, " This stone, which I have set up and consecrated, is that on which my head rested when I saw God and His angels. There He renewed His blessings on me. Believe me, this place is terrible. At first I knew it not ; but it is in very truth the house of God and the gate of Heaven. And now I have made a vow, and I have promised that if God shall be with me in my pilgrimage, this stone, this memorial of Divine condescension, shall be, as it were, the foundation stone of this entire city, which shall be called Bethel—the House of God—and I will offer there the tithe of my goods."

The inhabitants of Luza believed the words of the friend of the Lord, and their city was called Bethel, and became one of the holy cities of Israel.

2. *The Grave.*

Even after his death the saint continues to consecrate. His last remains are a link between earth and

Heaven. At his tomb meet the memories of his life and the regrets of his friends. He himself declared to them that it was another gate of Heaven. His last will is sacred, and the most sacred of its dispositions is that which keeps his body and his tomb for the Lord of his eternity. He has no other earthly possessions left. He knows that God accepts this last offering; he has consoled his children with this belief. From generation to generation, his descendants will come to lay their ashes by his; they will take pleasure in re-uniting the family by this mingling of their dust, which they will call the bosom of Abraham, thus adding to the sanctity of the place. Yes, we have known for 6000 years that the bodies of the just return, like those of others, to the dust of which all flesh is made; but for 6000 years we have asserted a resurrection from the inevitable decomposition. We know that God and His angels watch over those mouldering bones. He has Himself engraven in our hearts the desire of perpetuating the memory of those who were worthy of Him, especially in the place of their final rest. Little as may remain of their dust, holy souls feel there a sort of current of grace; there they breathe a perfume of life, and the faith which works miracles. Nay, it is not even necessary to be a saint to experience the power of the grave. Behold that violated tomb, still wide open—the tomb of the prophet Eliseus; a corpse is thrown in, just to get rid of it, and the corpse becomes a living man! (Kings iv. 13—20.)

A saint's tomb is the worthiest of altars for God

and men—reverence, love, religion, all join in making
it a sacred monument, an oratory. Hence arose the
veneration of antiquity for burial-places—a veneration
which degenerated into idolatry. But in this, as in
everything else, the exaggerations of error will always
fall short of the reality. No idolatry is capable of
reaching to the sublime grandeur with which God and
His friends have surrounded the tombs of the saints.

3. *The Church and the Priesthood.*

If one holy will closely united to that of the
Creator is sometimes sufficient for the sanctification of
a place, still more are several holy wills. "Where
there are two or three gathered together in My Name,
there am I in the midst of them" (St. Matt. xviii.
20). Without any extraordinary association, without
any miracle, let but a few men, influenced by the advantage and the desire of uniting in faith, prayer, and
adoration, yield to this attraction, and the Divine
Presence will be re-established in their midst. Graces
and favours will not be wanting. If this society continues, if prayer attains the form and force of local
custom, possession, and prescriptive right, the society
binds itself by a contract, or a quasi-contract, to set
apart and keep intact this particular spot, and if it
accept legacy or donation for such an intention, God
will not be ungrateful. He will sanction the vow of
this society. He will not be outdone in generosity.
Sanctification will follow man's desire as a fruit of

grace, and an engagement of honour and love entered into by Him Who is supremely faithful to His promises.

And if men raise monuments in memory of engagements entered into with Him, so He, too, builds invisibly, and blesses on earth an edifice whose completion will be in Heaven.

There are, there always have been, in the world men whose office it is to represent human society before God, and commissioned by God to represent Him to their brethren—Divine ambassadors accepted by men—human ambassadors accepted by God—chosen and privileged ministers of official sanctity; they may be unfaithful to the grace of which they are the guardians, because, before all things, they are men; but ordinarily God is pleased not to make their authority depend on their frailty. If they fail in their duty, it is the man who fails; the ambassador, with the treasures entrusted to him, remains the same; his hands are consecrated for blessing, his lips have drunk early at the source of benedictions, the whole man is, so to say, *sacramentalised;* what he chooses is chosen by Heaven; what he accepts is accepted, what he blesses is blessed, what he consecrates remains consecrated. The priesthood is the sanctifying authority, the guardian and security of sanctification. Holy in itself, independently of the person invested with it, everything which belongs to it in virtue of its Divine commission is sanctified by that very fact. It accepts in the name of sanctity, it confers sanctity. When an individual gives to God his field,

a city offers Him a temple, a prince his towns and
provinces; if these offerings are accepted, blessed, and
consecrated by the priesthood according to the fulness
of the powers belonging to it, then lands, buildings,
towns, and kingdoms are, by virtue of these acts, accepted, blessed, and consecrated by Heaven, and placed
under the sovereign ægis of the Saint of saints. They
are regularly *canonised,* so far as anything not in
Heaven can be canonised.

Apart from the priesthood, works of sanctification,
even miracles, may lack authority; private revelations
may be regarded as a dream, a saint may be mistaken
or misunderstood, the tomb may be but an unsolved
enigma; nations may lose the faith, the source of all
sanctity. Therefore, as a general rule, the sanctification of a place is doubtful till its consecration is attested
by the priesthood. But the priesthood, on its side,
founds its decision on the great chain of miracles and
revelations, on all that is purest in society and humanity,
on past and present sanctities, on the Word of God
Himself, and when it declares that a place is holy and
blessed, our part is to believe and venerate.

As a corollary to what has been said, we may add
that the fact of the performance by the priesthood of
holy ceremonies is enough to mark a place in the remembrance of God and men. When sacred acts, such
as prayer, preaching, and, *à fortiori,* sacrifice and the
celeration of the most august mysteries are regularly
performed within its precincts, it becomes linked to
the supernatural order; generally it is fitting to pre-

serve the memory of the Divine shadow which has brooded there, and to substitute permanent right for the passing fact.

CHAPTER V.

AUTHORITY AND LIBERTY.

ONE consecration gives birth to another. When the consecration of a place is, as it were, intensified, it becomes a centre for the sanctification of its neighbourhood, a kind of crystallisation, which spreads and forms a continuous network from point to point.

Nevertheless, it must not be imagined that the sanctification of places is in any way fated or necessary, like the chemical result of the union of two or three ingredients; it is almost always a matter in which both sides are free.

Sanctity, in itself, is independent of place. The Spirit "breatheth where He wills;" there is no asking whence He comes, or whither He goes, or whether He will remain. Grace is the cloud which follows Him, and none may fix its course, nor its place of halting. Hence, we can conceive the idea of sanctity gliding by without leaving any mark, or leaving only a remembrance, without taking possession. A mere momentary contact between God and man was enough.

Where should we stop if we were to mark and consecrate all the places where grace and mercy have followed, overtaken, struck, enlightened, converted, or con-

soled us ? We inherit the blessings of our fathers, and if
our souls were supernaturally enlightened, how often we
should have to exclaim with Jacob : "Truly this place is
all glorious with Divine revelations, and I knew it not !"

How many venerable spots, marked by the most
signal favours, are utterly forgotten ? Where are the
places dignified by the visions of Job and of the prophets ? where the stations of the Israelites in the
desert ? nay, where are the places which witnessed
our Lord's temptation, and the miracles of the apostles,
or the marvels of God's intimacy with His saints ?
Public or hidden, they filled the world ; yet the very
fact of their multiplication has made it possible that
they should in great part be forgotten with their local
circumstances. This is the natural consequence of
human weakness, and does not excite the displeasure
of God.

Not that He cannot, by right of His sovereign dominion, impose His Will absolutely. It belongs to His
freedom to be able to do so, and He has done it. In
Abraham's time the land of Canaan had its owners :
its cities and kingdoms had their rulers, but God consulted none when He said to the Patriarch : "To thee
and to thy seed will I give this land." He Himself
began the extermination of the Canaanitish nations,
and it was by His order and under His guidance that
the Israelites conquered them, and made choice of the
Levitical cities and the cities of refuge.

Wherever it has been His Will to choose and set
apart a sanctuary for Himself, He has touched its pre-

cincts as with the rod of Moses, and no one has been able to withstand Him; but it is only exceptionally that God exerts "the strength of His right Hand and of His mighty Arm" to win and to take possession. Generally speaking, He waits for the free-will offering of men, He is satisfied with their word, He keeps possession on their conditions. Even when He dispossessed the people of Canaan, it was only that He might give their land to the children of Abraham, and receive it again from them according to the niggard measure of their fidelity and gratitude.

Sanctification is almost always a matter of mutual consent, and is transacted, at least on God's side, with the utmost reverence. " Cum magnâ reverentiâ disponis nos," says the Wise Man. It is God Who respects our liberty, while we ourselves have the fatal privilege of indifference, of forgetfulness, of contempt for the power and love of God. Freer than Divine will in one sense, our liberty extends even to rebellion and sacrilege; so that the places which God has chosen for Himself are sometimes as much exposed to invasion, devastation, and ruin as the property of the most hopeless of the poor.

If ever there was a Place on earth of which God took possession by solemn words, it was that on which the Burning Bush stood. Yet it seems never to have been anything more to men than a striking instance of their power of oblivion.

It is enough to say that, if they are men of good will, our Heavenly Father gives His children all the liberty that they could desire to settle, as it were, *en famille*, everything as to the choice, manner, degree, and duration of sanctification.

Nevertheless, He cannot altogether exempt them from tribute, from rule, and from fitting observance. This would be deserting both them and the earth.

Their gratitude to Him on this point should ever find expression, more or less, by a triple homage :—

1. Belief in His sanctity, and acknowledgment of His sovereign dominion.

2. Filial confidence, which makes them feel more certain of pleasing His Divine Majesty, and of obtaining every petition from Him by conforming to the dispositions of His Will.

3. Worship and adoration, which, at the thought of a concentration of the Divine Presence, is itself concentrated in praise, love, and sacrifice, or breaks forth into devout hymns, ceremonies, and loving marks of care. A place is endeared to men for God's sake : they adorn it, they clothe it in beauty, they preserve it in a state of honour and decency; every privilege which is in harmony with the Divine idea is granted to it, and, so far as depends on human ability, they defend it for ever from all profanation.

CHAPTER VI.

IDEAL DEVELOPMENT OF SANCTIFICATION.

FROM what has been said, it may be seen that there are several degrees of sanctification—that places may receive a consecration more or less general, more or less absolute, according to circumstances, the requirements of religion, and the will of both God and man.

1. *Exorcism. Religious Labour.*

Speaking theoretically, the first degree consists in reclaiming a place from the powers of darkness; it is a purification—an exorcism—rather than a sanctification, properly so called.   The devils, by their sin, fell to a lower level than that of brute matter; but matter, in turn, fell under the power of the demons by the sin of man.   It is the work of humanity, divinely restored, to deliver the earth from this degradation and slavery.

The earth is, in some sort, humanised by labour.   It is subjected to mind; it returns to order.   But if labour is made supernatural by prayer and intention— if it is humble, penitent, and regulated by holy love— then the earth is not simply humanised; it receives the first of the blessings promised after the Fall.   The priest's benediction is only the complement and official sanction of this blessing on labour, and it is more especially with reference to the labourers of God, who water the earth with the sweat of their brow, that the priest blesses fields and meadows, mountains and valleys, vineyards and forests, wells and rivers, lakes and seas, roads, mines, buildings, and the whole of nature.

Unhappily, vice and the devil have their labourers also; but, in the end, the labour of the faithful must win the day, for they are the most powerful, united, and persevering. Full of hope, in sight of these blessings and this labour, the Church ceases not to sing daily: " O let the earth bless the Lord: let it praise and exalt Him above all for ever. O ye mountains and hills bless the Lord. . . . O ye fountains, ... seas, and floods, bless the Lord. Praise and exalt Him above all for ever."

2. *Transient Consecrations.*

But man is not satisfied with what is general; he wants to *specialise*—to concentrate—and this is the case with consecrations as with other things. In the world of thought there is the kingdom of prayer and meditation; in the world of science there is theology; in the world of affections there is the love of God; in the cycle of time and seasons there is the Lord's day and His festivals; in the realm of space there ought also to be His Holy Places.

And, indeed, the voice of all ages tells us that there are places set apart in a more especial way—the natural rendezvous of whatever is Heavenly in humanity. Happy musings, thoughts, aspirations, offerings, rest, affections, whatever tends towards God, naturally seeks its place where miracles, grace, custom, or simply fitness of place have fixed the attention and the hearts of men.

With the nomadic races of primitive times, however, prayer must have been as transient as everything else; there were places of temporary adoration, altars of a day, tents of the Lord. God condescended to adapt Himself to the life of men, and to be without dwelling-place, without local history, without local memorial. His grace was like the cloud of the Israelites, dark or bright, according to necessity, guiding the tribes from one encampment to another, submitting itself to the requirements of the little ones, and of the very flocks and herds, and leaving not a trace behind.

Nevertheless, even then memory had always a tendency to cling to the places where adoration had been offered—oracles, graces, or promises received. It was kept alive by the recitals which wiled away the night watches. The memory of primitive man, unencumbered by empty science and inutilities of all sorts, was marvellously adapted to take hold of the supernatural and miraculous facts, which stood out prominently, like the pyramids in the desert, from the monotony of their existence—a monotony often unbroken for centuries. They handed on the tale to their descendants, together with the description of the countries they had traversed, above all with the details of their sacrifices and thanksgivings.

3. *Permanent Reservations.*

But when men abandoned a wandering life, and built
themselves towns and cities, how could He, Whose delight it is to dwell with the children of men, remain,
as it were, a wanderer in the desert ?   When the stone
of the domestic hearth had become the symbol of the
family, how could there fail to be a fixed place for the
altar of sacrifice ?   When men had set up landmarks
to assure their own possessions, how was it possible for
those which belonged to God to be left without a stone
to point them out ?   When the poor had their houses,
and princes their palaces hewn out of the rock, or
towering aloft like mountains, and thronged by a crowd
of officers and servants, how should God remain without a dwelling-place for Himself and His faithful children ?

Men felt the necessity of combating their tendency
to forget; they felt their need of the Eternal on the
earth, and that they must be united to Him by something more than the memories of a day ; they felt that
all covenants with Him ought to have an eternal
character, so far as their infirmity permitted, and to
extend from generation to generation, in compensation
for the shortness of life.

Now there is, and there ought to be, no instability
in religion except what is accidental.   When love
bestows itself, it desires to bestow itself for ever ;
when it makes a sacrifice, the sacrifice is absolute ;
when it receives, it treasures the memory of the gift ;

and as gratitude clings to the places where mutual tokens of love have been exchanged, it would fain make the memory of the benefits eternal in those places. How is it possible that God should forget? He is the eternal Love, the eternal Gift, the eternal Gratitude.

Listen to the words in which He speaks Himself of one of the places of His predilection: "Can a woman forget her infant, so as not to have pity on the son of her womb? And if she should forget, yet will not I forget thee. Behold, I have graven thee in My Hands; thy walls are always before My Eyes."

When the prayer of a saint has caused God to descend on any place—*à fortiori*, when two or three, gathered together in His Name, have drawn Him down from the Throne of His glory in Heaven—He has no dearer wish than to remain with them, "even to the consummation of the world." When He "bows the heavens and comes down," His steps are the steps of His eternity. Everything that He blesses, receives an impress of eternity. Permanence and fixed possession is one of the gifts which He promises to those who serve Him, and He is pleased to attach this permanence to the benedictions He bestows upon a consecrated place.

In the course of time, God and men will, now and again, take pleasure in the unforeseen and the provisional—in a meeting in the desert, whose traces will, ere the morrow, have been effaced in the sands.

From time to time, too, they will take pleasure in a

simple memory, standing alone, without anything to keep it up. They will cling to it all the more fondly because it rests on no contract, possession, memorial, or any other external security.

The devotion to the *Via Dolorosa* is a tradition of this sort. A street in a Mussulman quarter is all that meets the eye; but to every Catholic it is indeed a Holy Place.

Close by rises Moriah, the mountain of the Temple, a spot still more desecrated by Mahometanism. All trace of Christianity, consecration, right, possession, seems lost for ever; but the remembrance is left. There is not a Christian sect—not even the most hostile to traditions—which does not turn thither its eyes, and seek to find the holy mountain beneath the pavement of El Haram es Scherif.

In this case the sorrowing and regret of faithful hearts are a homage full of delicate tenderness. The God of hearts permits profanations for the sake of the amends made by the saints. In His Eyes, their reparations are precious as temples.

These, however, are exceptions. Generally, the sanctification of a place requires something more than what is merely provisional, more than a simple remembrance—it pre-supposes the act of setting apart, of taking possession; whether God claims as Sovereign Master, or accepts an offering from men, the Holy Place is thereby raised above all common law, protected by the double *ægis* of the supreme dominion of

God and of the right men—it is committed to the religion and the faith of all.

This setting apart is commanded by reverence, gratitude, and love. Whether it be that a miracle has called forth thanksgiving and adoration, or that prayer has drawn down graces and blessings from Heaven, a communication is established between Heaven and earth, and mutual exchanges follow each other. God does not forget the place where He has looked down on men; and men, on their side, love to choose the place of grace as the place of sacrifice, and the centre of their religion.

Offerings are a part of worship. Now, naturally, the first oblation will be that of land (with privileges attached to it); it will be considered as an accessory to greater and more perfect sacrifices.

Nature herself teaches us the propriety of thus setting a place apart. If there is a situation which seems providentially pre-ordained for worship, it is that whose sublimity inspires terror, and thus escapes the profane uses of daily life. All nations have such sacred precincts set apart—their τέμενη. Later on, these τέμενη became temples.

What is the meaning of dedications and consecrations but this: that they are the deed by which Heaven and earth are called to witness the offering made to God of a special portion amongst those of the children of men; and, on the other side, the solemn act of accepting and taking possession in God's Name by His ministers?

4. *The Monument.*

The spot chosen for special benedictions ought to be marked by some external signs ; it is a necessity springing from our very nature, and consequently the custom dates from primitive ages.*

Man, feeling the necessity of defending himself from his own forgetfulness, at first made choice of caves, of bold promontories, of high places, of the parts of forests most suited to impress the senses.

Later on, not contented with what he found in nature, he piled up between Heaven and earth gigantic masses, capable of resisting the action of time and of the elements, in token of contracts, or semi-contracts, entered into with God.

Strange to say, it was an altar—a monument of death and destruction by fire and the knife—which was from the beginning, the sign of union between the Eternal and the creatures of a day. After altars came sepulchres, also monuments of our frailty. When altars or sepulchres were wanting, land-marks were set up, to endorsé or mark out the property of God as well as that of man ; but there was a feeling that these Men-hirs† should be worthy of the Divine Owner.

When Jacob had the celebrated vision of which we have spoken, he took the stone on which his head had

* Hence the word σῆμα, σημεῖον—sign, used for monuments.
† *Pierres levées*—erect stones, mazzeboth, &c.

rested while he slept, and set it up as a monument, on which he poured pure oil. This ceremony was according to custom, and was so well understood and accepted by men that, on this occasion, the neighbouring town changed its name of Luza to that of Bethel, or House of God.

These primitive monuments attracted attention, and awakened slumbering memories, but they had not the power of explaining themselves. For this popular tradition was required; and if war, emigration, or other scourges happened to break the chain, they were no longer understood, and ceased to be the "gate of Heaven." The way to prevent this profanation was to give them particular forms, and to mark them with symbolical sculpture and inscriptions. From the time of Job, it was to the hard flint stone that men entrusted the memories they wished to perpetuate.* Thenceforth, the inscriptions and wonders of sculpture gave to stone all the interest of which it is susceptible.

5. *The House of God.*

But, for the man of an advanced civilisation, it is necessary that the monument should be a real *House of God;* that the τέμενος should become a temple —a church. Amongst the dwellings of men God also must have His habitation, where man can find Him, unite himself to Him, enjoy Him, rest in Him.

The monumental edifice should be the solemn

---

* "Utinam celte sculpantur in silice."—Job xix. 24.

and more official realisation of God's promise to be with those who should meet in His Name, wherever it may be. It must be a place of assembly—a συναγωγή —where hearts and souls unite to invoke the Name of God, and to utter the Heavenly formulas which move the Most High to have His "delights with the children of men," and to pour down His grace and His Spirit more abundantly.

Man there must appear in that which is the chief dignity of his nature—in the form of an ἐκκλησία —in communion with the whole of humanity: with the past, into whose history he will inquire; with the present, availing himself of all its lights and helps, and good-will; with the future, examining into every induction and aspiration, every wise prevision, every prophetic intuition. It must be a school, in which man may learn to strip himself of self, and of the narrowness of the present. It must be something regular, as a college; great, as a forum; and attractive, as a hall adorned for a festival. It must be simple and beautiful, as the vault of heaven, and must breathe at once the awfulness and stillness of the grave, and the rapture of a marriage supper, given by God Himself, where He and His angels welcome the guests.

6. *The Metropolitan Church.*

The House of God must extend itself—it must have its radiating influence in keeping with the greatness of its destinies. It needs sacred ministers, guardians,

choirs of Levites and youths, and, in consequence,
houses, cloisters, schools, charitable institutions, forms
of government, and, also in consequence, funds and
property for all these various services.   All these
things receive, as it were, a character of sanctity by
reason of the purpose for which they are employed,
and nations rightly regard it as an act of sacrilege to
lay hands on them.   •

Beyond these immediate dependencies, the temple
radiates widely and freely.   Holy souls gather about
the sacred edifice, crowning it with piety, lustre, and
charitable works.   At one time, they go forth to bear to
a distance the Lord who lives within them; at another,
they return to plunge in the furnace of Divine union, to
issue thence once more with heightened fervour.   From
time to time, like bees when they find a young queen
reared by the efforts of the whole hive, they swarm,
they go forth to create secondary centres of piety and
sanctification in the towns and country districts round
about—chapels, houses of refuge or hospitality, of
silence and contemplation, of light and instruction; in
a word, works of every kind harmoniously grouped,
like brilliant satellites, round the metropolitan Church.

7. *The Holy City, the Religious Capital.*

The power of sanctification may go still further:
the city may belong to the Church.   This comes about
quite naturally, when it is indebted to the sanctuary
for its origin, its development, its entire being.   God
may choose for Himself also towns already built, like

the Levitical cities, and cities of refuge, which He set apart for Himself in Israel. Habitations of men, either singly or collectively, may be bequeathed, given, or conquered, and societies may choose their masters and governors. There is nothing, then, to prevent them, in certain cases, from becoming the portion of the Lord, and from belonging to His representatives on earth. Nay, there is a fitness in this, well understood by that great emperor who thought that there was no room left for him in the Rome of Saint Peter, because his presence there would only have the effect of cramping a power which was necessary to the world, and of eclipsing a Heavenly light by the earthly purple.

The holy city becomes, therefore, the sanctuary, the vision of peace, the lighthouse for a whole district and province, even for a whole kingdom. The idea of a place holy above others would require an imperial city —a religious capital of the whole world. Its royal sanctuary, otherwise called its *basilica*, the mother of all the sanctuaries in the world, ought to be like a mountain seated on predestined hills, towards which all eyes should turn—the rendezvous of all the nations.* There, uniting their prayers, and their treasures of life and intellect, they would be more powerful with Heaven, richer in the wealth of all, and better able to cause their own to overflow to the ends of the earth.

---

* " Preparatus mons domûs Domini in vertice montium, et elevabitur super colles, et fluent ad eam omnes gentes."—Is. ii. 2.

CHAPTER VII.

IS THE DEVELOPMENT OF HOLY PLACES A THING TO BE FEARED?

But, it will be said, if the possessions of sanctity ought to go on increasing in the world in this way, and if its right of possession rests ultimately on the supreme authority of God, what will remain for man? Will not the Church, in the Name of God, and un-checked by any secular control, absorb all possessions in herself? Empires, kingdoms, cities, towns, farms, fields, and forests, everything will, of necessity, fall into priestly hands. It will be, as in the seven years of famine in Egypt, when Joseph gained for Pharao all the land of the Egyptians, their furniture, their flocks, their money, their very persons. Why not at once frankly and confessedly set up universal theocracy, and put the rights and property of all in the hands of the Sovereign Pontiff?

To this we might reply: granted that this were so, are you so sure that the world would be the worse for it? But we have reason for believing that this ideal will never be fully realised. No theory ever is exactly realised. Absolute perfection is not to be reached in this world; but it moves before our eyes like a heavenly torch, showing us in what direction to turn our steps. As, in our private conduct, we must aim at perfection in order to gain the very poor results with which the Divine Mercy deigns to be satisfied, so,

in general questions, Christian humanity ought to
know its aim and direction without expecting to gain
every point. What is wanted is a theory; not an
imaginary system, but, according to the etymology of
the word, the sight—the contemplation of Heavenly
things.

Such a theory makes due allowance for humanity,
its wants and imperfections. With this qualification,
it may and ought to be realised. Yes; we say plainly
that we desire sanctity to possess the earth, and to
extend its rights everywhere—to be everywhere in
the ascendant, and to have supreme authority—to find
everywhere a *point d'appui*, enabling it to exert its
will and to make its influence felt.

But, at the same time, we believe that nothing can
be less arbitrary than this reign of sanctity, and that
its encroachments are the last of the dangers which
threaten humanity, for which it will always leave
room enough. The fear is, rather, its having too little
hold on the world, for, without it, men scarcely find
space except for mutually devouring each other. Far
from being injurious to the rights or the needs of
creatures, its natural effect is, on the contrary, to re-
establish order, in accordance with lofty and powerful
harmonies. No doubt, its first work is to satisfy the
spiritual needs of men, but it also contributes to their
material well-being. Inseparable from charity, it is in
the secret of all the great questions of political eco-
nomy, and of all the formidable problems raised by
the science or the folly of men. Even should its

empire be universally accepted, it would no more interfere with other possessions than the air around us is a hindrance to the functions of life. Its occupation of the earth is so pliant and so multifarious that it accommodates itself to every condition of things.

Yes, in one sense, we have the greatest reason to dread the sublime sovereignty of God; we should fear Him Who, to strip kings and nations of their power, has only to turn away His Eyes from them, and to abandon them to their own folly; Who can employ the elements to fight against the madmen of the world; Who has purified the earth by fire, sword, floods, and other scourges of His justice; Who has abandoned whole nations to wild beasts, and even to vile insects; Who employs barbarous nations as a rod of punishment, which He breaks after using.

If we have deserved to be swept from before His Face, we ought to fear, and to implore His mercy to deliver us from the blind instruments of His justice. Whether nations or individuals, we should follow St. Augustin's advice: " You fear God:—well, then, throw yourself into His Arms !"

When it is a question of His drawing near to us for the purpose of establishing His reign of love, God chooses to employ a meek Moses, a peaceful Solomon, His friends or His priests. He uses them in order to take possession, sweetly and mightily, of some spot of earth, and thence to send far and wide the light of His blessings. In this case, there is no reason for our vain fears.

Supremacy, placed in wise, strong, and gentle hands, in no way fetters the exercise of other and inferior rights of property: rather it acts towards them as guide and moderator, maintaining peace and equilibrium between town and country, rich and poor, labour and commerce, and, in general, among all the different powers which contend more immediately for the possession of the soil.

As to the direct possession of the soil by the representatives of God, there is, for many reasons, no fear of its ever occupying too much room; in the first place, as we have seen, the number of strictly Consecrated Places is essentially limited.

In point of purely personal property, sanctity needs but little, because its life has little about it that is earthly. It requires a foothold on the soil, especially for the sake of others. Riches are only a means of government and influence in its hands. Before all things, they are a means of sacrifice. Yes— it is for the purpose of ceaseless immolation that sanctity requires, not merely an altar, but fields, houses, funds, revenues. God is always demanding from it sacrifices in every possible way; it is His love for us which makes Him an insatiable exactor, and a consuming fire. It is for our sakes that He requires decoration of temples, and precious vessels. He requires them indeed; but marble altars are less important in His Eyes than the temporal and spiritual needs of His children. There are miseries and ignorances continually oozing out, there are acts of injustice to be redressed, there is nakedness to be covered. God also requires from sanctity sacrifice for its own sake; and for this reason He permits the triumph of the wicked. At every moment, whether it will or no, sanctity is required to pay the cost of the wars and revolutions made against itself. The fields which it sows for the poor, the house where it shelters the orphan, the orchard where it grows balsam, all are demanded of it. Its very temples and sacred vessels are seized; and then it is loaded with calumnies, and accused of coveting Naboth's vineyard, and of destroying peace and established order to obtain it.

Again, we have seen that Divine sanctity chooses to make its acquisitions by means of men, and after the manner of men; now there is no fear of men forgetting their own interests to such a degree as to strip themselves of everything for God's sake. All their follies, passions, wants—all the maxims of worldly prudence and wisdom combine to check the exuberance of pious generosity. Naturally speaking, the danger is that men will give nothing to God, nor for God, and that they will take back what they have given. It is by a lasting miracle that the Church is always acquiring new treasures, and so, in a sense, verifies the beatitude promised to the meek, that "they shall possess the land" (St. Matt. v. 4).

Men, too, are the guardians, farmers, administrators, and defenders of Consecrated Places. It is true that, under pretext of sanctity, ambition and avarice make their way into the sanctuary; but the very fact that

they must steal in under the mask of virtue, is a
security to begin with; and hypocrisy can never succeed for long; it has no support from God; He aban-
dons it to itself; it stumbles, and the mask falls.
Those whom God supports are those whom He has
prepared, chosen, and inspired to espouse His sanctuaries. He requires from them superhuman virtues,
such as chastity, religion, prayer, self-devotion, obedience, and, above all, disinterestedness. This is
enough in itself to drive away the crowd of servile
souls.

Ordinarily, Holy Places attract saints, whom they
help to sanctify. Pious souls will offer themselves for
the care of sanctuaries, and for all the works of religion
and mercy attached to them. Nations naturally ratify
these vocations by their approval, and the voice of the
multitude turns out to be the voice of God. "Vox
populi, vox Dei."

Such, as a rule, are the defenders of Holy Places and
of the Church and her rights; they are lambs in simplicity and innocence. They do their duty, indeed;
but, like St. Thomas of Canterbury, they know that
"the Church of God is not defended like a common
citadel." While merely earthly powers have stratagem
and violence at their command, the defenders of sanctity are bound to justice, gentleness, and rectitude;
their great stratagem is simplicity, which the world
cannot understand. When there is no remedy, they
say with the Maccabees: "Moriamur in simplicitate
nostrâ."

Sometimes their death is a triumph; but very often evil seems to win the day, and the weak remnant of the saints can only exclaim as they leave ruins impossible to be repaired: "O God, the heathens are come into Thy inheritance, they have defiled Thy holy Temple; they have made Jerusalem as a place to keep fruit. They have given the dead bodies of Thy servants to be meat for the fowls of the air: the flesh of Thy saints for the beasts of the earth: they have poured out their blood as water round about Jerusalem, and there was none to bury them" (Ps. lxxviii).

In theory, what is so strong as a wise Pontiff, whose authority is acknowledged by every power, and by all consciences, and whose smallest possession is covered by the ægis of Divine right? There is nothing grander than this authority of an Onias raising his voice from one end of the world to the other in warning against every Heliodorus: "Keep your hands from the treasures of the sanctuary; because they are the help of the widow and the orphan, as well as the glory of the earth; do not persist in your sacrileges, for the angels are there, ready to execute justice, and if they smite you my prayers alone will be able to stay their hand." In reality, what is weaker?

Alas! men, blind as they are where the ways of God are concerned, understand them only too well in things which they may use to lull their consciences to sleep. They know that the punishment of Heliodorus was miraculous, and that public miracles of justice are only wrought at long intervals, as solemn warnings.

Thousands of years pass, and the blow does not fall; and that is enough for those who think of nothing but enjoying the present. They know that, as far as the ordinary course of life is concerned, God is but a worm and no man, "vermis et non homo;" or, to quote the ancient law-term for a slave, "non tam homo quam nullus"—less a man than a nonentity which has no rights:—something between a forgotten ancestor, a waiting heir, and an absent person unable to defend himself. They know that the defenders of sanctity ought to be lambs; and they will remember it at the right time, when they feel inclined to be wolves.

No; the danger to society is not in property held by mortmain, nor in the inviolability of the rights of sanctity. The danger is when infidel societies enunciate as a systematic formula that the possessions of God, and the weak, may be seized, while Scripture is turned against God and His people.

If we study facts, either in the Old Testament, where we see sanctity connected with an earthly kingdom, or in the New, which, though apparently excluding the idea of such a claim, does but take possession of the earth in a far stronger and more extensive sense, we shall see clearly what we have to fear or to hope for from Holy Places, and what should be our thoughts and feelings with regard to them.

HISTORICAL SKETCH OF THE HOLY PLACES BEFORE
JESUS CHRIST.

1. *From the Patriarchs to the Schism of Israel.*

We will not repeat what has been already said of
the sanctification of Holy Places in the period anterior
to Abraham. The history of this patriarch and of his
first descendants gives us a pretty accurate knowledge
of the primeval transactions in this respect; for those
personages, at once so grand and simple, were commissioned to relay the foundation for the life of humanity,
and to start the work of a holy civilisation connected
with earthly dominion. The circumstantial story of
the facts which have combined to transform the land
of Canaan into a Holy Land, has, besides, this advantage: that it gives us the type of the sanctification of
the whole earth; for Palestine represents the universe,
and the Hebrew nation is the figure of the people of
God—of the Church.

The first development of the religious civilisation of
the children of Noe had been exceedingly rapid, but
it was almost immediately corrupted. When he
quitted the banks of the Euphrates, the father of the
faithful left behind him magnificent temples in Persia
and India. In his later journeyings, he found others
no less wondrous, on the banks of the Nile; but lying
idols had banished the true God, Who had once more
to make a way for Himself into the world. God,
by virtue of His sovereign authority, begins by pro-

mising the land of Canaan to the patriarch. It has
its owners, but He is the Lord of the universe. "To
thy seed," He said, near Sichem, "I will give this
land." Hardly has Abraham entered this Promised
Land, when he must leave it as a fugitive. He is
driven into Egypt by famine; but on his return, the
Lord appears to him on the mountain between Pen-
tapolis and Mambre, saying to him, "Lift up thy
eyes, and look from the place wherein thou now art to
the north and to the south, to the east and to the west.
All the land which thou seest, I will give to thee and
to thy seed for ever. . . . Arise, and walk through the
land in the length and in the breadth thereof; for I
will give it thee (Gen. xiii. 14—17). A third and a
fourth time God repeats His promise. He gives to the
holy nation all the country from the river of Egypt to
the great river Euphrates—all the cities and possessions of the hostile people. He multiplies His apparitions and promises, as the patriarch multiplies his sacrifices and acts of adoration. Notwithstanding all
these declarations, the father of the faithful was able
to say to the children of Heth, "I am a stranger and
sojourner among you." He repeated the same thing
after Sara's death. The burial of that admirable and
venerated woman is the first act by which he takes
possession. The children of Heth felt it an honour to
put at his disposal a place suitable for the purpose;
but he insisted on paying the price for it, and, for 400
sicles of silver, he purchased the field of Ephron, in
which was the double cave looking towards Mambre,

and surrounded by trees. Abraham, in his turn, rejoined Sara; his body was laid by Isaac and Ismael in the cave which he had bought.

The seed was sown; the holy root was in the soil.

But already the children of the patriarch, by Cetura, had removed to Upper Arabia; Ismael joined them there, and Isaac alone remained to keep alive the memories of Mambre. His own two sons grew up, and he remained alone. The eldest inhabited the mountain of Seir, in Idumæa, whilst Jacob fled before the jealousy of his brother. It was not till after the lapse of twenty years, that Providence brought Jacob back at the head of a tribe of children, servants, and numerous flocks. But when the time came to add the tombs of Isaac and Rebecca to the venerable recollections of Macphelah, when the whole land was filled with the memory of Divine blessings and promises, and the prophecy made to Abraham seemed on the point of accomplishment, the children of Israel had to leave memories, monuments, and burial-places to their own keeping for 400 years, like the grain which is left buried for the winter.

They went to Egypt. Did they sanctify the land of the ancient Pharaos? Yes, doubtless; as the conflicts of the just sanctify the world—delay curses—and prepare the way for a distant future. But, for many a day, Egypt was to be the type of the idolatrous and ungrateful world, drinking the blood and the sweat of the Saints, and only producing sanctity in spite of itself.

5

The peninsula of Sinai was more directly blessed; for forty years it was like a vast temple, the witness of an incomparable vision. The people of Israel had been in the land of the Pharaos like a bush preserving its verdure amidst the devouring flames of persecution. At the foot of Horeb, it was still to preserve the same character of vitality beneath a pillar of fire and amidst fresh trials. It is the mystery of which Moses saw the epitome at the beginning of his mission, when the Lord appeared to him in the midst of a burning bush, saying to him, "Come not nigh hither; put off the shoes from thy feet, for the place whereon thou standest is holy ground."

The entire peninsula was, indeed, sanctified by marvellous solemnities. When once they had quitted Egypt, very few external events disturbed the people during their long procession through the Desert; they were able to be completely under the influence of Heavenly marvels, from the time of their entering the naves of the long wadys, till they came to the sanctuary of granite, where Moses proclaimed the law; and till they ended it in the Promised Land.

Man must always be essentially a pilgrim on the earth. God teaches us this lesson repeatedly; but it was especially the teaching of the Desert. Thus, hardly were the Israelites at the threshold of Palestine, when the ground which had been whitened by the manna resumed its arid look under the footsteps of the Arabs, the miraculous fount of water was dried up, the chasm which had swallowed up Core, Dathan, and

Abiron was closed, the mountain of angelic thunderings and trumpets was nothing but a bare and silent peak, and the Bush was remembered no more now that its burning aureole had vanished.

To complete this transitory character, hardly are the Lawgiver and his brother in sight of the grand panorama of which Jerusalem was to be the centre, when their souls depart to God, and they leave their ashes on the threshold, as if to guard it.

Palestine, on the contrary, was to typify the permanent character of the kingdom of God on earth. Its situation fitted it admirably for this purpose. As the cradle, perhaps, of the human race, it was a suitable centre of the old world, a kind of connecting-link between the three continents then known. It was sufficiently protected by its position to ensure a long and easy security; sufficiently open to invite all present and future civilisations to intercourse; extensive enough to support multitudes of labourers, yet not to excite the cupidity of conquerors; rich enough to maintain its priests and men of letters, and keep up the worship of the true God with befitting splendour; but requiring order and labour as indispensable conditions for the superabundant fertility which merited for it the name of the "land flowing with milk and honey."

The Dead Sea, the deserts of Cades and Sinai, the mountains of Seir and Moab, the snow-clad peaks of Libanus and Hermon, the coasts of Joppe, Ascalon, and Carmel, formed, as it were, an enclosure round this sanctuary land. The names of Canaan, of Sodom and Gomorrha, and of the doomed nations, figured in the frontispiece of its history, as if to announce that fear is the beginning of wisdom. Other recollections, such as those of Jericho, Galgal, Hebal and Garizim, Gabaon, Bethsames, and Maspha, taught that confidence should temper fear. As a rule, the memories of peace and consolation, of glory and of Divine promises, were to predominate, and to be successively associated with mountains and valleys, streams and forests, towns and cities. Whilst on Sinai miracles had been, as it were, like seed unable to take root, they were to become naturalised on the soil of Palestine, like a crop which, season after season, shoots up, blossoms, and bears fruit. What sentiments of reverence and love are awakened by the mere names of Moria, Bersabee, Sichem, Rama, Bethlehem, and Sion.

The entrance of the people into the Promised Land was more like a religious solemnity than a conquest, so much so, that it forced from Balaam, on witnessing it, a cry of admiration at the beauty and order of the tents of Jacob. The same may be said of the passage of the Jordan, and the siege of Jericho; everything connected with the taking possession of this land was arranged with the precision of a ceremonial; the portion of the Levites was settled, forty-eight cities, with the suburbs and surrounding districts, were to belong to them; and six out of the number were to enjoy the privilege of refuge or sanctuary. It was also ordained that the Lord should not always dwell in the tabernacle of skins with which He had deigned to be contented in the Desert. "In the land which the Lord God of thy fathers will give thee," said the Lawgiver, "destroy all the places in which the nations, that you shall possess, worshipped their gods upon high mountains and hills, and under every shady tree. . . . You shall not do so to the Lord your God. But you shall come to the place which the Lord your God shall choose out of all your tribes to put His Name there, and to dwell in it: and you shall offer in that place your holocausts and victims, the tithes and first-fruits of your hands, and your vows and gifts, the first-born of your herds and your sheep. In the place which the Lord your God shall choose that His Name may be therein . . . there shall you feast before the Lord your God—you, and your sons, and your daughters, your men-servants and maid-servants, and the Levite that dwelleth in your cities."

The Lord required a centre of sanctification to ensure unity; but that unity was not to be an absolute monopoly. Galgal, Silo, Gabaon, Cariathiarim, and other places were older than Jerusalem so far as the possession of the ark and tabernacle was concerned. Yet, when David completed the conquest, there was no hesitation; the choice had to be made, or rather the spot already chosen by predestination had to become, not only the site of the great sanctuary, but the religious capital of the holy nation.

That spot was Jerusalem—and in particular the mysterious threshing-floor of Areuna. There—in the place prophesied of in the canticle of Mary, the sister of Moses,* near to the city of Sion, David prepared the site of the Temple. But it was reserved for his son Solomon to build and consecrate it in the presence of all the people. God sanctioned this consecration by His presence; and His glory appeared in the form of a mysterious cloud.

"O God," Solomon exclaimed in rapture, "I have built a house for Thy dwelling, to be Thy most firm throne for ever. . . . Is it, then, to be thought that God should indeed dwell on earth? for if heaven, and the heaven of heavens cannot contain Thee, how much less this house which I have built? But have regard to the prayer of Thy servant, and to his supplications, O Lord my God; hear the hymn and the prayer which Thy servant prayeth before Thee this day: that Thy eyes may be open upon this house, night and day: upon the house of which Thou hast said, 'My Name shall be there:' that Thou mayest hearken to the prayer which Thy servant prayeth in this place to Thee: that Thou mayest hearken to the supplication of Thy servant and of Thy people Israel, whatsoever they shall pray for in this place, and hear them in the place of Thy dwelling in heaven: and when Thou hearest, show them mercy . . . The stranger, also, when he shall come out of a far country . . . and shall pray in this place, then hear Thou in heaven, in

* Plantabis eos in monte hæreditatis tuæ; firmissimo habitaculo quod operatus es, Domine: sanctuarium tuum, Domine, quod firmaverunt manus tuæ.

the firmament of Thy dwelling-place, and do all those things for which that stranger shall call upon Thee: that all the people of the earth may learn to fear Thy Name, as do Thy people Israel, and may prove that Thy Name is called upon in this house which I have built. If Thy people go out to war against their enemies, by what way soever Thou shalt send them, they shall pray to Thee towards the way of the city which Thou hast chosen, and towards the house which I have built to Thy Name. And then hear Thou in heaven their prayers and their supplications, and do judgment for them. If they sin against Thee (for there is no man who sinneth not), and Thou, being angry, deliverest them up to their enemies, so that they be led away captives into the land of their enemies . . . then, if they do penance in their hearts in the place of captivity, and, being converted . . . pray to Thee, towards the way of their land which Thou gavest to their fathers, and of the city which Thou hast chosen, and of the Temple which I have built to Thy Name : then hear Thou in heaven, in the firmament of Thy throne, and forgive Thy people that have sinned against Thee . . . for they are Thy people. . . . That Thy Eyes may be open to the supplication of Thy servant, and of Thy people Israel."

After this prayer of Solomon, there is no longer a cloud, but a flame, a fire coming down from heaven, and consuming the holocausts which have been prepared. The feast lasted seven days, for the victims were more than could be reckoned, and the people

came in great multitudes "from the entrance of Emath
to the river of Egypt."

In conclusion, the Lord appeared to Solomon by
night, and said to him: "I have heard thy prayer,
and I have chosen this place to Myself for a house of
sacrifice. If I shut up heaven, and there fall no rain,
or if I give orders, and command the locusts to devour
the land, or if I send pestilence among My people:
and My people . . . being converted, shall make supplication to Me, and seek out My Face, and do penance
. . . then will I hear from heaven. . . . My Eyes shall
be open, and My Ears attentive to the prayer of him
that shall pray in this place. For I have chosen and
sanctified this place, that My Name may be there for
ever, and My Eyes and My Heart may remain there
perpetually. . . . And if thou walk before Me . . .
and keep My justice and My judgments, I will raise
up the throne of thy kingdom as I promised to David
thy father. But if you turn away, and forsake My
justices and My commandments which I have set
before you, and shall go and serve strange gods and
adore them, I will pluck you up by the root out of My
land which I have given you: and this house which I
have sanctified to My Name I will cast away from
before My Face, and will make it a by-word and an
example among all nations. And this house shall be
for a proverb to all that pass by; and they shall be
astonished, and say: 'Why hath the Lord done thus
to this land, and to this house?' And they shall
answer: 'Because they forsook the Lord, the God of

their fathers, Who brought them out of the land of Egypt. and laid hold on strange gods, and adored them, and worshipped them, therefore all these evils are come upon them.' "

2. *After the Schism, Decline, Fall, or Slavery.*

Strange to say, we seem to be seeing the first beginnings of the Temple and the holy city, and already they have reached the zenith of their glory. The period of decline is about to begin, and the threats which we have just heard from the lips of Solomon are to have their earliest fulfilment in the person of that prince himself. The wisdom which he so early displayed had led him to make his capital the City of God. He had time, during his long reign, to taste the sweetness of the rewards promised to those who faithfully accomplish God's great designs with regard to nations and kingdoms. All eyes were fixed on him; the glories of his throne were inseparably associated with those of the Temple which he had built. His sway extended from the river of Egypt to the Euphrates. In the eyes of his countrymen he was the representative of the race of David and the patriarchs, which was to give birth to the Messiah; in those of foreigners he was the embodiment of wisdom, power, and religion.

The period of decline dates from the day when indulgence in unlawful pleasures brought him in his old age to apostasy. In the beginning of his reign, his people had felt only pride and pleasure in contributing to the pious and useful, as well as magnificent, works in which he was engaged; but when taxes and contributions were levied for pompous undertakings, for the whims of an idolatrous seraglio, for the temples of Moloch, Chamos, and Astarthe, disaffection and rebellion sprang up on all sides, and God, in His anger, declared to the guilty prince that his fair heritage should be torn to pieces, and only a weak remnant be left for his son. The aged king saw the gathering clouds, and when he closed his eyes in death, the storm burst—the schism of Israel began—and its first act was the profanation of Bethel, and the worship of the golden calf at each extremity of the new kingdom. More or less, all the kings of Israel did evil, and prevented the ten tribes subject to them from obeying the law of the Lord, and freely celebrating His feasts. After solemn warnings and partial chastisements, the ten tribes were carried into captivity by Salmanasar.

We are not told that Roboam, or the other kings of Judah, profaned the Temple; but it is not enough to abstain from actual outrages. "*Noblesse oblige;*" and the proverb is equally applicable to the sanctuary. They did not understand this sufficiently; and the Scripture tells us so, when it says that they did evil " in the sight of the Lord," that is, under His Eyes, in the holy city, and before the Temple. Roboam, after being punished by the loss of nearly the whole of his kingdom, suffered the humiliating invasion of Sesac, who made him his vassal, and carried away the treasures of the Temple and palace. One of Roboam's

successors, Joas, at first shówed some zeal in repairing
the House of God, which the impious Athaliah had
despoiled to adorn the temple of Baal; but he did not
persevere in the right path : he and his countrymen
again forsook the House of the Eternal God for the
groves of the idols, and the high-priest, Zacharias,
was stoned, by order of the ungrateful prince, in the
very porch of the Temple.

In the reign of Amasias, the Israelites themselves
threw down the walls of the holy city, and robbed the
Temple of its treasures. The same insults came from
the Babylonians, in the reign of Manasses, who was
carried away captive, and afterwards from Nechao, in
the reign of Joachaz. Lastly, three successive times,
the armies of Nabuchodonosor fell upon the miserable
remnant of Judah, and left the Temple, the city, and
its walls a heap of ruins, a fit subject for the immortal
Lamentations of Jeremias. Kings and people had
alike caused these profanations, never to be surpassed
till the day when this same Jerusalem, restored, but
guiltier than ever, was to fall once more beneath the
blows of Titus.

Jerusalem and its Temple were indeed rebuilt after
the seventy years of captivity, but never regained
their bygone splendour. Old men, who had known
the first Temple, bewailed the inferiority of the new
buildings. The glories of the kingdom are over;
there is an end of peaceful independence. Herod is to
be king. Connected, in some degree, with the nation
and the Asmonean family, he will set on foot gigantic

works in the Temple. But his reign will be a bitter mockery: he will always be the hateful Idumæan—the slave of Cæsar—the great desecrator—the first of anti-Christs—the persecutor of whatever is innocent or generous.

With a few intervals, the condition of the Temple from its rebuilding was nearly always one of conflict and servitude. The Jewish race had increased in cosmopolitan importance; but the kings of Assyria, Egypt, and Syria, impious men for the most part, ruled Palestine in turn, and considered the Temple and city merely as something subject to them. Now and then, they affected a certain respect, by way of gratifying the common people, who also regarded the Holy Places as their patrimony, but, in reality, they had no object but to humble, rob, and make profit of that glorious Temple whose treasures and dignity were only defended by the respect which it inspired, the strength of its walls, and the devoted attachment of a few Levites. Violence, stratagem, intrigues, one after another, broke down the patience of its defenders. Yet, in spite of all, to the very end, the Temple found servants and sacrifices. It was supported by an Invisible Power, and in case of need, as we have seen, the very Herods undertook to repair its walls.

3. *Mysterious Reaction.*

Contemporary with this decline of the human glories of sanctity from the time of Solomon, are the germ, development, and growth of a new order of things which initiates us into the mysteries of sanctity as explained by Christ. "Blessed are they that weep!" More blessed than Solomon are the thousands of faithful souls, scattered through the ten tribes, who never bowed the knee to Baal, or to any other idol. Blessed were they who lamented the transgressions of the people, and bewailed their own captivity. Blessed was Jonas, who, from the abysses of the deep, spoke of seeing the holy Temple again, because it was his habit to defy every obstacle that he might go up and pay to the Lord the annual tribute of his obedience. Blessed were the prophets, whose eyes were ever turned towards the holy mountain, and who resisted evil with a "forehead of brass." They had not heard the doctrine of the Beatitudes spoken in favour of those who suffer persecution. The law only promised temporal blessings as the reward of their fidelity, and yet the Apostle Saint Paul tells us that "they had trial of mockeries and stripes, of bands and prisons. They were stoned, they were cut asunder, they were tempted, they were put to death by the sword, they wandered about in sheepskins . . . . being in want, distressed, afflicted; of whom the world was not worthy; wandering in deserts, in mountains, and in dens, and in caves of the earth."

Was it cursed, then, or blessed, this land of Jerusalem, which drank so much innocent blood? Were they cursed or blessed, those tops of Carmel—those ridges of Libanus—those hills of Galilee—silent witnesses of so many holy desires and pious tears? They

were both the one and the other; but in the ways of
the Lord, mercy triumphs over justice. The benedictions on the patience of the Saints extended far beyond
the limits of Solomon's kingdom, and the sighs of the
scattered Israelites brought a blessing on the world
before the knowledge of Christ.

When a procession is forming in a town, we do not
wonder at the sanctuary being deserted for a time;
and it is some comfort, in the desolation of Jerusalem,
to see men like Daniel, Tobias, and so many others,
heading the great procession, and sowing beforehand,
on all the ways to be one day trodden by Jesus and
His Apostles, the pearls and rubies of their tears
and blood—jewels despised by men, but prized at their
true value by the angels and their Divine Master.

The ruin and humiliations of Sion compelled elect
souls to lift themselves up to the vision of greater and
more Heavenly cities. "Thou art great, O Lord, for
ever," exclaims the aged Tobias, "and Thy kingdom
is unto all ages. For Thou scourgest, and thou savest.
. . . . He hath chastised us for our iniquities; and He
will save us for His own mercy. . . . Bless ye the
Lord, all His elect. Keep days of joy, and give glory
to Him. Jerusalem, city of God, the Lord hath chastised thee for the works of thy hands, but thou shalt
rejoice in thy children. . . . . Give glory to the Lord,
and bless the God eternal, that He may rebuild His
tabernacle in thee, and may call back all the captives
to thee, and thou mayest rejoice for ever and ever.
Thou shalt shine with a glorious light; and all the

ends of the earth shall worship thee. Nations from afar shall come to thee, and shall bring gifts, and shall adore the Lord in thee, and shall esteem thy land as holy. . . . Happy shall I be if there shall remain of my seed to see the glory of Jerusalem. The gates of Jerusalem shall be built of sapphire and of emerald, and all the walls thereof round about of precious stones. All its streets shall be paved with white and clean stones, and alleluia shall be sung in its streets."

The prophet Aggeus, seeing the Jews discouraged in the work of rebuilding the Temple, reveals to them, in order to inspire them with fresh vigour, that, however inferior the new building may be to that of Solomon, there is in store for it a glory with which nothing can compare. " Yet one little while, saith the Lord of hosts, and I will move the heaven and the earth, and the sea, and the dry land. . . . And the Desired of all nations shall come, and I will fill this house with glory. . . . . Great shall be the glory of this last house, more than of the first, saith the Lord of hosts. And in this place I will give peace."

Daniel goes still farther. The holy city and mountain are waste and desolate, when the Archangel Gabriel announces to him that the desires of his heart have been granted. He does not hesitate to speak plainly to that strong and humble soul, and to show him how sharp and intense the struggle will be. The deepest profanation is to follow close upon the footsteps of the highest sanctity, and for ages it will be a hand-to-hand conflict. Something like the mourning and the awfulness of a divine death must cling to the places where God has centred the treasures and the inventions of His life of sanctity. " Seventy weeks," says the archangel, " are shortened upon thy people, and thy holy city, that transgression may be finished, and sin may have an end, and iniquity may be abolished, and everlasting justice may be brought, and vision and prophecy may be fulfilled, and the Saint of Saints may be anointed. . . . From the going forth of the word to build up Jerusalem again unto Christ, the Prince, there shall be seven weeks and sixty-two weeks. . . . After which Christ shall be slain, and the people that shall deny Him shall not be His. And a people with their leader that shall come, shall destroy the city and the sanctuary; and the end thereof shall be waste, and after the end of the war, the appointed desolation. . . . . The victim and the sacrifice shall fail ; and there shall be in the Temple the abomination of desolation; and the desolation shall continue even to the consummation and to the end." Never was there a more forcible announcement of local miseries, which were, nevertheless, linked to the promise of the speedy coming of the true King of Israel and of Juda, the Desired of all nations.

CHAPTER IX.

WAS CHRIST INDIFFERENT TO PLACES?

IT is certain that the New Law is, compared with the old one, a law of grace, a more spiritual law. It is the Spirit of God infusing Himself into humanity, in order to help it to shake off the corruptions of the flesh and the fetters of matter. But we must not conclude that, because Christ's kingdom is not of this world, the Divine Saviour has established a sort of Manicheism, and once more delivered over matter to the devil. On the contrary, He came into this world, as He said Himself, "*to save that which was lost.*"

1. *Two objections.*

It is idle to say that our Lord Himself has given us a great lesson of indifference with regard to places of worship in His words to the woman of Samaria : "Woman, believe Me that the hour cometh when you shall neither on this mountain nor in Jerusalem adore the Father. . . . But the hour cometh, and now is, when the true adorers shall adore the Father in spirit and in truth."

There is in this text both a principle and a prophecy. Our Lord is contrasting the spirit of centralisation in the Old Law with the spirit of liberty which was to be the predominant characteristic of the new. Under the law of fear the attachment of the Jews to their Temple was, for the most part, a servile and jealous feeling,

6

whilst national jealousy led the Samaritans to the
schism and actual disobedience of the worship on Mount
Garizim.   Under the Law of grace the centralising
precept is abolished, or, more correctly speaking, happily modified, the spirit of the worshippers is changed.
The Catholic may and ought to pay the tribute of his
adoration and love in every place; he glories in filling
the universe with it.   But he is at the same time perfectly free to let his memory linger in the places where
he has been visited by grace, or in those where our
Lord vouchsafed to enrich all mankind with the blessings of His Divine Presence.

There is nothing to prevent him from repeating, at
this time, the words of holy King David : " If I forget
thee, O Jerusalem, if I make not Jerusalem the beginning of my joy, let my right hand be forgotten, let my
tongue cleave to my jaws."   Nay, he can repeat them,
perhaps, with even more strength and illumination than
the Prophet who only looked into the distant vista of
futurity.

To him, Jerusalem is the city of unspeakable memories.   The earthly Sion, in her depths of abasement,
touches his heart only the more profoundly, while
giving him, at the same time, a clearer vision and a
keener desire of the City which is eternal in the
heavens.

We said that the words of our Lord to the woman
of Samaria contained a prophecy; and, as a matter of
fact, how many times in history do we find that the
Samaritans have been unable to offer worship on

Mount Garizim? Lost in Naplouse, the most thoroughly Turkish city of Palestine, living there oppressed and despised, reduced to fifteen families, nothing remains to them but a stealthy rite on a deserted hill: they have no national worship worth mentioning. As to the Jews—their condition at Jerusalem is well known. Never, since the days of Vespasian, have they worshipped upon their holy mountain; but, shut up in their unhealthy suburb, under the outer wall of the Temple they have, no longer their place of adoration, but their " *Wailing place;*" thither they come to crowd together, and to die.

The learned author of the work entitled " Sinai and Palestine," raises another objection.* " The Cave of Bethlehem," he says, " and the house of Nazareth, where our Lord passed an unconscious (! ! !) infancy and an unknown youth, cannot be compared for sanctity with that 'house' of Capharnaum which was the home of His Manhood, and the chief scene of His words and works." As our Lord has permitted Capharnaum to fall into such utter oblivion that its site is a subject of mere conjecture, Dean Stanley concludes, from that fact, that Bethlehem and other places have only been saved from a similar oblivion by chance or human caprice, even supposing that these places are really authenticated, a question with which, in his opinion, Providence has concerned Itself only that it may be confined to the speculations of the learned. This is not the place for discussing the theology, or rather the

* Page 472.

G—2

Arianism of Stanley on the subject of Christ's "*unconscious*" Infancy. His principles lead him to measure the relative importance of the places of Divine abode, by the manifestations of the Sacred Humanity. For ourselves, we will not precisely say that we judge in an inverse ratio to appearances, but merely that we cannot judge according to them.

We said that God is free in the consecration and preservation of Holy Places, and that, unless He has bound Himself by special promises, it is not for us to call on Him to explain His manifold reasons for bestowing or withdrawing His predilections. As to Capharnaum, not only was there no promise of Divine preservation, but a positive prophecy to the contrary. The complete oblivion of Capharnaum, Corozain, and Bethsaida, is the consequence of a Divine judgment, on indifference and ingratitude—crimes sometimes more insupportable than malice itself. There was a promise of forgiveness for Jerusalem, even though she was to fill up the measure of her iniquity. But as to Corozain and Bethsaida, and Capharnaum, exalted up to heaven by the presence of the Word, they shall be more severely judged than Tyre and Sidon: they shall become an enigma for the wise, and a warning to nations and individuals who harden themselves against light and grace. What conclusion can possibly be drawn from them applicable to places where it pleases God to preserve for Himself a domain of remembrance and of grace?

2. *Did the Word become Biblified, Systematised, or Incarnate?*

The starting-point for us Catholics is not what may please this or that thinker, nor what may agree with this or that human system. We have to see, first of all, what God has willed—what He has done. Has our Lord, in becoming incarnate, entered into the conditions of humanity in all respects? If He has done so, has He attached, and is it His Will that His disciples should attach, any importance to the fact?

Protestantism would have us believe that Jesus Christ has not localised, but *biblified* Himself. Nothing is more opposed to the Scripture itself than this theory, which gives to ink and paper a pre-eminence degrading to the person. The dead letter would be a poor substitute for the Incarnate Life. It is a pasture which only feeds the sheep of God just in proportion as it is watered by the Divine Shepherd. Being, as it is, a weak and unintelligent image of the Word, it requires not merely a Divine power, but many human sciences to explain and comment on it, among others, topography, and if the Scriptures did not exist, Providence could have made sacred topography suffice for the preservation of traditions.

Christ has not been *biblified*, neither has He made Himself a *system* or an abstract doctrine. If this had been the only result He intended, where would have been the need of the Incarnation? It would only have been an unnecessary and embarrassing complication. It would have been enough to inspire the sages of old and form them into a school for the amelioration of the human race. At the most, He might have vouchsafed to show Himself in a vision, as on Sinai and elsewhere. All that was needed would have been to appear, like a Divine Plato on Cape Sunium, in the fulness of age and of doctrine!

But Eternal Wisdom had different designs, in which the Bible—systems—philosophy are only accessories, more or less necessary.

3. *The True Idea of the Incarnation: its Local Consequences.*

The Word was made Flesh; and His first object was to dwell amongst us—that is to say, to take His place amongst us, and to take it for a long time.

To localise Himself for us. This was the first grace He bestowed upon us, long before opening His sacred mouth, or uttering a single word. All the rest of His life was in conformity with this great fact. He came, it is true, to teach a life altogether Heavenly; but our Divine philosophy was to begin by stooping down and finding its starting-point on earth. Our adorable Master, therefore, began by submitting to the precept laid upon man—to honour the earth—*colere terram*—and to gain His bread by the sweat of the brow. From His contact with the earth, and even with the depths of the grave, He has willed that His doctrine should spring, almost as much as from His

Divine words. Jesus is the Teacher, the Head of the great school, the Supreme Truth; but it is only by going down with Him into the abyss of our nothingness that we can rise with Him into the perfect light In Him the Teacher is almost lost in the Priest of Divine Love; the earth is His altar: Book and tapers are there giving light to the wondrous Liturgy.

Once more. What is the Incarnation? It is the Word of God making Himself visibly subject to the conditions of humanity; and, in consequence, to those of place and of space—it is the Word of God localised. Before the Incarnation, God allowed His Divine Eyes to be attracted to the earth; it was only the emanations of His mercy which were bound by local sanctification. Now it is His whole Self which He suffers to be chained by the bonds common to the race of Adam, that He may draw to Himself and carry along with Him the companions of His bonds. " Funiculis Adam traham eos." No longer will He be to men either the unbeginning Ancestor, or the Heir as yet unborn. He will have His own place on earth, His country, His birth-place, His· abodes, His memories. His history will be attached to privileged spots; He Himself will linger there by a Presence of unutterable intensity and power for those who are able to consider it, a Presence which passes every other, in comparison with which all our visible presences are only shadows, whatever appearances may say. It is the sense of this truth that has made Christian artists represent

the Infant Jesus holding the world in His Hand, like a
plaything—"ludens in orbe terrarum." And we find
the same idea in the image of Our Lady of Victories,
in which the starry globe is the footstool of the Child,
Who is held lightly on it by His Mother, as He gives
His blessing.

Jesus is divinely present, He is supremely man.
Nay, no one is so utterly human as He is; for He took
possession of the properties of humanity in all their
perfection, and, as a general rule, He was pleased to
rest on them alone in His action upon the world. He
is the $Aὐτόχθων$, the authentic fruit of the only one
virginal generation; and when we say that the Word
descended from Heaven to take root in the garden
of Mary, this descent, or rather this condescension, is
not a change from one place to another—it is the union
of an Omnipresent Person with a nature limited by
space, not the withdrawing of His presence from elsewhere. Jesus is the only One of the children of men
Who chose His birth-place, and Who chose it with perfect knowledge and supreme wisdom. Will any one
venture to say it was undesignedly that He chose
the place of great religious memories, the country in
which His family had roots of such incomparable
dignity ? He declares to us that He came not to destroy, but to fulfil these memories of the Law. He
made His family a shadow of the Heavenly Trinity,
and the land of Judah a kind of reflection of His
Heavenly home.

The memories of this earthly Trinity are inseparable

from the place where it abode. They are the complement of, the whole of sacred history—that is to
say, of the history of God in Palestine.

CHAPTER X.

SOME REASONS FOR THE CHOICE OF THE PLACES SANCTIFIED BY CHRIST.

1. *Influence of Places on Life; Natural and Mystical Harmonies.*

WHY did Jesus continue His life there ? No doubt
the years He passed at Nazareth teach us the humility
of His hidden life ; but there must be more in this
than a moral lesson—there is a collection of facts connected with the great plan of the sanctification of
the world. It was there that Jesus physically knew
abode and departure, presence and absence, journeys
and weariness, restriction and liberty. With the force
of perception of His deified organs, He felt, more perfectly than all others, the sense of comfort, the sense
of inconvenience, and the like. They were all, to
Him, the occasions of an innumerable multitude of
acts, which were most pure, most perfect, most holy,
and consequently most worthy of the adoration of the
angels and of all intelligent creatures. Till a theology
is shown to us, at once more Divine, and more
human, we will adore the Word in the predilec-

tions which made Him choose certain places in which
to be born, to live, to dwell, to work, to teach, to love,
to suffer, and to die; we will visit those places which
were the scene of free actions, or of long and voluntary
captivities; those places watered with tears, and sweat,
and blood; those places, lastly, where Jesus did and
suffered everything possible to human nature, except
imperfection, caprice, moral weakness, error, and corruption.

If, in order to be men of a particular country,
we must have fixed our lives and affections there, and
struck such firm root as to withstand the force of
winds and tempests, then, certainly, Jesus chose to be,
in the order of time, the Man of His country, before
being the Man of humanity.

All the local relations and predilections of Christ
have their reasons—reasons, for the most part, mysterious and incomprehensible; but those which are
within the reach of our comprehension, are admirable
in the eyes of those who know how to study them; they
are reasons of grand historical harmony, and of sublime propriety with regard to the glory of the Father;
reasons of justice and retribution; reasons of illumination for the whole Church; reasons of charity and
Divine condescension for weak, and of complacency no
less Divine for good and perfect souls.   In the choices
of Christ, all human reasons, family reasons, reasons of
circumstance and of antecedents, genealogical, political
reasons, reasons of every kind are adopted, purified,
and made Divine.   It is impossible to deny them; far

drawn from them a multitude of lessons full of depth and profit to the spiritual life. So far is the *composition of place* from being an indifferent thing in the contemplative life, that Saint Ignatius, that great master of divine psychology, gives it an important place in the preludes of meditation ; he would have us re-compose the Divine scenes before fathoming the mysteries wrought there. Now, if an imaginary re-composition may be of some advantage to the soul, much more the reality for which it thirsts. We examine into the smallest circumstances which may help to understand the actions of Jesus ; those actions reveal to us His Heart, and by that Heart we penetrate even to the treasures of His Divinity.

We must needs be satisfied with an ideal, if we want to have an approximate image of the transfigured world, or of the glories of Heaven ; but when the question before us is that of the scenes in which our Saviour's earthly life was passed, or the facts of Biblical history, the mind and the heart are satisfied with nothing short of the reality, as it appeared to the eyes of contemporaries ; in this case, the only use of the ideal is to clear away ruins, or modern orna-mentation. If we cannot entirely reproduce the scenes in our minds, we like, at all events, to know the sur-rounding landscape, the general look of the country, the outline of the mountains. I grant that this know-ledge of details belongs rather to the luxury of devo-tion than to the necessaries of faith. Our fathers were often, and without any serious disadvantage, contented

to invent or to paint imaginary scenes for Biblical
events; but it is not the less true that the moral sense
and a judicious reverence lead us to desire that there
shall be nothing fantastic or false, even in these accessories of worship and devotion. I believe, too, that
the ignorance of our fathers about the Holy Land has
been greatly exaggerated. Doubtless, they possessed
none of our modern artistic resources, still less of our
scientific pretensions; but they knew the places so
well described in the Bible by the tradition of pilgrims,
and by the instinct of the heart.

It is not unintentional on the part of the Holy
Ghost, that the Scriptures, without aiming at picturesque descriptions, are, nevertheless, so graphic in
their details. They initiate us into the scenes and objects of Eastern life far better than many books of
travels. From our childhood, they have made us
familiar with the splendour of a Syrian sun, with the
palms of the desert, the vines of Engaddi, the tere-
binths of the valleys, and the cedars of the mountain.
We may have imagined the Mount of Olives less pale
and scorched than it is at the present day; but it was
not always under the rule of the scimitar. The childlike love which we imbibed from the Scriptures for
the "land of light," is, surely, not without influence on
our love for the Incarnate Word, and on the way in
which our whole life turns towards the heavenly
country where the sun never goes down. We are not
afraid to say that the Holy Ghost has always kept up
in His Church a certain knowledge of these lands,

sanctified by a thousand memories. Instead of being lost, this knowledge has increased, and become richer from age to age. Now—thanks to the progress of archæology and to modern inventions—we are, perhaps, better acquainted with Palestine as it was in the time of our Lord, than its inhabitants were 1500 years ago.

2. *Transition between the two Testaments. Teaching of the Divine Saviour.*

Every connection of ideas between the Old and New Testaments is full of salutary lessons. Teachings and memories are so intertwined, that they have become inseparable. The well of Jacob is still there, amidst the fertile fields of Samaria, but mingled with the memories of the ancient patriarch's pastoral life is that of the Shepherd of souls conversing with the woman of Samaria. The Jordan, rushing rapidly between its two borders of oleanders, slackens its course in the plain of Jericho at the spot where the ark passed at the head of the twelve tribes; but the pilgrims who come to bathe there do so chiefly in remembrance of the new Josue who made His baptism by John the inauguration of His public life; their souls seek the heavenly Dove, and call on the Voice of the Father; they look for the Guide Who is finally to lead them into the true Promised Land. If Nazareth and a few other places belong especially to the Gospel, and show that a new order of things has arisen, Bethlehem, Jerusalem, and the Temple preserve their former im-

portance, though their ancient glories are eclipsed by
those of the Presence and the merits of Jesus.

Let us study the lessons of the New Lawgiver, especially in what concerns the Temple. In one sense,
that sanctuary had lived its time at the moment of
the Incarnation. The Blessed Virgin was the new
Temple of the true God, or, rather, the Sacred Humanity Itself was eminently the true living Temple,
not built by the hand of man, but made and consecrated by the Spirit of life, so that Jesus was Himself to say: "Destroy this Temple, and in three days
I will raise It up."

And yet, consider how our Saviour acted with regard to the old Moria. The first act of the gospel-
drama takes place in its sanctuary. It is the announcement of the coming of the Forerunner of Christ to his
father Zachary, as he was praying before the altar of
incense. Jesus was not yet incarnate, but we must
recollect that it is He Who said, "Before Abraham
was, I am;" He Who governs all things by His Providence, and Who guides His saints as well as the stars
of heaven. We may, and ought, therefore, to ascribe
to Him the choice of the Temple for the promise of the
Precursor, the choice of the Golden Gate for the meeting of St. Joachim and St. Anne, and that of the sacred
cloisters for the life of retirement led by the Blessed
Virgin. After His Birth, He chose to be carried to
the Temple, and there to be proclaimed to the world
as the Great Victim by the lips of the holy old man
Simeon, and of the prophetess Anna. Again, He chose

to be taken there, when twelve years old, for the Pasch there to show Himself as the Teacher of the teachers of Israel, and to declare that there He had "to be about" the great "business" of His Heavenly Father.

When thirty years old, He goes there Himself, and His first exercise of authority is to use a scourge of cords to drive out the buyers and sellers: "Take these things hence," He said, "and make not the house of My Father a house of traffic." And we are told that His disciples remarked in this the fulfilment of the words of the holy King David: "The zeal of Thine house hath eaten me up" (St. John ii. 16; Ps. lxix. 9). Shortly before His Passion, He manifests the same zeal with still greater vehemence and authority, implying that His Father's house was His also: "Is it not written," He says, "'My house shall be called the house of prayer?' but you have made it a den of thieves" (St. Matt. xxi. 12; St. Mark xi. 17; St. Luke xix. 46). In the interval between these two acts of authority, He frequently chooses the Temple for the scene of His preaching and miracles. He teaches and acts as Master. As the time of His Passion approaches, He is there still oftener—and at last He teaches there daily. On the day of His triumphal entry into Jerusalem, He stops on beholding the city and Sanctuary, and weeps over those objects of His predilection. He turns His steps towards the Temple: He purifies it, He cures the blind and lame in it; the acclamations which had greeted His entry are redoubled, to the indignation of the chief priests: they ask Him to silence

7

the chorus of Hosanna; but instead of disclaiming them, He quotes their own canticles: "Have you not read," says He, "'Out of the mouth of infants and of sucklings Thou hast perfected praise?'"

The next day, and the next again, He returns thither, and prolongs His discourse to His disciples. It is as though He cannot abandon to His enemies the place of the great priesthood; and, in fact, He does not abandon it; the Jews themselves determine the scene of the great sacrifice and of the new covenant. Even when speaking to His disciples of the closing period of the world, it seems as though His attention were mainly fixed on the approaching fate of the Sanctuary. They call on Him to admire the strength of the building; but it only draws from Him words of sorrowful lament: "Jerusalem, Jerusalem . . . how often would I have gathered together thy children, as a hen doth gather her chickens under her wings, and thou wouldest not? . . . Verily I say unto you, there shall not be left a stone upon a stone that shall not be thrown down."

After His Death and Resurrection, He did not curse the place, which, nevertheless, He might well regard as the stronghold of deicide; He did not forbid His disciples to enter it; nay, long after, we see the apostle St. Paul praying and fulfilling his vows there; and St. Simeon, in spite of the memories of the Cœnaculum and of Calvary, passing his nights and days prostrate in prayer in the Holy of Holies. It was not till the last moment, when all the Christians had taken refuge

at Pella, that God allowed His angels to exclaim, " Let
us depart—let us depart hence."

Calvary is our new Moria: it deserves to be considered by itself. There, perhaps, recollections of the
Old Testament are not absolutely wanting; but the
grand figures of Adam and Melchisedech are only
seen in the dim distance, so as not to distract our
thoughts from the one Great Victim. Other places
may speak to the powers of the soul, Calvary
appeals in a special manner to the inmost depths of a
heart illuminated by faith. There is no place, no
temple, nothing in the world, that has received a consecration to be compared with that of Calvary. The
cave of Gethsemani was, indeed, watered by the bloody
sweat which was forced through all the pores of the
body of the Man-God; so, too, the hall of Scourging
received torrents of the Blood shed for the salvation
of the world; but no spot can be compared with Calvary for the solemnity of that baptism of Divine Blood
and its unbounded prodigality. It is no longer the
beginning of the sacrifice in the silence of the night,
and in the horrors of that dreadful hall; it is the offering of the holocaust in the full light of day, and before
the whole nation assembled for the Pasch. Judging
from the title on the Cross, there were Greeks and
Latins, as well as Jews present—the court of Herod
as well as that of the Roman governor: their troops
took part in the execution; hell had representatives
there; it was, apparently, its hour of triumph. . . .
But our Blessed Lady, too, was there, mingling her

unutterably sacred tears with the Divine Bloodshedding.
. . . John was there, and the holy women, and the
disciples, dumb with grief : the centurion and his band
struck their breasts, and owned the Divinity of Christ
in the immense humiliation of which they were witnesses, as well as in the stream of Blood which gushed
forth from the dead body.   In truth, that Blood came
from the Sacred Heart, not by the ordinary action of
human life, but by that of the Divine Person Who
still remained united to the body : the separated Soul
had gone down into the heart of the earth to visit the
souls of the just ; and it seemed as though the Divine
Blood rushed forth to follow it, and longed to penetrate no less far and deep that it might reach both the
living and the dead.

Behold Jesus on His Cross !—the stem rooted on
that barren hill.   It is the stem of Jesse, with its
Flower—the Tree of life, with its Fruit.   The Flower
is gathered, and the Fruit falls.   And the Mother of
Sorrows tenderly takes to herself that bruised Fruit.
Joseph of Arimathea assists at the solemn harvest.
He sows and buries in his garden the Divine Grain,
so soon to spring up and multiply throughout the
earth.

O Earth and Rocks of incomparable dignity, ye
have abundantly replaced the ancient Temple.   Ye
are now the religious centre of the world, and the
meeting-point of all the nations !   O Tomb of Jesus !
does not the whole universe flock to thy glorious
gates, to listen to the voice of Jesus echoing from thy

depths, and saying to all ages, " I am the Resurrection
and the Life. Every one that liveth and believeth in
Me shall not die for ever ?" Who will venture to contest the right of the Son of God to this land, purchased
by His Blood ? Certainly, the good Joseph of Arimathea would not be the one to assert his claim to his
garden and his tomb! And if those words are true,
" Blessed are the meek, for they shall inherit the land,"
who was ever so meek as the Lamb of Calvary, and
who, therefore, ever had so much right to possess the
earth ? And as He nowhere manifested His meekness
more than at the place where He was sacrificed, so
there is no spot more rightfully His than Calvary. It
ought to be the highest, the strongest, the most perfect of possessions. This would seem to be the logical
conclusion; but is it so in reality ? Have Calvary, the
Sepulchre, or the Cœnaculum, enjoyed the privileges of
the ancient Temple ? Have they taken its place ?
Have they become the metropolis of Christendom ? Is
Jerusalem itself the capital of the world, as it was of
the kingdom of Juda ? Yes, truly; but in a sense
which is not that of the world.

We cannot go through all the places mentioned in
the Bible, which were beloved by our Lord. It is only
necessary to read Guide-books to Holy Places, or even
passages in Protestant authors, to catch a glimpse
of the depths of holy contemplation presented by the
concordance of the Old and New Testaments, when
observed on the spot. Let us take, as our last instance,
the top of the Mount of Olives, with the panorama

spread below, and let us ask ourselves honestly whether it is likely that the scene of the Ascension was chosen undesignedly, and whether the study of its details can be a matter of little consequence to Christian knowledge and devotion.

Let us carry back our thoughts to the last lesson of our Saviour. He teaches us that those heavens, which are about to open to receive Him, will, in like manner, re-open on the Day of the Final Judgment.

The disciples, whose eyes are fixed on Him, see, in the background, the Mount of Offence, now waste and desolate, formerly the scene of the revelries of that king, the most ungrateful of all, because he might have been the holiest of the ancestors of Christ, and His most glorious type. Further back, their gaze wanders over the valley where Sodom and the other guilty cities once stood, now "a kind of gulph, at the bottom of which the Dead Sea gleams like a lake of molten metal."* Further still, under curse almost as heavy, stretches a long wall of mountains, in whose clefts lie the cities of Moab, and their magnificent tombs, which the Arab shares with the jackal. Mount Nebo alone breaks the hard line, whereon may be read the anathemas of the prophets, declaring that the only sign of life left to them shall be the howlings of wild beasts in the ruins of their cities. To the left, a line of verdure marks the course of the Jordan, and the boundaries of the Holy Land, properly so called. This is the background on

* Mgr. Mislin.

which His disciples see the figure of their Lord. Behind them, and beneath the Eyes of the Divine Saviour,
under His last blessing, lies first the Valley of Josaphat, associated by the prophets with the thought of
the Last Judgment, and that of Tophet, which recalls
the horrors of the eternal Gehenna. There are the
olive trees of Gethsemani, rows of tombs, the brook
Cedron. Then comes the Temple of Jerusalem—the
Temple over which it would seem that Jesus wept in
vain, and which nothing can save. Ah! if there were
any true and watchful souls in that Temple, they
would seek Him—they would know that He is there
before them, and that He is about to ascend in glory
—but there are no faithful, loving looks turned towards Him. Beyond the Temple are the streets along
which He went, shedding blessings on every side, and,
last of all, His Blood. There lies the much-loved Sion.
There, among the buildings which surround the Sepulchre of David, is hidden a new Temple, destined to
outlive the old one; the upper chamber, the first
Christian Church, in which Jesus Himself celebrated
the Pasch and the Holy Sacrifice. Farther off,
on the same side as the Tower of David, that
dark hill, almost lost amid houses and palaces, and
yet marked clearly by three crosses, is Calvary,
where was offered the first Sacrifice for the redemption
of the world. Rome lies in that direction; and when
Jesus blessed His apostles before rising, borne on the
bright cloud, He at the same time blessed our lands of
the West, and the future See of His Vicar on earth.

The mountains of Ephraim and Samaria complete the picture.

We will stop here. The little that has been said is enough to show how mysteries and memories crowd around the closing scenes of the Life of Jesus—how present, past, and future seem to meet together, and attend His last hour on earth.

The Christian world looks on Jerusalem as its country—its inheritance—and the metropolis of its affections. And yet, in the lapse of almost 1900 years after Christ, how often has she been, I do not say mistress and queen—I do not even say free and honoured —but merely exempt from the worst insults of slavery? It is not too easy to count the years in which this has been the case. There is a mystery, or, rather, a series of mysteries, strange, indeed, but closely answering to those of the life and death of the Son of God. These mysteries belong to an order of things, according to which Rome is a new Jerusalem, occupying the place between the old and the eternal one; the metropolis of the Holy Places of the whole world, as the ancient one was of Juda. Jerusalem can never be forgotten. She will always have her emphatically Patriarchal dignity. Her fate will always oe full of interest to Christendom. She will always be an object of loving meditation for holy souls. But it is by studying this new order of things in its completeness, that we shall best understand her exalted position.

CHAPTER XI.

HOLY POSSESSIONS UNDER THE NEW LAW.

1. *Mystery of Detachment.*

THE Incarnation of the Word brings us face to face with the most surprising contrasts. The coming of the Son of God destroys all the ideas and hopes of the carnal Jews, who were expecting a conquering Prince. Instead of a Jewish Nebuchodonosor or Alexander, succeeding the others as the founder of a fifth and last great empire, we see the Messias coming silently amidst the din and pre-occupations of Roman civilisation.

He had, as the Son of David, father, mother, and genealogy, yet He chose to be, in one sense, "without father, and without mother" (Heb. vii. 3), and His noble lineage was lost in the nameless gulph of poverty. He has not where to lay His Head; He does not consider Himself, or His own interests; He preaches detachment from riches and honours, both by word and example: He hides Himself when men wish to make Him a king; at the time of His Passion He declares His Kingdom not to be of that world, which He allows to take His last covering, reserving for Himself nothing but a Cross, a Crown of thorns, and a borrowed Tomb. In the Temple of Jerusalem He is in His own House, and no authority could have disputed His right to be worshipped there, and to speak as absolute Master:

and as a matter of fact He did drive out the sellers : in like manner if He had been pleased to enter the palace of His ancestors as its Lord, and to realise the dream of the Jews by the temporal conquest of the world, who would have opposed Him ? The nation would have been in His favour on the ground of the time-honoured rights of birth and of the yearnings of the world. Who would have thought of objecting to His rights, those of Rome and its governors, so recent, and so unscrupulously acquired ? Or, to go farther back, who would have put in opposition to Him the equivocal, inconstant, and more than doubtful authority of an Antiochus, a Ptolemy, or a Herod ?

He chose to die, because death is a final sacrifice, a final abnegation, a final detachment from earthly things. When He rose, it was not to lead a life again in the world, He revealed to His disciples a Heavenly life with new detachments. Shall we speak of His Eucharistic life ? There He appears without human form or power, incapable of exercising any rights, even that of defending or possessing Himself.

2. *Nevertheless, Sanctity may and ought to possess the Earth, under the Law of Grace.*

Has sanctity, then, less power over matter and space after the Incarnation than before ? Is it possible that the Incarnate Word has left a memory of Himself in certain spots, and imbued them with sanctifying power, without protecting any part of them from profanation, oblivion, or caprice ? Has He for ever abandoned for

Himself and His people, every heritage and gift, reserving not an inch of ground, not even a refuge which He may share with the poor and the orphan? Is He to have a home nowhere? Has He refused for Himself all share and exercise both of ordinary possession, and of that supreme possession which touches the earth from above, reaches it from afar, and harmonises with the rights, interests, and welfare of the multitude? No, I read nowhere in Scripture that the Man-God has formally renounced the exercise of the powers which He assumed in order to make Himself like men, and to live with them. He wills the end, and the ordinary means of attaining it. Doubtless He has Divine means of establishing peace and harmony amongst those whom He calls His brethren, for maintaining the poor and the rich, the weak and the powerful in a happy union, for organising talent, industry, and all vital forces, for promoting great undertakings, and guiding human society towards its end. But, as a rule, He prefers obtaining all these objects by human means rather than by miracles. His Divine Sovereignty, then, is not satisfied with a few grains of incense, but He takes and receives, at the proper time and place, from the love and free offering of men, His useful, just, and suitable share of possession and earthly sovereignty. He might have chosen to disdain the support afforded by human influence; but He prefers to sanctify it as well as everything else; it is His pleasure that there should be holy rights, holy kingdoms, possessions of every sort specially belonging to sanctity—sanctity in every form, and, above all, in its most exalted types. It would have been contrary to the fitness of things, if, after His coming into the world, there had been absolutely nothing to mark the virginal dominion of sanctity over matter. No, it was not in vain that He took His place among persons with a capacity for enjoying, possessing, and reigning: His design was to elevate that capacity into the power of a Divine capacity, and its human rights to the power of Divine ones.

As the High-Priest, Jesus was to sacrifice all things, to offer up all creation to His Heavenly Father. Now in order to sacrifice all things, one must possess them all. Men, it is true, may sacrifice vain hopes, chimerical unrealities. But when the Word Incarnate is concerned, unreal offerings cannot be. He came, therefore, with titles and rights which He might have made use of, but some He has offered in silent adoration, whilst others He has proclaimed before men to make His surrender of them more solemn and authentic.

We know from Scripture that God His Father has given Him all things by a comprehensive promise. The nations are to be His inheritance, and the ends of the earth His possession: He is the Heir of all things; the Son of Adam, of Abraham, and of David; all blessings of humanity, of descents, and of royal inheritance, meet on His anointed Head. He chose to be born, even proving by miracles that He was born in the royal city of Bethlehem, of the house and family of the kings of Juda: He chose that His coming into the world should be hailed by the worship of angels and Magi in that city of His ancestors. He drew to Himself gifts, hearts, and wills: He declared Himself to be a King, and born for a Kingdom—"Ego ad hoc natus sum." He passionately desired, even at the price of the Cross, the dominion which was promised Him as King of kings and Lord of lords, not only of souls, but of humanity as a whole.

True, He said that His Kingdom was not of this world, and when the people of Galilee resolved to make Him a king, He fled into the mountains; but this was to teach us that His authority is not originally derived from below, and that He does nòt choose to establish by merely worldly means a power which is not, like the world, transitory. Neither He nor any of His followers ever consented to play the part of a common pretender, who imposes upon the enthusiasm of the crowd, deceives them by intrigue and audacity, forces himself between the Herods and the Cæsars, seizes first one city, then another, then a province, robs treasures, pays troops, and defeats his adversaries.

He does not say one word to condemn or even to disclaim the idea of the Galilean multitude : He merely "passes on," having at the time a fuller and sublimer mission to fulfil. His Kingly dignity comes out in fiery characters even in the depths of the insults of the Passion. It is upon this point that the accusations of the Pharisees rest: "Art Thou a King, then ?" Pilate asks Him. "Thou sayest it," answers the Saint of saints, "for this was I born." There is not even a circumstance in the brutal sports of the soldiers without its character of unintentional prophecy in this direction. They clothe Him in a ragged purple garment, they place in His Hands a reed for a sceptre, and a crown of thorns on His Head, and they prostrate themselves before Him, saying, "Hail, King of the Jews." Pilate unconsciously goes on with the idea, and writes on the title over the Cross, "Jesus of Nazareth, the King of the Jews."

"Le Roi est mort: Vive le Roi!" After Jesus, King of the Jews, comes Jesus, King of the Catholic world. His Death purchases the prerogative of drawing all to Himself, and the still more amazing one of surviving Himself, and of being His own Heir. "He will give the ungodly the charge of His Burial," the prophet had said, "and the rich for His Death . . . because His Soul hath laboured, He shall see and be filled. . . . The multitude will be allotted to Him, and He shall divide the spoils of the strong" (Is. liii.).

Not till the root of Jesse shall be set up as a standard are the nations to be gathered together: it is then that the sacrifice and oblation of the holy Victim is to be multiplied from east to west; and whilst, during His mortal life, He was only sent to the lost sheep of the house of Israel, and that within the ordinary limits allotted to men, Jesus the Victim is to know no limits save those of the ends of the earth. He loses nothing of His personality nor of His rights by being hidden under weak appearances: He is none the less recognised by the faithful as present in all His majesty

human and Divine; capable of possessing, and "worthy
to receive all power, and glory, and honour" (Apoc.
v. 12). And so, wherever He finds souls that are prepared He enriches them with the priceless gifts of His
grace, and receives in exchange, sometimes the shelter
of a day, sometimes a temple to last for ages, sometimes
a humble alms, sometimes royal munificence. He receives, according to need, opportunity, or devotion,
the hospitality of a catacomb, or that of a basilica.
Every Christian city, every village must possess the
Heavenly Guest, and assign a sanctuary to Him. For
Him Constantine will make Rome a new Jerusalem
and Italy a new Palestine more open to the movements of the world. The Middle Ages will assign to
Him in the person of His visible Vicar a high dominion : they will recognise the Eucharistic King as
being by right, and for ever, the Liege-Lord of Christendom and of the world. Such, indeed, Jesus ought
to be, and such He will be whenever princes care to
rest their rights on something more than the force of
bayonets, the intrigues of diplomacy, the stones of a
barricade, the calculations of a vain balance of power,
or the trickery of finance. Such He will be, according
to all appearances, when the great reign, before the
end of the world, shall come.

It would be to the interest of the kings and people
of all ages solemnly to renew this homage. But how
few there are who are able to take in in one glance the
things of the world and those of faith. Without denying the Eucharistic King, the great ones of the world

see with the eyes of the flesh that He is weaker than a child, and that He reigns as though not reigning. Now and then they condescend to be His foster-fathers and guardians, but only on condition of keeping Him in a perpetual minority.

As to His complete emancipation in the person of His ministers, they will not hear of it; they will not hear of His supremacy in politics, in finance—anywhere; they are afraid of it; they employ legions of sophists to put hindrances in the way.

Year after year, century after century, the faithful soul continues to find Jesus, as at Bethlehem, wrapped in swaddling clothes, and in this nineteenth century she still sings—

> " Poor and lowly is He born,
> Though all the world is His."

Still, as at Bethlehem, kings and shepherds make their offerings to Him, but very often those made by the first are for decency and form's sake. The powers of the world may not always go so far as to refuse to the Vicar of Jesus Christ the shadow of temporal power necessary for his independence and free action; but they take care to make more or less ridiculous the rag of purple which they grudge him, and are ready to rob him of it a moment afterwards.

But, in spite of all, the Eucharistic King continues His meek conquest of the world; He multiplies His chapels, His altars, and His saints. His rule extends beyond that of kings; with or against their will, He passes through their kingdoms, and proclaims the independence of sanctity in the wigwam of the savage and the snow-hut of the Esquimaux.

CHAPTER XII.

THE WONDERFUL VARIETY OF THE HOLY PLACES.

WE say, "I believe in the *Holy Catholic* Church." From her infancy, the Church has spread the network of sanctity in every direction, multiplying its knots and strengthening its cords as time went on, so that nothing might escape her influence. We believe, or rather we see this, and therefore we have faith in her. From the ever-increasing and ever-renewed diffusion of the sanctifying power, results an exceeding beauty, an infinite variety of forms, of memories, and of associations of ideas. It is an outward clothing, indeed, but the clothing of a queen, in which the variety of the pattern can only be compared with the richness of the texture.

We have already seen how the memories of the Old and New Testament blended together in the ancient soil of Judea. Now eighteen centuries of pilgrimages, of devotion of every sort, of painful, constant, and loving labour have, so to speak, added their embroidery to the fabric which was so fair already.

And, turning to the rest of the world, we see the Divine Gardener transplanting on every side, into every city and every climate, the traditions of Bethlehem and Nazareth, of the Temple and Calvary; in a word, all the names and memories of Juda. On lofty mountains, in deep defiles, on the sea-shore, in the desert, in great cities, the holy associations of Judea are intermingled with new lights, new legends, new traditions. What histories are those of the catacombs and churches of Rome! What bibles are the annals and works of more than one monastery! The daily chronicle of certain places of pilgrimage is a real gospel, with this difference: that formerly "Jesus *went about* doing good;" now He *remains*, and can say to those who visit Him, "Go and tell the world what you have seen and heard—the blind see, the lame walk, the lepers are made clean, the deaf hear, the dead rise again, to the poor the Gospel is preached; in a word, all the diseases of body and soul are tended and cured." Poor labourers of Lyons, poor shepherds of the Alps, poor sufferers in the Paris faubourgs, do not complain that Jerusalem is so far off, that there is no Pool of Probatica for you, and that the times of Jesus are past. See, there is Fourvières, Laus, Einsiedeln, Nôtre Dame des Victoires, and many other shrines, less famous, but scarcely less favoured. O Canterbury, when will thy ways rejoice again?

Not to speak of places of pilgrimage, how many outposts and citadels of sanctity there are, even in the heart of our modern Babylons! Here it is the hospital ward, that sanctuary of holy death-beds, tended by brothers and sisters who have become our angels, and by angels who have become our brothers and sisters. Farther on, it is the private oratory, the refuge, the garret, sanctified by a combination of poverty, patience, and charity. Outside the city, I find the way-side cross and the village church; nay, even the fields and houses are made holy to me by labour, innocence, and the domestic virtues, although there is nothing official and patent in this sanctification.

There is, too, the variety with which every period, nation, civilisation, and climate, stamp religious monuments. Look at our cathedrals, those wonders of art and genius, aided by the riches and inventions of centuries; their aspect tells of the ages which have passed over them, and of the indefatigable zeal of the saints for the House of God. Away with the narrow spirit which would fain represent its one stiff arch, its grotesque heraldic figures and gargoyles, as the complete *ne plus ultra* of religious art!

Christian art is genius directed by knowledge and piety, which says to itself, "I will use the lessons of the past, the progress of the arts and of industry—all forms and all treasures; I will borrow ideas and methods from the Greeks, the Egyptians, the Hindoos, from ancients and from moderns; above all, I will study nature and her infinite fertility of form; I will strive to produce something nobler, grander, and lovelier than the eye of man has ever yet seen; and when all is done, it will be but an unworthy dwelling—a Bethlehem—for Christ; but others after me will do better things."

There are natural harmonies between art and different climates, works, and nations. The " hypæthra " would be as much out of place in Lapland as a northern church would be out of place under the equator. Or—not to go so far—place an Italian church, with its light and frescoes, in the centre of one of our foggy, smoky, northern capitals; before five years are over, our dim light will fall on black and gray, and you will seek in vain for gilding and colour. If it is a private chapel, a nobleman may be able to give himself the pleasure of restoring the whole from time to time; but for a cathedral, what is required is decoration by stone, and marble, and stained glass. which defies time, and withstands the wear and tear of the elements. Does not nature herself, by her distribution of materials, teach us to vary them, and not to use brick, granite, or cedar, exclusively and everywhere ?

Apart from these natural reasons, there are a multitude of others, which prove that, according to the intention of Providence, there ought to be an incomparable pliability in Christian art, which should adapt itself to everything. In its way of treating Holy Places, it should be, as it were, a universal poem, full of rhythm and unity, sung by the Church in praise of her Spouse. The subject of the great epic is, and always will be, the Life of her Beloved in this world —the lowly Birth, the Life, the Retirement, the

Patience, the Death, the Tomb, the Resurrection, the Immortality, the Expansion, the Glory, the Eternal Youth, the Eternal Love of Christ.

Variety is produced by the continuation of this same life of Christ in His mystical members, that is to say, in other lives, other climates, mingled with different and endless perfumes, loves, and memories.

One of the providential reasons for this variety in Holy Places, their forms and associations, is, that it is intended to act physiologically on young souls. It has an influence on their conceptions of piety and of the things of God. It gives them *the flavour of the soil.* Combined with the differences of race, of temperament, and of vocation, it helps to give both to bodies and individuals their special stamp—their originality of spiritual life and of sanctity.

CHAPTER XIII.

PERMANENCE AND INVIOLABILITY.

THE same variety which we have remarked in the mysteries and forms of the Holy Places of the New Law is to be found also in their degrees of permanence. As in the human body there are bones, flesh, and fluids, as in the globe there are granite, dust, and water, so, too, in the providential distribution of Holy Places, some convey to us the idea of solidity and stability, while others represent the mobility, expansion, and liberty of life.

We need not repeat what has been said in general of this permanence and liberty, but both the one and the other have a particular aspect under the Law of grace; and the means by which permanence is secured are especially worthy of our study.

To the missionary peculiarly belong the joys, the sorrows, and the consolations of the ancient nomadic patriarchs, those of Jesus and Mary, in their journeyings; to infant missions, to new convents, and new works of all sorts, Bethlehem-like joys, dawning hopes, hired stable, and poverty. To Christian communities of old date belong the sunset glories of Sion, the grand ruin and rebuilding; the rock-tombs, whence a revived sanctity will emerge.

Naturally, everything belonging to men and their institutions passes away, grows old, changes, fades, and is forgotten. Monuments and titles would not be sufficient to rescue places from this general law. A special providence and the care of the Church are requisite. The means of preservation resemble those of acquisition. On the part of God, it is by continuing and multiplying His presence, by answering the prayers of the faithful, by enlightening and consoling them, by increasing in every possible way the stream of His ordinary or miraculous favours, that He preserves His titles, written more lastingly in the hearts of men than in stone, and inclines those who love Him to maintain His rights. Elsewhere, He bends wills and events, and makes even the opposition and the passions of His enemies a means of defending

His Church from invasions, covetousness, and destructive fury.

The Church is, by its constitution, a visible and regularly organised society, to which God has committed the guardianship of holy things. Thus she must of necessity be concerned with Holy Places. Doubtless, she places her main reliance on Him Who rules and directs chance events, and the capricious wills of men. She believes in Providence, but she also knows that Providence requires our co-operation, and does not dispense us from the obligation of doing our duty. The Church, then, has taken possession of Holy Places, as of a Divine treasure falling naturally to her guardianship. In the first place, she claims those which are, in a sense, above all consecration, because they have been solemnly marked by Divine acts. As to the rest, she verifies their origin, and regulates their consecration. She has in her liturgy various formulas drawn up with regard to their degrees of sanctity, and in conformity with their destination. She fixes which is to be the object of an ordinary benediction, and which demands a higher and more irrevocable consecration ; what can be done by a simple priest, and what is reserved for the bishop, or even for the Bishop of bishops, the Vicar of the Eternal High-Priest.

Even when less important benedictions and temporary consecrations are in question, she will have nothing completely left to arbitrary choice or caprice. What has been once withdrawn from common use, ought not to be lightly and inconsiderately given back to it.

Once in possession of a place, the Church regulates its purpose and destination. She gives the greatest liberty to the arts and to various tastes; but, at the same time, she has her own especial tastes, laws, and traditions, by which she gives to her works a stamp of venerableness and of duration. She watches over their honour and their preservation; and, in order to defend them each in its degree of sanctity, or of social and religious importance, she surrounds them, as it were, with a rampart of holy laws and institutions.

Next to ecclesiastical doctrines and persons, there is nothing that the Church has guarded by severer warnings and penalties than her sanctuaries, and those establishments where devotion is combined with charity and science.

She has defended them, not only by laws, rules, and anathemas, but also by all other means in her power: she has not spared the life, the treasures, and the blood of her children in this cause. With this object she founded religious orders, and orders of knighthood, preached the Crusades, encouraged leagues of St. Sebastian, blessed and sanctioned the holy pertinacity which acknowledges and defends at any cost the rights of the Lamb of God. The "seides" of violence may come and unite with legions of lawyers and disputants to contest the claims of Christ and His Church, yet simple souls will continue to regard the acknowledgment of His rights as the safeguard of all others, of all possessions, and of all lives. They will answer all sophists by identifying themselves more and more with Christ, so as to reign with Him by love—possess the world with Him, or die on the Cross in the attempt.

CHAPTER XIV.

TEACHING OF THE RITUAL IN THE CONSECRATION OF SANCTUARIES.

THE best way of understanding the mind of the Church in this matter is to turn to her ritual and other canonical books. It is from her authenticated, authorised, traditional prayers—prayers inspired by the Holy Ghost Himself, because it is His Will to hear and to grant them—that we are most sure of understanding her intention.

1. *Plans and Preparations.*

Let us see how she regulates the consecration of a church. Everything is arranged beforehand, with a view to security in the future, and to making a deep impression on the people. No other ceremony, not even the ordination of a bishop, occupies so large a space in the liturgical books.

As the first step, the bishop of the diocese must be consulted. He has to give his approbation to the site, the plan, the dimensions; to settle the amount of the dowry to be given to this *Bride*, who, as yet, exists only in intention. The site is usually a central spot,

and yet sufficiently isolated to be undisturbed by all
profane sounds.   As a rule, it is surrounded by the
quiet churchyard.

The church herself is a sweet and fitting burial-place
for her ministers and dearest children; and the altar
ought to be, more or less, a holy tomb.   The assembly
(Ecclesia) of the living, the mediatrix between the
suffering and the triumphant Church, will take her
place on the surface of the earth, as it were, between
the two kingdoms.   Its walls and arches should be
adorned, if possible, as an image of Heaven, a reflection of the Heavenly Jerusalem, the kingdom of the
saints and angels.   On them the virtues and the conflicts of these friends of God ought to be fitly represented.

Another important point is that there should be
a living body of ministers, to act as the visible
angels of the church, and as they are subject to the
necessities of mortal life, it is the prelate's duty to pro-
vide, with the help of Providence, for their honourable subsistence.

2. *The First Stone.*

The second preliminary is the blessing of the first
stone by the bishop or his deputy.   This chosen block
is the type of that foundation-stone of the Corner on
which rests the spiritual building of the whole Church.
It is waiting there, as Christ waits for His ministers,
in all His mysteries of grace.   The officiating bishop
first takes possession of the land, by sprinkling holy

water, to "deliver it from all possession of the unclean spirit, and to replace all terror of the infernal serpent by the gracious presence of the Holy Spirit," and then by planting the wooden cross.

He prays to the Lord God Whom heaven and earth cannot contain, and Who, nevertheless, deigns to make His dwelling-place among men ; he implores Him, "by the intercession of the Blessed Virgin, the saints, and the intended patron of the church, to look with an eye of mercy upon the newly-chosen spot, to purify it by His grace, to preserve in it this supernatural purity, and to bring to a happy issue the intentions of His servants, as He brought those of His well-beloved David by the hands of his son Solomon."

In another prayer he passes on to more recent memories, and reminds our Lord that He is Himself the Corner-stone, the Foundation-stone, hewn out of the mountain by no human hand ; and not the less so, because He was the Stone rejected by human madness. He beseeches Him Who chose the apostle St. Peter to be, with Himself, the firm foundation on which He builds His Church, to make his undertaking a part of that Divine scheme, whose beginning dates from the creation, and whose end shall be consummated in glory.

Remembering that, "unless the Lord build the house, they labour in vain that build it"—(Ps. cxxvi.) —the servant of the Lord lays, in his Master's Name, the first stone of the new building to be cemented by faith, the fear of God, and brotherly charity.

After a second sprinkling and more prayers, the

choir is emboldened to sing the words of Jacob at the moment of the great vision of Bethel: " How terrible is this place! this is no other but the House of God and the gate of Heaven." And then the visions of the old and the new Jerusalem mingle together in its memory, and it sings, with holy King David—" Her foundations are in the holy mountains. The Lord loveth the gates of Sion above all the tabernacles of Jacob. Glorious things are said of thee, O city of God. Rahab, Babylon, who know me, the Philistine, Tyre, and the people of the Ethiopians found in thee their meeting-place. Shall not Sion say: A Man is born in her, a Man the Highest Himself, Who founded her. The Lord shall tell in His writings of peoples and of princes, of them that have been in her. O holy mansion! the joy of all seems to rest in thee " (Ps. lxxxvi.).

" May eternal peace from the Lord dwell in this house," the bishop continues : " may the Word of God, the Everlasting Peace, be Himself the peace of this abode; may the Merciful Paraclete be Himself the pledge of this peace."

He entreats the Lord, Who, without any infringement of holy unity, multiplies dwelling-places in His Heavenly kingdom, to be pleased to bless, sanctify, and consecrate the future building; then, supported by the choir, he sings—

" I rejoiced at the things that were said to me : we shall go into the House of the Lord. Our feet were standing in expectation in thy courts, O Jerusalem !

"Jerusalem, a well-planned city in every part ; its treasures are enjoyed by all.

"For thither did the tribes go up, the tribes of the Lord, the testimony of Israel, to praise the Name of the Lord.

"All sitting as judges, all enthroned as kings in the house of David.

"Pray for the things that are for her peace. O Jerusalem! plentifulness is for them that love thee.

"Let peace be in thy strength, and abundance in thy towers " (Ps. cxxii.).

The ceremony ends with the "Veni Creator," the pontifical benediction, and the proclamation of indulgences.

All this is only a preparatory blessing; the Holy Place is as yet but a bare field, and one cannot help asking, what more can the bishop say when he returns to consecrate the building in all the freshness of its first beauty ?

3. *The Consecration.*

At the head of the clergy and people, the consecrating bishop reaches the place where lie the relics destined to be placed beneath the altar.

After the Psalms and Litanies, he sprinkles the outside walls of the church, while the choir chants the anthem of the prophet's vision—

" The mountain of the house of the Lord shall be prepared on the top of mountains, and it shall be exalted above the hills, and all nations shall flow unto it . . . and say: Glory to Thee, O Lord! The new comers shall come with joyfulness, carrying their sheaves. They shall say, Glory to Thee, O Lord!"

On arriving at the great door, the bishop knocks at it with the foot of his crosier; and using the words which David puts in the mouth of the Everlasting High-Priest when entering Heaven, he lifts his voice in His Name—

"Lift up your gates, O ye Princes, and be ye lifted up, O eternal gates! The King of Glory demands entrance."

A deacon from the inside—"Who is this King of Glory?"

The bishop—"The Lord Who is strong and mighty; the Lord mighty in battle."

Thrice the bishop finds the door shut, thrice he repeats the sprinkling of the outer walls, knocks at the door, and recommences the dialogue; but the next time all the clergy, lifting their voices with the bishop's, repeat—

"It is the Lord of Hosts: He is the King of Glory! Open, open, open!"

Then the bishop, making the sign of the Cross on the door, says, by himself, "Behold the sign of the Cross! let every hostile spectre vanish!"

The door opens, and he enters, saying, "Peace be to this house!"

The choir—"From the Lord, may everlasting peace reign in this house; may the Word of the Father, the

Eternal Peace, be Himself the Peace of this dwelling; may the Merciful Paraclete be here Himself the Pledge of Peace. Zaccheus (and all you, sinners like him, who desire to see the Lord, I invite you in His Name), make haste, and come down, for this day I must abide in your house; this day is salvation come to this house from God. Alleluia."

Then follow the "Veni Creator," the Litany of the saints, the "Benedictus," and the accompanying prayers.

Next, two lines of ashes having been sprinkled diagonally on the pavement of the church, the bishop writes in them the Greek and Latin alphabet, as though to express that henceforward the very dust of that place is to preach the Alpha and Omega, the elements of the Faith, to the Greeks and the Gentiles. Everything, from the roof to the pavement, from the baptismal font to the sanctuary, from the pulpit and the tribunal of penance to the tabernacle, is to instruct the souls of the faithful.

The bishop now moves towards the high altar. Thrice, each time in a louder voice, he invokes the assistance of God, and then mixes together water, salt, ashes, and wine, to sprinkle the sanctuary, where, henceforward, souls are to be purified, not only by the tears of repentance, but still more by the salt of heavenly doctrine, by the consuming annihilations of adoration, and by the inebriation of eucharistic love. He blesses each of these different ingredients individually, then altogether; and raising his soul to the

Source of all pure and fruitful benediction, he prays that this place may be "the effusion of His spiritual treasures, the destruction of the powers of hell, and the protection of the angels of light."

"May Thy blessing," he says, "secure the duration of this dwelling, begun in Thy Name, and completed by Thy assistance. May this roof be sheltered by Thy protection. May these doors admit Thee, and this sanctuary receive Thee. May the light of Thy Countenance be an assurance of stability to these walls, and of Thy favours to the worshippers within them."

He next signs the door twice inside with the sign of the Cross, chanting the blessings it has gained us; then, after sprinkling the walls with holy water, he proceeds to bless and consecrate the altar. He prays the God of all sanctification—the God Who embraces in the bosom of His mercy the blessings of Heaven and of earth—to vouchsafe Himself to dedicate, illuminate, and glorify this building destined to the celebration of the sacred mysteries. May He deign henceforth graciously to receive every one who shall come here to worship Him. May He grant his prayers! May He protect and cover him with an everlasting defence, so that the faithful, happy, and contented with the bonds of religion may persevere in the confession of the Holy Trinity, and in the Catholic Faith.

He invokes the blessing of the Holy Ghost on this house of prayer, of prayer which shall be heard:

" O Holy and Blessed Trinity, the Purity, Beauty, and
Loveliness of all things; O Divine Majesty, filling, containing, and disposing all things; deign to stretch
forth that Hand whose office is to sanctify, to enrich, and to bless.   May this church rejoice in the
treasures of an inexhaustible sanctification !   In this
centre of priestly sacrifices and of general supplications,
may the sinner be eased of the load beneath which
he groans !   May sin be expiated !   May disease, sickness, leprosy, blindness of soul and body, find here
their perfect healing !   May the devils be put to flight,
and all things be made new by the meeting of every
kind of misery with the Sovereign Mercy of God !"

The holy water before mentioned is used, not only
for the different aspersions, but also for preparing the
cement which is to fasten up the relics in the altar.
The relics and the holy chrism are fetched, during
which time antiphons are chanted, commemorating
the mysterious relations which exist between the
Church of the Saints in Heaven, and the churches
built by the children of men.

Before re-entering the building, the bishop gives an
instruction to the people crowding round the entrance.
Enshrined in the ritual and language of the Church,
it is preserved from the influences of time and circumstance, and, soaring above the material or legislative
ruins accumulated by revolutions, heresies, and other
human accidents, it countersigns the aspirations and
the thoughts of Catholicity in every age.   Here it is:—

" The sacred canons, the laws of the Church, and the

universal practice of worship, as understood by the
mind of the faithful, combine to teach us, dear brethren, how reverently we ought to regard churches and
other places consecrated to God. The holy sacrifice
ought to be regularly offered in all solemnity to the
Lord in His sacred temples; for, according to His command, given to Moses, the tabernacle, with the tables,
the altar, and the brazen vessels, were to be consecrated
before being employed in the Divine worship. The
tabernacle received unction and consecration, and none
but the holy priests and Levites, clad in sacred vest-
ments, were permitted to touch the Divine symbols,
and to offer oblation for the people. In after times, the
Hebrew kings had their temple, and Christian princes
basilicas built by their care. They held them in the
highest veneration, and desired that no noise of the
world or stir of business should come near them, no
common or secular affairs disturb the house of prayer.
Privileges and immunities were attached to them,
guarded by the severest penalties; for it was justly
considered that the dwelling-places of the Most High
ought not to be exposed to audacious presumption,
and treated, according to the expression of the Truth
Himself, like a den of thieves. It is, in fact, a place
of safety—a harbour for the shipwrecked—a haven
during the storm. It is a place of supplication, where
every right prayer is granted. It is a place of refuge,
where the criminal finds impunity for his misdeeds in
the prayer of the priesthood. With great reverence,
therefore, dear brethren, ought we to approach the

sacred temples of the Lord ; and the hearts which offer oblation to this Divine Master should be pure from all sin. Among other churches, you have requested us to consecrate this one (enriched with privileges by the sovereign Pontiffs, and built by your care). Moved by your pious wishes, we dedicate it to the service of Almighty God, of the Blessed Virgin Mary, of all the saints, and especially of its blessed patrons, N. and N.

"I take this opportunity of pointing out to you the obligation of paying to the churches and their priests the just dues which God has reserved to Himself as a sign of His universal dominion.

"'Tithes,' says St. Augustine, 'are the tribute of needy souls.' In return for this offering you will receive, not only the abundance of the fruits of the earth, but also health of soul and body; for the Lord your God desires your service far more than your riches; and if He Who has given you everything condescends to receive any offering at your hands, it is for your sake rather than His own. Hence, what is a sinful refusal, or even a mere delay in paying to God His portion of your wages, your gains, your labours, but a defrauding of yourselves, through avarice, of a double blessing for earth and for heaven? And do you know how God, in His justice, usually recalls transgressors to their duty? What has been withheld from the priests you will abandon to the impious soldier. What has been refused to Christ shall be consumed by the exchequer. 'Return to Me,' says the

9—2

Lord, by the mouth of a prophet, 'and I will return to you. And you have said, Wherein shall we return? Shall a man outrage God as you did outrage Me? Wherein, you say, do we outrage Thee? In tithes and in first-fruits. And you are cursed with want, because you outrage Me, even the whole nation of you. Bring all the tithes into the storehouse, that there may be meat in My house, and try me in this, saith the Lord, if I open not unto you the flood-gates of Heaven, and pour out a blessing even to abundance. And I will rebuke for your sakes the devourer, and he shall not spoil the fruit of your land: neither shall the vine in the field be barren, saith the Lord of Hosts. And all nations shall call you blessed: for you shall be a delightful land, saith the Lord of Hosts' (Mal. iii. 7—11). Keep these words in mind, dear brethren, and let your readiness show that you understand them. Learn by the small sacrifice of your worldly goods to merit everlasting rewards."

The archdeacon reads then the decrees renewed by the Council of Trent concerning the rights of property of churches, setting forth that whosoever, cleric or laic, even if he were of imperial dignity, through fear, violence, or artifice, shall dare to divert from their object, or to usurp any goods, rights, or revenues whatever, belonging to churches, is, *ipso facto*, under anathema, and deprived of every privilege till such time as he shall make restitution.

The bishop resumes. He addresses the founders, and explains to them that their liberality must not be an isolated act with no bearing on the future. A church cannot be left to itself: it requires the priest-hood, the sacred ministry chosen from among men. She is a bride with her attendants; a bride to be dowered and maintained according to her rank. She will not be ungrateful: she has privileges in store for her fathers and guardians, and she will remember them at the fitting time.

The procession re-enters the church. The bishop takes the holy chrism—that oil which consecrates the hands and head of the bishop—and begins, at the entrance-door, the successive anointings, which he will continue to the altar-stone, and even to the walls of the building, as if to declare that hence-forth this place is to be regarded as occupying on the face of the earth the same standing which the priesthood does in human society, and that there is in it a continuation, a dependency, an extension, of the eternal priesthood, of which Jesus Christ is the source and the fulness.

The officiating prelate places the relics in the "*tomb*" of the altar, and fixes with cement the stone which is to secure them, recalling to the mind of the choir the Divine altar of the Apocalypse, under which St. John heard the martyrs crying with a loud voice for the appointed time of the Lord. " How long," they say, " dost Thou not revenge our blood?" And this was the Divine reply : that they should rest " for a little time, till the number of their brethren should be filled up."

After again anointing the altar, both with the oil of the catechumens and the holy chrism, he continues the anointings all round the church, at each of the twelve places marked by a cross, according to the number of the gates of the mystical Jerusalem. He returns to the altar, sprinkles it again, and at the same time burns, at the five crosses of anointing, grains of incense and little candles, crosswise, symbolising the union of the mysteries of adoration and prayer with that of the Great Sacrifice. These transient symbols do, in fact, herald the great eucharistic holocaust, and the bishop beseeches God to have respect, by anticipation, to the Divine sacrifice which is to be offered on this stone.

' Then comes another solemn preface. The bishop addresses the Eternal Father, Who regards the interior clothing of faithful souls as the chief ornament of His temples. He implores Him to vouchsafe to flood this church and altar with His blessings and graces of holiness. He invokes the help of the angels of light, and the illumination of the Holy Spirit. He calls to mind the blessings granted of old to Abraham, Isaac, and Jacob, and begs of God to hear the prayers and bless the offerings made in this place, and to cause those blessings to return to those who make them.

"May the title of this church, which is Thine," he continues, "be eternal! May it have a table always spread for the heavenly banquet of souls. Do Thou, O Lord, by the words of Thy Divine Mouth, bless the oblations laid on this altar. After having blessed them, do Thou accept them, and may we find, by a close union with them, the gifts of eternal life."

The last anointing is given to the altar and its base, where it joins the rest of the building; for, thanks to the Holy Spirit, every part is consecrated together in the plan of Divine Love, which begins by the edification of the Church, and is perfected in eternity.

4. *Other dispositions.*

If we pass from the ritual to the liturgical books, we find in them the magnificent offices of Dedication. It is the desire of the Church that we should preserve the remembrance of the solemn consecration. In order that we may better appreciate the lowly house which God has been graciously pleased to accept from us on earth, she transports us in spirit to our heavenly country, and there shows us the " vision of peace," the glorious Spouse of the Everlasting Bridegroom, the Jerusalem of the angels, built of living stones, in the number of which we are to find our secret place according as the blows and trials of life have shaped and polished us like precious stones.

We might go on multiplying the liturgical testimonies, but those already quoted are sufficient to show the mind of the Church with regard to the respect due to her consecrated sanctuaries, and to their inviolability. But, it will be said, the fact remains that the Church, with or against her will, has to yield to time and human progress. She decrees, indeed, that her churches

and other property shall be eternal, much as ancient
Rome did with regard to the temples of her gods; but
death removes her benefactors, one nation displaces
another, wars and dissensions arise, ideas and requirements change; the elements, too, do their work, some
slowly, like the worm eating away in secret, others
with the rapidity of lightning; councils may utter
their anathemas, but the manufactory and the market
take the place of the convent and the church all the
same; the manufactory and the market-place pass
away in their turn, and nameless ruins are left.

This is what we see with our eyes. The Church
knows all this—she knows better than any one that
the fashion of the world passeth away, and that the
whole earth is to be destroyed by fire; she knows that
miracles of preservation are exceptional cases, the secret
of which is revealed to her only in part. She knows
that ruins, like scandals, are necessary; but she is constantly re-acting upon both scandals and ruins; she is
eminently conservative. As far as she is able, she preserves in its freshness the mantle of beauty which was
always intended to cover everything holy. And—
when there is nothing more that she can do, she does
her best to reserve desecration itself to the pious and
reverent handling of her children as she does with
funerals. She watches over ruins, she embalms memories, she waits for seasons of restoration.

From this time till the world is drowned in a deluge of
fire, churches will be the gates and images of the heavens,
which may indeed be veiled by clouds and storms, but

which are always there. We can even catch a glimpse of a great reign of the saints on earth before the end of time, and, consequently, of a splendid glorification of all Consecrated Places. Even after the great conflagration, there is nothing to prevent our supposing that a last tear, a last prayer of the Virgin of virgins may win, at the last day, a sort of restoration of the surface of the earth for the benefit of children who have died unbaptised, and other victims of merely original sin. Their eternity would be filled by the remembrance of the smile given by Jesus to His Mother in the midst of the company of the saints, and by all that the angel of the earth would tell them of the spots marked by the footsteps of God and of His servants, the only ones spared by the flames. A revelation made to the Sister de la Nativité favours this view.

CHAPTER XV.

CONFLICTS OF THE CHURCH FOR HER SANCTUARIES.

IT is only natural that the enemies of Christ are always the enemies of the Holy Places. It requires no great effort of genius to discover that the point at which religion touches the earth may be attacked with advantage; and in the absence of genius, covetousness alone would suggest this line of tactics. And so, from the earliest ages, we see the Roman emperors, prefects, and pro-consuls open the way for the expropriations of all future centuries. The charity of the early Christians, and their zeal for the objects of worship, made them appear enormously rich to these covetous and luxurious men. Repeated disappointments failed to correct the error. So nothing is of more frequent occurrence in the acts of the martyrs than the fury of avarice cheated of its expectations, and fearing to be again deceived. The greedy proconsul is seen taunting the Jesuits *en robe courte ou longue* of his day, and pressing them on the plea of evangelical counsels, detachment from the things of the world, and the love of poverty, which makes men like the Crucified Jesus. He carries on the jest to the last extremity, and by capital punishment places his victims "in possession of the heavenly treasures which they desire." Confiscation is only named as an accessory, but who can doubt that very often it was the only object of the persecutor?

To the pagans succeeded the Arians and other heretics, and the barbarians of the north. We keep the name of Vandal to express destructive rage and profanation; but Huns, Normans, Tartars, Saracens, alike employed brute force to destroy the last traces of the worship of God.

What is the history of the Church but that of a long challenge between the children of the God of peace, and those of the flesh and the devil? the former lavishing time, life, wealth, labour, and genius to build up, to give God a standing on earth, to surround Him with peace and safety, to adore Him in the gladness and the splendour of a heavenly festivity: the latter eager to level all things in blood, luxury, and ruin. The flesh and the devil seem to be always triumphing— they shout, "Victory!" but the Church always rises again, like the flowers which appear above the snow, heralding to the conquered winter the sunshine and the perfume of spring.

In the sixteenth century, more than ever, she seemed to be building peacefully, extending her dominion on every side, and possessing all things; but the Reformation was approaching, and it was an era of Vandalism. Worship in spirit and truth, without body, temple, or altar, was the dream of the more active portion of these sectaries. They carried destruction everywhere, and saw nothing around them but Amalekites to be destroyed. Still, the Reformation preserved the Name of Christ and the Bible; and with the exception of certain fits of madness, it was rather iconoclastic than Vandalic. It was more convenient for the Reformers to take possession of the churches, than to burn them in order to build "temples." Tho French Protestants had a predilection for this word, the reason of which it would be difficult to explain by strict logic, for the Temple at Jerusalem was not meant to have a successor; and the Bible is equally silent as to the Temple of Charenton and the Church of Nôtre-Dame. However, there was a certain Biblical flavour in the name. It was better than that of *synagogue* which the Jews had monopolised, and it had a more dignified sound than that of *dining-room*, or *upper chamber* mentioned in the Gospels and Acts of the

Apostles as the places of meeting for the early disciples: and it was fit to distinguish the buildings in which the "Lord's Supper" had taken the place of the papistical Mass.

However this may be, the idea of a mere meeting to hear sermons, and of the commemoration of a supper, tended greatly to lower the ideas attached of old to the grand word "temple;" it was no longer the awful place not to be approached without trembling, no longer the gate of Heaven, nor even of the Holy of Holies, the veil of which hid an adorable Presence enthroned above the holy ark. It was merely a place of assembly, a συναγωγή under a dignified name.

Thus was the way prepared for that modern naturalism which the revolution has announced as the received principle with regard to sanctuaries. All power, all authority emanates from the nation; public churches are the property of the nation, and it is the nation which appoints to them what destination it pleases; it consecrates them, if there is any meaning in the expression; it permits Catholics to use their churches, Jews their synagogues, Protestants their temples, Mussulmans their mosques, and actors their theatres, so as to meet the wishes of important fractions of the community, and in deference to good order and a policy of toleration. But the nation has the power of altering these dispositions; it can expropriate when it pleases, if, indeed, to take what is its own can be termed expropriation; it is answerable to nobody; it knows its own will, and that is enough.

If there is a Sovereign Ruler above, it does not concern itself about Him.

Alas, poor nation! Who made her a goddess? Who endowed her with omnipotence? And if she is omnipotent, what need is there for her to lean on the arm of any adventurer who may claim to call himself the State? What need to lavish on him her treasures for his revelries, to sacrifice her children to him? Of what use is her power, if she only employs it for her enslavement and her ruin?

And again; ought this noisy mob, which calls itself the nation, to be believed on its own word?

The nation, the daughter of Heaven and of Christ, is that queen in mourning robes, whom I see weeping in the sanctuary; and she who comes to insult her and drive her from that refuge, to turn it into a bazaar or a theatre—what is she?

CHAPTER XVI.

CONSTANCY OF THE CHURCH ILLUSTRATED.

THERE are two places especially which represent the invincible constancy of the Church in her struggle for Holy Places under two aspects—the one, that of the extremity of desolation; the other, of an ever-renewed hope.

1. *Palestine.*

The first is Palestine, the land of Juda, formerly the land of obstinate and unruly minds; but ever since the thorn-crowned Jesus has become the King of the new Jews, this obstinacy has become a tender and heroic perseverance.

There was a strange problem to be solved in this land, in which the curses of Mount Ebal had answered the blessings of Garizim. In spite of the warnings and the threats of the prophets, the people and their rulers had chosen the curses, and had continued for centuries to heap them up.

Isaias, Jeremias, Our Lord Himself, uttered sadder lamentations over this land than over the destruction of Ninive, Babylon, and Egypt.

On the other hand, while the clouds of wrath were gathering as dark as those which overwhelmed Sodom and Gomorrha, this land became the land of Jesus and of Mary, the land of the Holy Family, the country of the apostles, and consequently the cradle of grace, salvation and joy for the whole universe. There was no curse which could be put in comparison with the new blessings.

The very Deicide which drew down upon Jerusalem a destruction which was the type of the Last Judgment and the final desolation, could not prevent the Divine Blood from being at once the sovereign curse and the sovereign blessing.

This is the explanation of the state of Palestine in our day. A land of ruins, of oblivion, of devastation, of slavery, of infinite horror and agony ; a soil burnt, waste, stained, and, to quote Châteaubriand, "ploughed by the wrath of God ;" and at the same time, a land of

ineffable and imperishable love ! One destroying generation has followed another—"the locust hath eaten
that which the palmer-worm hath left; and that which
the locust hath left, the bruchus hath eaten; and that
which the bruchus hath left, the mildew hath destroyed" (Joel i.). To the fire and sword of the Roman legions, succeeded the ravages of the Persians,
and lastly came those of the Mussulman races.

For a short time, in the tenth century, the Crusades
rescued the Tomb of Christ. It was a protest by anticipation against the masonic, Josephist, pseudo-
liberal, indifferentist, and other crotchets of our time.
Modern parliaments would be unable to comprehend
under what pretext it could be possible and lawful
to attack a nation of a different creed, which had
for years possessed towns and territories round the
Jordan; but in those days of faith, it would not have
been thought possible that Christian nations should
grant to unbelievers the permanent right of blasphemy,
persecution, and profanation, under the pretence of
conquest, liberty of conscience, or equality of worship; it would not have been thought possible to acknowledge a prescription against God and His rights.
For nearly 200 years, the one idea of the whole of
Europe was the vindication of the rights of Jesus
Christ to the country of His ancestors. Her treasures
and the flower of her chivalry were lavished in this
cause. No one was uninterested in it. The clergy
and the monks preached; convents, mothers, brides,
offered to God the sacrifices of their prayers and tears.

And, in fact, the cause was greater even than it was thought at the time. The defence of the Holy Sepulchre was the defence of all sanctuaries; the defence of Palestine was the defence of the world; the defence of the rights of Christ was the defence of all rights and all property; to defend a Christian in the object of his veneration was to defend mankind in its relations with God; to defend the pilgrim of a day was to rescue the future from all transient social follies. " Dieu le veut," was the Crusaders' cry; and, in very truth, what proof is there that it was not the Will of God ? Will any one allege failure as a proof? But the success of God is often hidden under a disaster. Principles have been laid down; that is enough for the Church, who can afford to wait, because she will live till the consummation of ages. Even at the present day, we are in the thick of the Crusades, and there is no better motto for our banners than the old one of our fathers, " Dieu le veut."

Since the Protestant Reformation, Christian kings and people seem to have conspired to abandon Palestine, or, rather, to fetter her to her desolation, and to keep her under the nameless degradation and wretchedness of the Mussulman yoke. Every one of our modern follies in turn, if it has not diminished the rights of Christ, has at least dimmed and confused them: one after another these various follies,—Biblical, absolutist, parliamentary, Jansenistic, Gallican, philosophical, national, revolutionary, economic, social, democratic, republican, diplomatic, and many others, have made the

clouds darker. The last phase of the masonic progress
of the question has been the discussion and regulation
of the interests and rights of Christendom between a
nominally Catholic sovereign, the Czar of Russia, and the
Sultan of Constantinople, without reference to the Sovereign Pontiff, or the Church. Regard was had to political
facts, not to rights founded on Divine truth. But in
vain have a thousand revolutions passed over Palestine,
in vain she seems to have reached the last stage of
ruin and degradation, in vain have the rulers of Christian nations acknowledged the mockery of legitimacy
which gives to the son of the seraglio what ought to
belong to the Son of the Virgin ; faithful hearts do
but profess more loudly that this land ought to be the
land of God and of holy love, the fatherland of all.
They would still gladly give their blood for its deliverance.   For us Palestine is still the " Holy Land,"
and to the end it will be the epitome of the world
and the type of the kingdom of God on the earth.   If
there, more than anywhere else, Christ possesses as
though He possessed not, He is for that reason only
the more like Himself.   Jerusalem is the proof that
the Church knows both how to possess and how to
renounce, how to deprive herself of everything for the
sake of peace, and how to abound for the sake of charity,
how to be stripped, like Jesus Christ, by brutal soldiers, or how to be clad in her robes of glory.

What a subject for meditation is this indestructible
possession amidst spoliations ! We might compare it
to one of those phantoms imagined by the Middle

Ages, which were supposed to wander about their ancient possessions, threatening misfortune and vengeance to the descendants of the usurpers, and prophesying the restoration of the rightful stock.

2. *Italy.*

The second centre of conflict is Rome and Italy. Rome is another Jerusalem, the new Sion, the eternal city in which Christ, risen to die no more, lives with His Church, and preaches the gospel with her.

Rome has the patience, the vitality, the perseverance of the ancient Jerusalem. She inherits her glories and her promises for the future. Jesus is there—He will be there always, the sovereign Ruler: there He ever reigns, with His sceptre of a reed, His crown of thorns, His ragged purple robe. But it is a reed which bends the wills of millions; it is a thorny crown whose splendour shines far and wide ; and that ragged purple robe is the protection of the world from the anger of God and the rage of the wicked.

The Balaams, who come to insult and curse Rome, find that unbidden praise and blessing rise to their lips in the midst of their blasphemies: and the men of power who condemn her cannot forbear from stamping her brow with the title of royalty, saying with Pilate, " What I have written I have written."

O Rome! city of the catacombs, city of the trophies of triumphs over paganism, city of glorious basilicas, city of relics unrivalled! within thy walls I have adored, not only the greatest number of Eucharistic sacrifices, but also the Holy Crib, the Cross, the Lance, the Column of the Scourging, the Santa Scala! Within thy walls I have venerated the chains of Peter, and the relics of countless victims whom Jesus has joined to His mystical Body. Blessed for ever be thou because thou hast set all these treasures in gold and precious stones, and lavished, together with thy blood, the marvels of art and industry to preserve them for future ages! The sword of greedy persecutors has never for an instant been able to turn thee from thy labours and ecstasies of love! Be filled for ever with the acclamations of thy children! They come from the ends of the earth to adore Jesus in His most exalted representation, in the choicest manifestations of His mystical life — and the Holy Spirit does not suffer their expectations to be disappointed. As thou guardest the soil of thy sanctuaries, so, too, dost thou guard the groundwork of faith: as thou guardest the relics of Jesus and His saints, so, too, thou guardest the treasures of Divine knowledge, the secrets of a life of sanctity, and the marvels of holy love in the soul :—" Salve, magna parens frugum. . . . Magna virûm. . . ."

There is, perhaps, a hidden mystery in the fact that the rock of the Crucifixion and that of the Holy Sepulchre have remained at Jerusalem, while the Holy Crib has found a resting-place in the Liberian basilica at Rome, and the Holy House of Nazareth on the soil of Italy. The Church in Palestine is Rachel weeping over the grave of her children who are not. At Rome,

she is the fruitful mother rejoicing in her sons. And
yet, at Rome, as at Jerusalem, there is always the
struggle going on. Success is more evident at Rome;
but, in reality, its temporal acquisitions are slow, like
the growth of the oak, while its spoliations are sudden
and terrible. Where are the donations of Constantine,
of the Countess Matilda, and many others? How
many provinces are the subject of an annual protest
which would be absurdly weak from any other court
but that of Rome? What was left of the patrimony
of St. Peter had long been merely a bait for covetous
neighbours irritated at seeing a corner of the earth, defended by an old man, resist their attacks for ages. But
now even this corner is no longer in his power. Violence, progress, and so-called civilisation, have invaded
everything. The old man's only freedom is in the
loftiness of his soul: his only majesty is that of his
justice: his only pomp that of the truth: he has no
exchequer but his influence over hearts: no power but
the Sovereign Love, whose representative he is. His
footing in the world is little more than the fictitious
point of mathematics. But from it he still defends
his rights and those of sanctity. To the world this
omnipotent weakness has always been, and always
will be an enigma: it cannot understand why to-day
the Church gives up her coat to him who only asks
her cloak, and why to-morrow she defends that coat
to the death, and succeeds. How can there be, at one
and the same time, so much attachment and so much
contempt for earthly dignities and goods: so much

liberality in one case, and so much tenacity in the other? We have already fathomed this enigma in what has been said of the freedom of God and men in the choice of Holy Places. In the first place, God does what He pleases, and the Church knows the mind of her Sovereign Spouse: she understands His wisdom and the mysteries of His love. Even if she did not understand, she would not question them. At a sign of His predilection she would sacrifice everything in defence of a single nook of earth, as an act of homage and adoration.

In the second place, she is herself a sovereign. After God, she is the supreme judge *de commodo et incommodo;* she knows what is useful or necessary for the interests of her children, and of all mankind. She knows that sometimes resistance unto death is necessary. She knows when it is well to preach detachment, and when to proclaim aloud the sovereign rights of God. And, after all, the enemies of sacred rights and property are supremely foolish and bungling in their demands. Saints, such as Pius IX., like nothing better than to strip themselves, and enrich others, when it is a spontaneous act of their exuberant charity. Why require them to do it in a cowardly way, and in alliance with robbers? Deceive them, if you will: make use of diplomatic delays and chicanery: mingle as judiciously as you please threats and promises, the brutality of violence and the interchange of favours:— perhaps you may succeed by such means in inducing a Sovereign Pontiff to cede to you a county of Avignon.

. . . But if you are so ill-judged as to bring in a question of dogma or morals, if you demand the sacrifice of a principle, if you exact an inch of land in the name of the supremacy of fashion or policy, you will be told that true Christians love country, monarchy, nation, liberty, and all that is good, better than you do; but that they despise and detest the absurd idols which foolish and ambitious men disguise with these titles.

Away with the harlequin rattling the bells of his bauble of '89, in the name of which he demands the key of my church or my presbytery! I will shut the door on the madman, even though he break my windows! Away, too, with the clever and prudent prince who aims at the same end by wiser means! If he is powerful by the art of governing, he is, for that reason, only the more dangerous in his plans of invasion.

Be you who you may, ask of Pius IX., of all the bishops, of the humblest priest worthy of the name, a crime, an act of injustice or of baseness, and you will find either heroes or victims, and certainly a wall of brass fronting you. The clever men of this world can never bring themselves to believe in the reality of our principles of faith and truth. Accustomed as they are to the weak and debased characters around them, they imagine that every one is to be bribed and can be made to yield.

Hence it is, that they are put out and irritated when they meet with one of these gentle victims on whom violence is wasted, as the power of an ironclad vessel

when stranded on a sandbank. And yet they ought
to know us by this time.

CHAPTER XVII.

THE LATEST ENEMIES.

CENTURY after century, the war against the Holy
Places has become more scientific and more crafty.
Doubtless, in every age, men of violence and rapine
are the adversaries of the kingdom of God on earth;
but they are not the most dangerous enemies. The
Mussulmen themselves, even while breaking the
crosses, and massacring our priests and pilgrims, retained strong instincts of faith and reverence: they
respected the greater part of our sanctuaries. If they
excluded Jews and Christians from the Haram es
Scherif, it was from exaggerated veneration for the
Temple of Solomon.

The attacks of heretics and free-thinkers tended to
destroy the very idea of a consecrated place. But the
master-stroke of the enemy is to turn these privileged
spots into an occasion of mockery and of accusations
against the Church and Catholicism.

What would it avail us to have a magnificent theory
on the subject of local sanctification, if men, with the
torch of science and of history in their hand, found
nothing in the archives of our most famous sanctuaries
but fable, absurdity, falsehood, and superstition?

If our temples are merely new editions of those of

Baal and Serapis, with their secret passages, their hiding-places, and their ventriloquising priests; if the Holy Sepulchre is not where Christianity affirms it to be, but under the Mosque of the Sakkra; if Saint Peter never set foot in Rome; if it is impossible that the holy house of Loreto could adjust itself to the grotto of Nazareth; if the canons of St. Januarius are tricksters of the same stamp as the "bishop of fire" among the Greeks; if the events of La Salette, and of Lourdes, are juggleries, and if the legends of Auray, of Liesse, and other great places of pilgrimage, famous from their origin, rest on no more respectable foundations; what can we say of the soundness of our judgment, or of our good faith with regard to the sanctity of our other sanctuaries? If we are the victims of our imaginations and of our own impostures, in the case of places miraculously visited by God, how can we be infallible in maintaining the efficacy of our own benedictions? If we are sure of nothing, or if our assertions are founded on absurdities, is not the state right in placing us on a level with Mahometans, Jews, Buddhists, or even with children and persons of weak intellect, to whom they give official guardians, and who are put back into their proper place by force, if they lay claim to any superiority?

Thus we come to the question of authenticity.

PART II.

THE QUESTION OF AUTHENTICITY.

CHAPTER I.

SUPERNATURAL AUTHENTICITY.

WE have seen that every idea of local sanctification should have for its basis some supernatural facts. Directly or indirectly, there must be a Divine revelation for all sanctity in its origin.

St. Paul, in his Epistle to the Hebrews, points out to us, this genealogy, so to speak, of manifestations and sanctifications all linked together. He shows to us, at first, "God at sundry times and in divers manners speaking in times past to the fathers by the prophets and angels, and confirming this word, so that every transgression and disobedience received a just recompense of reward; then, in latter days, speaking by His Son . . . the Heir of all things, Whose declarations were confirmed to us by them that heard Him; and lastly (for these also), bearing witness by signs

and wonders and divers miracles, and distributions of
the Holy Spirit according to His own Will."

This is not the place for a treatise on direct revelations, such as miracles, prophecy, dreams, visions,
heavenly voices, interior illuminations, etc. It is
enough to say that the Scriptures speak of Holy
Places, and mention supernatural operations as a proof
of their sanctity. As a matter of fact, we have no
other test, and we cannot conceive, much less demand,
any other.

To those who deny everything, we say, look around,
and try to solve these Divine enigmas. Facts have
taken place, in the Name of the Divine Revealer,
which the world or human science can only explain
by the bravado of a future progress which never
arrives. *We* explain them by the omnipotence and
the other perfections of God. We are melted in love,
adoration, and gratitude before these gleams of light
and infinite condescension.

Divine evidences, carrying their proofs with them,
produce a supernatural authenticity. The authenticity, then, which I call supernatural, is that which
rests on Divine revelation, or, in general, on reasons
recognised by faith. If Jacob believes in the sanctity
of Bethel, it is because he sees something extraordinary
in the dream which God has sent to him. If we believe in the sanctity of a consecrated church, it is not,
indeed, by special and direct revelation, but in consequence of a series of miracles and other antecedent
manifestations, which have shown us that the power

of blessing and consecrating is given to the priest-hood.

Natural authenticity rests on human reasons, recog-nised by science, such as titles, inscriptions, popular traditions. Thus, we are certain that the dome of St. Peter's, at Rome, was constructed after the design of Michael Angelo, and we have only human documents as a basis for that conviction.

Most frequently, in the case of religious monuments, these two kinds of authenticity are allied—grafted one on the other—and mutually strengthening one another. Thus, simple tradition teaches us that the prince of the apostles was crucified at Montorio, and buried in the Vatican. Faith makes us ascribe a special blessing, and providential destinies to these primitive facts, and a high authority to the tradition itself. Lastly, the miraculous graces, which have been since granted, form a new body of traditions and documents coming in support of the original fact.

Still, the two kinds of authenticity are frequently independent of each other. There was no need for Moses to consult any document, any human evidence, before believing in the burning Bush; neither, to quote a more recent example, was there any such need for the little peasant girl of Lourdes, before receiving her heavenly vision. They saw, they heard, they believed.

CHAPTER II.

ON THE VALUE OF EXTRAORDINARY SUPERNATURAL EVIDENCE.

1. One solitary evident Fact may be sufficient to establish Authenticity.

As we said before, the great principle which consecrates a place, is the same which perpetuates its consecration. As God is able to set apart a place for Himself, and to make the fact of His having done so acknowledged, there is nothing to prevent His continuing and renewing His action and His revelations in this respect.

Strictly speaking, a single Divine intimation, well known and well attested, would be sufficient authority for regarding a place as consecrated and authentic, till there was a proof that God had deserted it. According to this principle, we should require nothing more to make us perfectly safe in our veneration for the Holy Sepulchre, than the prophecy which declares that " the Tomb of Christ shall be glorious."

I can imagine a deist, or any other infidel who rejects the Sacred Scripture, rejecting at the same time this prophecy, and all the consequences which I might draw from it. But I do not see how a Protestant, who admits the inspiration of the prophets and their general interpretation, can call in question the site of the Holy Sepulchre.

It may, perhaps, be said that the fact of the Resur

rection is enough, in itself, to make the Holy Sepulchre glorious. That would be a very poor fulfilment
of a very great prophecy, and the Holy Ghost, Who
cannot be accused of not foreseeing consequences,
would have exposed the Church to an inevitable error.
The true Sepulchre, the "Glorious" Sepulchre, which
saw no corruption, which will have nothing to give up
at the last day—that Sepulchre watched over by angels
and visited by the disciples, the holy women, and the
Blessed Virgin—must have been, directly after the
Resurrection, completely forgotten by God, angels,
and men. And, at the same time, the place actually
venerated for eighteen centuries as marked by prophecy, and as the great memorial of the purification
and regeneration of mankind by the Blood of God—
that scene of so many mysteries of love, justice, and
mercy, would be no better than a gigantic mistake, a
lie, a profanation !

The extravagances of Messrs. Robinson, Fergusson,
and Co. were needed to undeceive us, and to teach us
that, in spite of prophecy, the Sepulchre has been forgotten by God and man, and another place taken for it,
ever since the day of the Resurrection, or very little
later !

We have already said that God may sometimes permit forgetfulness, error, and profanation from man,
when His word is not pledged. But, otherwise, He
does not allow oblivion or profanation, and if He promises and gives His word, that word ought to be
enough for us.

2. *Multiplication of supernatural testimonies.*

When it is expedient for the protection of the sanctity of a place from oblivion and error, God is not satisfied with a single manifestation. He multiplies wonders, and then one miracle confirms another; prophetic declarations, supernatural favours, graces of every sort, are linked together, and form a body of evidence which cannot be withstood, except by accusing God and His Church of unworthy and incredible trickery.

Let us take, as an instance, the story of La Salette. Taken by itself, the original fact would be open to more than one objection. It rests upon the evidence of two children, whose veracity might be questioned without any great injustice. Let us admit, in addition, that the announcement of the coming chastisements may have been suggested to them by the first signs which they saw, and that the appearance and continuance of the fountain may have been a mere coincidence due to natural causes.

But people come in crowds to make pilgrimages to the spot. A church, and a centre of apostolate, rise up in manifest connection with the apparition; and God gives His sanction to all these things by prodigies, by conversions, by striking and countless graces. It is no longer an isolated fact—it is a series of miracles, by the help of which we judge of the past.

I know that there are Catholics who have said, speaking of the miracles of La Salette, " We are certainly obliged to confess that there is an extraordinary concourse of people to that place, who must be drawn thither by motives of piety, and that God grants them miraculous favours and cures ; but, in doing so, He rewards good faith, simplicity, and fervour, without in any way sanctioning the story of the two peasant children, which is nothing but a farce and an absurdity."

I beg pardon of those persons who have been able to speak or write in this strain, but I must say that I regard such an assertion as blasphemous, unless it is excused by want of consideration. In the mind of the people, the pilgrimage and its fruits depend on the fact affirmed by the children. God knows this—God foresaw it ; He is perfectly unfettered in His choice of places, and as to circumstances ; He has thousands of opportunities for rewarding good faith; He is able to inspire pious souls to perform thousands of recognised practices, and afterwards to recompense them ; and yet we are to believe that He shuts His Eyes, sanctions error, and makes profit of it on a large scale! In other words, the Holy Ghost is treated as a kind of Simon Magus, inconsistent with Himself, turning everything to advantage, getting out of a difficulty at all risks, without concerning Himself about the truth and reality of our objects of edification !

And in case the error should be discovered, how will the Holy Ghost get out of the difficulty ? Will He work fresh miracles to throw dust in men's eyes, and to silence their tongues ? No—the Very Truth has no need to make use of falsehood even if it were in order to close the mouth of hell. So soon as the Hand of God is seen in a question of authenticity, from that moment the question is settled.

I know that Providence makes all things, even the malice of men and devils, subserve Its designs; but there is a radical difference between that sovereign guidance which compels the enemies of God to bring about the work of His glory in spite of themselves, and a positive and miraculous sanction given to folly and imposture. God allowed Himself to be worshipped in idol temples; but He entered them openly, as a Conqueror. When He took possession of the Pantheon, He did not, as it were, insinuate Himself into them beneath the mask of an idol, He did not employ His Blessed Mother, His angels, and His saints as supernumeraries or fellow-actors in a disgraceful comedy.

If you can make up your mind to be a deist, a materialist, or an atheist, you will be acting consistently with yourself in shutting your eyes to every supernatural fact. But, once admit the Christian idea of a miracle, and you must not tell me that it can possibly be mixed up with the tricks of a juggler, and appear on the same stage with them.

CHAPTER III.

ON THE VALUE OF MORE ORDINARY SUPERNATURAL EVIDENCE.

BESIDES the supernatural facts already mentioned, namely, direct revelations, prophecies, miracles, visions, heavenly voices, and other similar facts, which strike the mind of a well-disposed man and immediately force upon him the logic of his faith, there are others which, without being so evidently Divine, possess, notwithstanding, a great supernatural value, and which must be taken into account in the question we are discussing. Such are the continual and extraordinary impetration of spiritual graces and temporal favours—the popular movements among Christians—the instincts and what may be termed the "clairvoyance" of the saints, the authority of the Holy See, and of bishops : nay, even the witness borne by evil spirits. All these elements, so far as they are manifestations of the Holy Ghost, form a body of authority which tend to strengthen other testimony. We will now take a brief survey of them.

1. *Outpourings of Graces bestowed on Holy Places.*

Graces and favours, either temporal or spiritual, do not disturb the natural order of things, and are not regarded as an exact proof of Divine interposition. Spiritual favours, moreover, are the secret of the soul, and, for that very reason, it is impossible to bring

11

them forward as a demonstration. In one sense, there is no more striking miracle than a conversion : it is in an especial manner the work of God, it is the resurrection of a soul, the healing of blindness, paralysis, leprosy, and all other mortal diseases; but who could venture to affirm that any particular conversion is sincere, real, supernatural, and, above all, lasting ? Nevertheless, if there is a regular and constant stream of graces and conversions of every kind in any particular spot, if the voice of praying multitudes affirms that a more direct, efficacious, and infallible answer is granted to petitions offered at a certain spot than anywhere else, then I see in these facts, taken together, a proof of Divine approval which is, to my conscience, equivalent to the highest order of miracles. At the same time, it is a proof which appeals to the heart, and which cannot be made use of for the purpose of convincing the incredulous.

2. *On the value of a Popular Movement towards Holy Places.*

It may be said that pilgrimages, and similar devotions, often have their origin in a popular impulse, and that the mass of men have often been deceived by ignorance and prejudice. The words of the founder of the Oratory in England might even be quoted against me, on this head, in which he says that " the religion of the multitude is always vulgar, abnormal, marked by fanaticism and superstition." But these words require a wise interpretation. If by " popular religion" is meant the " religion of the populace," of the dregs of our seaports and suburbs, mines and manufactories, then I confess that the religion of those who are almost without any must be a corrupt religion; but if the religion of countries and multitudes who have kept up practical faith and simple manners is spoken of, then I assert that the purest and brightest manifestations of the Holy Spirit are to be found in these upright and vigorous souls. They have a surer guide in Heavenly instinct than can be given by the torch of science; and while the learned theologian is liable to go astray in the maze of his own ideas and arguments, the poor Irish maidservant, or the peasant of the Agro Romano, strong in their Catechism and their Credo, have a habit of supernatural feeling, which is their safeguard against all doctrinal error, false spirituality, or any touch of a doubtful devotion. The question might be raised, on what soil religion is the most liable to corruption. The upper ranks of society, we should certainly answer, if they only concerned themselves enough about it! As it is, I am inclined to fix upon certain middle regions, abounding in embittered and erratic minds. As to the poor and lowly, even granting that they are carried away by the masses, their fall is less deep, at any rate; they have the gift of simple faith and the other seeds of spiritual resurrection. As a rule they are kept from religious corruption, because God takes pleasure in them, and reveals to them the things which He hides from the wise and prudent. The faith, the religion, the devotion of the mass of Christians are

pure and lofty ; otherwise it could not be said that the
Holy Ghost enlightens His Church. The difference
between the *teaching*, and the *taught* Church consists,
not in the quality of the light, which is the same in
both, but in the power of reflecting its rays. Very
often the absorbing is in an inverse ratio to the reflecting power ; and this explains the fact that we more
often find the gift of supernatural feeling and clairvoyance among simple souls than among theologians
and men of learning.

3. *Scholars and Saints.*

It is not innocent and simple minds only who visit
Holy Places, who study them, guard them, make
them more or less an important centre of their
lives. Once let the religious attraction to a place become sufficiently habitual to draw to itself a considerable portion of the Church, and one may feel certain
that those who are eminent from their virtue and
purity will be of the number. There will be savants,
philosophers, historians, artists, antiquaries, leading
men in every line, not to speak of those whose business it is to study the subject. To them it belongs to
supply what is wanting in the less enlightened masses.

The most favourable condition for judging of questions relating to Holy Places, would be a union of
supernatural gifts and human knowledge ; but, at all
events, a familiarity with the ways of God is necessary. Sanctity is not to be examined by a magnify-

ing glass, nor probed like a geological stratum. Mere physical science and criticism are not enough for its appreciation. The light of faith and the tenderness of devotion must come in to elevate learning and to direct criticism. Now it cannot be said that God has left the spots which He intends to endow with a peculiar sanctity without this two-fold advantage. We have our scholars, historians, and antiquaries, whom we need not blush to compare with those in other fields of science. The spirit of faith and other supernatural habits, make their insight keener, their intuition more powerful, their labours more philosophical in tendency, their deductions more absolutely certain. They are our true guides in Holy Places, as everywhere else.

4. *Clairvoyance.*

As every place of pilgrimage is frequented especially by pious persons, it is certain that many of the number will unite, with knowledge and sagacity, supernatural lights and a peculiar instinctive feeling of what is holy. If there were a mistake or a deception, such as Protestants and incredulous persons assert that there is in the miracles of the liquefaction of the blood of St. Januarius at Naples, the saints would be the first to perceive, to point it out, and to denounce it. We read in the history of St. Martin, that there was, in the neighbourhood of Tours, a place venerated by the people as the tomb of a martyr. The great bishop, who believed nothing too readily, asked the oldest of the clergy to show him the name of the saint, or the date of his death, and finding no certain tradition on the subject, he deferred going there for some time ; but at last he did go, with some of his brethren, and standing before the tomb, he prayed to God to reveal to him who lay buried there. Then he saw, on his left hand, a dreadful phantom, whom he recognised as a robber who had been executed for his crimes. St. Martin had the altar removed, and delivered the people from this superstition. We see, from this instance, that God does sometimes permit a popular delusion ; but this is not the case of a devout population, but of a village only half-converted from Paganism—it is neither a general error, nor one of long duration.

As regards the Holy Places of Palestine, we have not only a more than probable conjecture that they must have been visited by persons supernaturally enlightened, but we know as a positive fact that they have been so visited by numerous saints recognised as such by the Church, and whose clearness of vision has been verified. Not to speak of St. Jerome and his constellation of associates, St. Bridget saw the events of the Gospels displayed before her in the places consecrated by tradition. Other saints, who were not at Jerusalem, have seen the whole history from a distance, and their descriptions have been proved to answer minutely to the places pointed out by tradition. The visions of the venerable Sister Emmerich are of this kind. There are illuminations which, if less direct, are not therefore, less convincing. Take, for instance, that of the venerable Curé d'Ars, with regard to the events of

La Salette. His soul is disturbed by an equivocal in-
cident, but only regains its tranquillity and clearness
by abandoning itself completely to the spirit of faith.
The mass of pious persons, without possessing any
manifestly supernatural lights of the first order, feel
in the Holy Places' sensations of joy and peace, too
strong and too universal to be attributed to merely
human causes, or to the movements of an emotional
and superficial devotion.

The pleasure of reaching a picturesque place of
meeting, of being with pious companions, and with a
free and light heart, in an atmosphere of lights, and
flowers, and incense, adds, no doubt, to the popular enthusiasm of a pilgrimage, but it will not explain everything. Certainly, besides all this, there is something
beyond any charm of sense in the attraction of Holy
Places—something of the "Nonne cor nostrum erat
ardens in nobis?" called forth by a nearer presence, a
more intimate association with God.

5. *Ecclesiastical Authority.*

To form a judgment concerning Holy Places, there
must be something more than the good sense of the
body of Christians, the knowledge of enlightened men,
and the clairvoyance of souls in union with God. In
the example of St. Martin, just referred to, there was
more than the man of rectitude and simplicity, more
than the wise or learned man, more than the man of
faith gifted with supernatural illumination; there was
the man of authority, the man appointed by the Holy

Spirit to govern the church and the district. Neither the priest in his parish, nor the bishop in his diocese, are infallible; neither of them is able to make a place an article of faith. Still, the bishop has grace given him to ascertain, verify, and confirm the belief of those committed to his charge. So long as he is not plainly at variance with his superiors in the episcopate, the safest way is to doubt where he doubts, to believe, approve, and reject as he does; at all events, to suspend all contrary judgment—*à fortiori*, every expression of blame or of disagreement. In regard to questions concerning some holy spot in particular, the bishop of the diocese is on his own ground; he is the competent, although not the only or the final judge.

6. *The Authority of the Holy See.*

Although any question concerning a Holy Place is in the first instance a diocesan business, it is in the very nature of Divine grace to be expansive, and to diffuse itself more or less through the whole world. The attractions of a place of pilgrimage make themselves gradually felt and communicated. At La Salette, the two children attract the village, the village the diocese, the diocese the province; lastly, the whole religious world in France is interested—all its dioceses have their representatives at the spot which our Lady has appointed; princes of the Church, missioners from distant countries, illustrious converts come, year by year, to mingle with the crowd, and to represent in a more sensible manner the catholicity of the movement.

Images of La Salette are multiplied, churches are built and dedicated under its privileged title. And so, after the bishop of the diocese, those of the most remote countries have to deliver their judgment on the subject, *à propos* of blessing chapels, approving or condemning books and doctrines, permitting and encouraging pious practices, verifying graces and miracles.

Eleven bishops, not to mention priests and laymen, have proclaimed and defend the wonderful tale. Meanwhile, the matter comes before the Apostolic See. Far from condemning, the Sovereign Pontiff listens favourably, grants graces and indulgences, and approves of an arch-confraternity. When things have grown to such a height, a cause may be considered over. What more can be required? Will the Church be asked to pronounce more definitely than it is her custom to do in such a case? Must the Sovereign Pontiff, for the satisfaction of every small personage who considers himself of the first importance, summon a general council, prepare a dogmatic bull, and give every authentic devotion a place in the Credo?

The Church has never thought fit to give judgment in this manner on such subjects, and we have other means of ascertaining her mind.

Whenever a considerable movement takes place in religion, when this movement finds an expression in popular acts, and when it evidently carries with it the majority of good priests and bishops, we cannot suppose it possible that it can escape the vigilance of the Apostolic See; and when the Vicar of Jesus Christ, instead of ignoring, or maintaining reserve, approves, encourages, and sanctions, by repeatedly granting privileges and solemn rescripts, then we are able to see in all this a sufficient expression of the Church's mind. Even when the Church does not deliver an explicit judgment, we admit her infallibility in the choice of her principal devotions. She is the mother and mistress of all churches, and, I will add, of sanctuaries. She does not lavish her caresses on base-born children. The aid of the Holy Ghost gives her what may be called a collective and incomparable clairvoyance.

The discernment of an individual saint may be called in question; such and such instances or modes of supernatural sight in St. Bridget, or blessed Mary of Agreda, may be discussed lawfully; but every Catholic is bound to admit that the great Spouse of Christ is never without the guidance of the Holy Spirit, and that He preserves her from all serious error in worship and discipline. " Holy Church," says one of our great lights, " neither admits nor encourages, even by silence, anything contrary to truth, virtue, or piety." " Ecclesia Christi quæ non sunt consentanea virtuti, pietati, aut veritati, non consentit, nec tacet aut approbat." Her favours, her solemnities, her indulgences, her rescripts, the sound of which is echoed throughout the world, are never granted to any devotion marked by error, imposture, imprudence, or superstition.

This is the argument of the learned Quaresmius, on the subject of the Holy Land :—" The universal

Church," he says, "believes with the Eastern churches, that the places in Palestine with which we are concerned, are those same Holy Places in which the mysteries of our redemption and the other Biblical events took place ; and, consequently, she offers them to the veneration of the faithful. In order to stimulate this feeling, and make it more affectionate, the Sovereign Pontiffs, Christ's vicars on earth, have lavished indulgences and privileges of every kind, which they would not have done, unless they had been convinced that they were not deceiving the faithful by proposing falsehood as truth. And we, the friars minor—we, the special children of the Catholic and Roman Church, the one universal mother of the faithful—we aid her representatives, when, by our day and night offices, our visits and processions, by the fidelity of our guardianship, above all, by the fervour of our devout affections, we show our veneration for these consecrated places mentioned in the sacred Scriptures. The different Eastern churches, Armenian, Jacobite, etc., not only separated, but wholly estranged from the Roman Church, do the same, as far as they can. And what did they not do when they were united, as in the days of St. Jerome ? It may be seen by the details of the holy pilgrimages which he gives us."

CHAPTER IV.

1. *Their Formal Testimony.*

THE learned Quaresmius directs our attention to another supernatural testimony which is seldom wanting to the authenticity of Holy Places. It is that of the evil spirits, which is, in some sort, a test of the Divine approval.

"The evil spirits," he says, "after having been once driven from the Holy Places by Christ, cannot endure to be in them; they fly from them, and by so doing show us what we ought to think about them. The abhorrence shown by the enemy of man for a place which does not belong to him is a proof of the ownership of his Adversary; and the secret power which compels Christ's deadly foe to go out of the bodies of possessed persons when they take refuge in these places, is, in like manner, a witness to their sanctity." Here Quaresmius quotes St. Jerome's letter to Marcella on the Holy Sepulchre. "If we do not believe from our own evidence, we may, at least, trust that of the devil and his angels, who, whenever they are cast out of the bodies of the possessed, before the Holy Sepulchre, behave like criminals before the judge's tribunal, trembling, howling, regretting their having crucified Him Whom they are forced to dread." In another place, the holy doctor says, speaking of the

tombs of Abdias, Eliseus, and of the holy Precursor of
Christ, that St. Paula was terrified by the prodigies
which she saw wrought there; for the evil spirits,
through the medium of the possessed, roared, barked,
howled, hissed, growled, like wild beasts; forcing their
victims to shake their heads violently, to throw themselves backward till they touched the ground with
their foreheads, hanging them by their feet in the air,
showing by all these unnatural movements the real
sanctity of those tombs which made them unsupport-
able to their humbled pride.

I am aware that these quotations from St. Jerome
will not find much favour in an age which has very
slight belief in bodily possession or obsession. We,
who believe the Gospel, know something of the ways
of the evil spirits; and we know that the whole Church
history on this head, as on all others, is the continuation of the inspired books. In the nineteenth,
as in the first century, the devil is an unclean, de-
graded spirit, without self-respect—the opposite of all
sanctity and Christian dignity—only, his operations
are less sensible and frequent in our days for two
reasons.

In the first place, his liberty is more limited in the
Christian world by the influence of the sacraments,
and other spiritual safeguards. He has lost his nearly
ubiquitous power and habits in places, elements, and
persons. From the time of our Lord we see examples
of this limitation; we can follow its progress in the
course of ages, whether in the extinction of oracles, or

in other facts no less remarkable. The ground which hell has lost is not always completely gained by sanctity; but at all events it is more or less left free to men. The second reason why the operations of the devil are less sensible and frequent is this: in ages of infidelity there is no occasion for the devil to prove the truth of his existence to a generation of materialists, nor to confirm by facts the statements made about him in the Bible. He does not trouble himself with credulity or incredulity, so long as he can get possession of souls; but he prefers the false philosophy which is more fatal to them. Why should he expose himself to the scourge of the exorcists, so long as he can cross his arms and leave the Voltaires and Renans to turn the mill instead of himself? The presence of evil spirits is but too evident from their works in our great cities; and no over-scrupulosity would prevent certain members of our learned institutes from giving us representations like those of Simon Magus. But in Paris, London, wherever the Faith has taken possession, the evil spirits, even with the aid of every human power, can never recover their former audacity; they are neither free, nor powerful, nor at home there; they act under some equivocal disguise of mesmerism, table-turning, spiritualism, or other similar impositions; but they never show themselves as lords and masters, as the gods of men and of nature, as they did of old in the pagan temples and highways, as they still do wherever the Cross has not been planted by the Christian missioner. Certainly we have too good reason to know that the place does not make the saint any more than the cowl makes the monk. We have terrible instances of travellers whose weak faith has been entirely broken to pieces against the stone of the Holy Sepulchre, the walls of Loreto, or Nôtre Dame des Victoires. The miserable "Fire-bishop" and his accomplices, the Greek monks, are not sanctified by living near the Holy Sepulchre. Year after year, the wretched impostor waits for Easter Day, and lurking in the sacred tomb, like an infernal spider, weaves his web, in which every conceivable scandal, profanation, and impiety seems combined to ruin souls on the very scene of their redemption.

In such instances as these, man, already ruined, brings back the evil spirits to the places which, if they were free, they would shun. The parts are changed; it is no longer the bodies of men which are invaded, possessed by evil spirits of a nature superior to their own; it is the evil spirits who are possessed by men, whom mysteries of regeneration have made superiors in spite of their transgressions.

With or against their will, the fallen angels are compelled to submit to the ascendancy of humanity, and no longer to appear save under the veil of human flesh.

This explains the infernal hatred of certain persons for the Holy Places. The reprobate man attacks them with a rage and fury which pass the bounds of common natural feeling; he cannot tear his thoughts from them —it is a perfect nightmare; he denies them, hurls sarcasms at them, spits upon them; but he returns to them incessantly; he is not satisfied with pillage, he wants destruction and annihilation. Garibaldi and his followers must have " Rome or death !"

2. *Silent Witness of the Demons.*

The devout son of St. Francis points out to us another proof of the power of the Holy Places over evil spirits. It is one, the force of which may frequently fail of appreciation in detail, but is none the less powerful as a whole; and we may fairly trust on it, because of the word of saints and men of prayer. It is the deep instinct of the faithful in general as to the weakness of the great tempter in consecrated places. There he has less power to distract, to weary, to harass, to grieve, to debase, to deceive souls, to overshadow them with darkness, to inflate them with empty vapours, to fill them with dangerous visions. True, as has just been said, the place does not make the saint, and it is possible to be a Satan to one's self everywhere; but it should also be said that the experience of simple upright souls is to feel better, freer, purer, when they abandon themselves to the influence of consecrated places. In some persons this experience may be vague and obscure, but it is too general, too significant, too unanimously attested, not to be taken into account. And, further, if this feeling of spiritual welfare and liberty is but faintly developed in ruder souls, it is because it is reserved for purer ones fully to enjoy its delights, and appreciate the weakness of the fetters with which the enemy would fain bind them. Souls elevated to a state of sublime prayer generally possess a clearer perception of the defeat of the evil spirits, and are able to give us a stronger and more definite testimony than soft and dissipated souls. They are not deceived by an affected silence, by seeming absence, by stratagems of war; they can, in case of need, compel the lying spirits to quit their hiding-place, to abandon their hypocritical neutrality: when a soul is steeped in Divine light, like that of the Curé d'Ars, then no dissimulation, no ambushes, no tactics of any sort are any longer possible or lasting for the enemy of man. There is no resource left him but the rage of an evil being who feels humiliated, wounded—stripped of his disguises in broad daylight, and hurled back to everlasting horror. In this way extremes meet, and we see some saints become habitually the masters of evil spirits, lead them captive like real magicians, with this difference, that the latter seek evil for its own sake, while the saints only call up the powers of hell in order to do battle with them, and to snatch from them souls and bodies, time and space.

CHAPTER V.

ON NATURAL AUTHENTICITY.

APART from every religious question, the authenticity of a monument or a local recollection may rest on four kinds of direct proofs: archæological proofs, inscriptions, historical data, and written documents, and, lastly, tradition.

1. *Archæological Proofs, properly so called.*

These are drawn from the examination of places and monuments. Buildings, and other remains of the industry of the past, bear the stamp of the age, the nation, and the race which have bequeathed them to us. From the cutting of the stones, from the stroke of the chisel, from the materials employed and their combination, those learned in the subject are able to discover the origin and transformations of a building, to retrace its history, and, up to a certain point, that of the generations and people who were its architects or masters. In this study the archæologist neglects no circumstance; he examines the marks of violence and destruction, the different strata of *débris* accumulated by centuries; he allows for the corrosive action of time and of the elements; he weighs and discusses the smallest signs; bits of stuccoes, marks shapeless to the eyes of all others, are to him so many aids in forming conjectures, and sometimes positive assertions. In this way he recognises ages of faith or of irreligion, of rudeness or of luxury, of opulence or poverty, of greatness or decay, of elegance or bad taste, of ruin, transition, or renaissance. In a word, to him the stone is a book of which he can read the characters.

2. *Inscriptions.*

There are two things which the antiquarian examines

in inscriptions—the form and the meaning. The form, the beauty of the characters, the care with which they are traced, are in the province of archæology, for the letters and the orthography vary like the languages themselves, and are more or less perfect according to the time: even the faults committed by ignorant or foreign workmen are worth noticing. Then the materials employed must be observed : for instance, inscriptions on porphyry and other hard stones show that steel, which was supposed to be modern, has been employed, or some other process lost in our time.

When we come to their signification, inscriptions enter the department of history, or, rather, they are history embedded in archæology, which neither the negligence of copyists nor the whims of learned men have altered.

From primitive times we may hear Job, the man of nature, express the wish that his complaints might be " written with an iron pen in a plate of lead, or graven with an instrument in a flint stone." No one denies the importance of a name, a word, engraven on stone. Among inscriptions may be classed symbolical sculptures, emblems, characters partaking, more or less, of the nature of hieroglyphics, as well as medals, and coins when found under certain conditions.

3. *Written Data.*

After the discovery of a clear and significant inscription, the great thing for any one desiring to study a monument is to find its archives—to follow up its ancient traditions preserved in legends, confirmed by public or private transactions, embodied in the history of a people, supported by literary works, and chronicles of the neighbourhood. If the chain is well connected and has an indisputable origin, if the stream of testimony is swelled by incidental confirmations drawn from other histories and literature, conviction follows, and the result is scientific evidence.

4. *Traditions.*

The proofs we have just mentioned are, more or less, material. It would be a body without a soul, if all were not bound together, vivified, explained, commented on by tradition.

Inscriptions may be obscure, mutilated, or worn; history may be wanting, or not have the requisite link of connection with such or such a ruin. In these cases, one feels the importance of a living guide; such a guide is found in popular tradition. When preserved by primitive people, whose recollections and customs are unchangeable, it may be a reliable substitute for slabs of granite, and its authority is greater than when mingled with the troubled waters of a more advanced civilisation, rich though civilisation is in other resources. It is the part of the linguist to discover the identity of names in spite of the alterations they undergo from the vicissitudes of ages and conquests; it belongs to the critic to discern the foundation of truth hidden under the fables which may be built upon it.

5. *Accessory Proofs.*

Besides the sources of direct demonstration of which we have spoken, there is a multitude of accidental proofs which may come in triumphantly to the support of ancient memories.

Such may be afforded by medals, coins, and other objects of art found in the ruins of a building; such are the indications of distance or orientation which are accidentally revealed to us by history or collateral traditions. Almost every science may contribute these proofs, and accessory demonstrations may turn out as decisive as others. They can all be referred, more or less, to one of the four kinds which have been specified, so we need not linger over details. We will content ourselves with giving an instance of authenticity, decisively confirmed by nautical observation. It is taken from the magnificent work of MM. Conybeare and Howson on the Life and Letters of St. Paul.

Every one knows that the great Catholic tradition makes the island of Malta the scene of the shipwreck of the Apostle. Near the bay which bears his name, is shown the little chapel built in his honour, under the cave where the shipwrecked sailors lighted a fire, and where the barbarians saw the viper revive and fasten on the hand of the man of God. All these places, says a traveller, are venerated by the Maltese almost as much as the history of the events, and every spot supposed to have been trodden by the messenger of truth is regarded with respectful reverence. At

Floriana, between Valetta and the cavern, a church bearing the name of San Publio, shows the site of the house of the magistrate converted by his preaching.

In spite of this tradition, the Dalmatians, ever since the tenth century, have claimed for their island— Meleda, in the Gulf of Venice—the honour of having been the scene of the shipwreck; and some Benedictines of Ragusa have naturally been eager to lay hold of this claim, and to support it formally.

Here was a lucky chance for the enemies of tradition. This is what is said by Coleridge, in his "Table Talk":—"The belief that Malta is the island on which St. Paul was wrecked is so rooted in the common Maltese, and cherished with such a superstitious nationality, that the government would run the chance of exciting a tumult, if it or its representatives unwarily ridiculed it. The supposition itself is quite absurd. Not to argue the matter at length, consider these few conclusive facts: The narrative speaks of the 'barbarous people,' or 'barbarians' of the islands. Now, our Malta was at that time fully peopled and highly civilised, as we may surely infer from Cicero and other writers. A viper comes out from the sticks upon the fire being lighted; the men are not surprised at the appearance of the snake, but imagine, first a murderer, and then a God from the harmless attack. Now, in our Malta, there are, I may say, no snakes at all— which, to be sure, the Maltese attribute to St. Paul's having cursed them away. Melita, in the Adriatic, was a perfectly barbarous island as to its native population, and was, and is now, infested with serpents. Besides, the context shows that the scene is in the Adriatic."

As to the last point, it is sufficient to remark that poets, historians, and geographers of the period give the name of the Adriatic to all that part of the Mediterranean which lies between Sicily and Greece, without confining it, as we do, to the Gulf. As to the word "barbarians," used by St. Luke, every one knows that the Greeks were accustomed so to designate any foreigners not speaking their language. Neither is the argument drawn from the absence of vipers in Malta more conclusive than the others, when it is remembered that, considering its extent, that island has become one of the most populous spots in Europe, and that there is not a corner of it which is not cultivated. There are no serpents in Malta now, for the same reason that there are none in the Champs Elysées in Paris, or in our London parks.

But instead of discussing objections any longer, let us pass on to the proofs which are the subject of this chapter.

An officer of the English Royal Navy, Admiral Penrose, and another well-informed writer, Mr. J. Smith, have made it their business to verify St. Paul's voyage, particularly from the nautical point of view.

Bearing in mind the state of navigation under the first emperors, they have followed, day by day, and almost hour by hour, the circumstantial details given by St. Luke. Without any communication with each

other, they agree as to the course which the ship must
have taken from the Good Havens, in the island of
Crete, coasting the little isle of Clauda, to the scene of
the shipwreck. They think that a vessel of that time,
heavily laden, disabled, and driven by the storm, must
have taken thirteen days to reach the lee-shore of
Malta; that on arriving there on the fourteenth night,
the practised ear of the sailors could have recognised
the sound of the breakers even before coming in sight
of shore; they found that in the direction of St. Paul's
Bay, the soundings must have given a depth, first of
twenty, then of fifteen fathoms; that the bay in question must have offered a good hold for the anchors,
and, in the morning, a good beach on which to run
ashore; that in this place a shelter was afforded by an
islet dividing the sea—"locum dithalassum." In short,
they found in the details of soundings and other calculations, the most exact explanation of St. Luke's
words. Whereas, if the attempt be made to prove
that the vessel's course lay along the Illyrian coast, we
meet with endless difficulties, contradictions, and disagreement with the sacred text, the meaning of which
it becomes almost impossible to determine.

CHAPTER VI.

ON THE COMPARATIVE VALUE OF THESE DIFFERENT TESTIMONIES.

UP to a certain point, we might fairly confine ourselves to Divine authenticity as regards places consecrated by the memories of the Church. When God makes a sanctuary the scene of His wonders, and the centre of His Divine operations, I need no documents nor inscriptions to tell me that its great and principal sanctity rests on no deception. A holy obscurity would be enough to give me perfect confidence in venerating the traditional place which has for its vouchers the blessing of Heaven, the approbation of bishops, and the reverence of nations. Still, as a rule, it has not pleased God to deprive the Holy Places of the glory of those noble and ancient origins which set forth their title deeds and indisputable proofs of their authenticity in the face of men.

Wherever the Church herself attaches the sanctity of a place to the memory of a great event, it is to be believed, not only that she does so on good grounds, but that she is in a position to justify her traditions and practice in the eyes of well-disposed persons.

If I am able to believe in the details of my religion, as a scholar, an historian, an antiquarian, there is no law which compels me to believe blindly. It is well for the simple Christian to be able to give reasons, and to prove that his devotion is well founded. Priests, bishops, doctors, theologians, should know, in case of need, how to wield the sword of human knowledge in defence of the rights and practices of the Church. They should put us in a position to repel the attacks of ignorance, and the wild assertions of error. The true business of the Christian antiquary is to furnish us with arsenals for this purpose. In this lies his dignity; without such an aim, I confess I can only look upon him as an industrious idler, or a scientific charlatan.

Whether religious or profane monuments are in question, both scepticism and rashness are to be avoided. Archæology is still an infant science, and, usually, is not hard of belief. A traveller reaches a ruin, observes its style and architecture, examines its environs and situation; he discovers some traces of inscriptions or carvings; he questions his guide, and, putting together these data, he launches his conjectures abroad. The authority of his name gets credit for them; his carelessly formed suppositions gain for him a glory which the contradictions of more careful observers will hardly overcast. As a matter of fact, it would be unjust to require from the man of learning more than he is able to give. His ingenious guesses are frequently the result of long and patient study; and this must be counted to his honour, even although it has not led him to absolute proof. We all know the disputes of the learned concerning the site of Alesia, the last bulwark of Gaulish liberty which fell before

the armies of Cæsar. No matter what antiquarian
work we open, it is full of discussion and uncertainty.
Whole cities are a riddle to us. Their mutilated ruins
are a confusion of different periods, and of styles
barely recognisable; their inscriptions are effaced, or
partly obliterated; and the difficulty is increased by a
variety of names and vague traditions. Hence the in-
terminable disputes in books of travel.

How often have ancient inscriptions been found in
the ruins of comparatively recent buildings! and, on
the other hand, inscriptions of the time of the Ptole-
mies or Cæsars on temples and tombs of an earlier
date—earlier, perhaps, by a thousand years. The
learned have attributed hundreds of buildings to one
and the same Rameses, or Sesostris, and have suddenly
awakened to the fact of there being several of the
name to be distributed among as many centuries.

We find the same obscurity, the same disputes, when
tradition is in question. Very often it appears like
one of those fantastic and all but invisible threads
which float on the autumn breeze, and which are
broken by a breath. It depends only on oral trans-
mission and on the recollection of generations, and
there appears to be no security for it.

Every one knows that, as a rule, very little reliance
can be placed on popular tales, which are a mass of
exaggeration, and in the end become mere fiction.

Sometimes, the first link in the chain is missing in
a local tradition, and it is in this way that the mere
guesses, or even questions, of travellers have become

transformed into traditions. " Is this Elim ?" asks a
traveller of his Arab guide, who, piquing himself on
knowing everything, replies in the affirmative, and,
some day or other, says to another traveller, " This is
Elim." Question and answer, confused together, are
handed on, till the scientific discovery of the true Elim
shows that a false track has hitherto been followed.
Usually, travellers are not more particular about
traditions than about other proofs. A name more or
less altered by the natives of a country is sufficient to
make them decide on the site of an ançient city after
ages of oblivion. It may be all very well, so long as
there is no proof to the contrary ; but this easy way of
settling matters has given rise to more than one mistake.

It is undeniable, also, that topographical tradition,
like all human things, may die out, or become corrupted ; and that, if it is lost to sight for many centuries, to re-appear, only mingled with absurd fables,
and unsupported by history, it loses at least a portion
of its credit.

But here, again, we are met by the exaggerations of
critics. A metal may be depreciated by alloy without
losing all its value ; sometimes, even, a little rust does
but serve to enhance the price of a medal ; and, in the
same way, a fable, or any other accidental error, does
not destroy a tradition ; nay, it may even be a confirmation of it, so long as it does not injure its
foundation, so long as it is only the rust of centuries. Thus, all the romances which have made
Charlemagne's nephew almost a fabulous personage,

strengthen, rather than destroy, the tradition of Roland's death at Roncevaux.

It may happen that a fable, or even a series of fables, sets us on the right track, explains and confirms the truth to us. This is perfectly acknowledged in profane science, and the learned consider their time well employed in disentangling truth from falsehood in periods where history verges on mythology. In this manner, the imposture of the "sacred fire" of the Greeks is a pain to our religious feeling, without in any way shaking our faith in the authenticity of the Holy Sepulchre. It proves that the Greeks, eager as they are to find the Latins in fault, have not been able, even in the days of their deepest degradation, to divest themselves of the universal belief on the subject of its site.

Is it fair to conclude that there is no such thing as perfectly conclusive evidence, from the fact that it is, perhaps, rarer than is generally thought ? Surely not. A man must be mad to suppose, on discovering a building at Thebes or Memphis answering to the dimensions and descriptions given by Diodorus Siculus, nearly 2000 years ago, that those colossal ruins had actually been made on purpose to fit in with the figures of the Greek historian. Who has ever heard a doubt of the authenticity of the Coliseum, of Trajan's Column, or of the Arch of Titus ?

Numbers of inscriptions and ruins bear on themselves irrefragable proofs of their authenticity. Very often, a single proof is sufficient to compel conviction.

How much more when they are multiplied! When monuments are explained by history and tradition, and they, in their turn, are confirmed by clear, numerous, and well-grounded archæological observations, to doubt would be folly, or bad faith. But such a concurrence of proofs and evidence is rarely to be met with in things which antiquity has consecrated, without respecting them more than other human works.

For the most part, revolutions, disasters, and the rust of oblivion wear away the long chain, till only some broken links are left; still, such as they are, these links may have a certain value. No savant or antiquarian ever requires accumulated proofs of different kinds. One definitive proof is sufficient. Some monuments and inscriptions explain themselves. Certain archives lead the reader to the very commencement of a building, and give us, so to say, its plan and photograph; and there are traditions which are as reliable as archives, and which carry conviction to the mind of every fair judging person.

The value of these different kinds of proof is so independent of their combination, that it is possible that in one instance they may, all together, be too weak to bring conviction; while in another a single proof is enough to satisfy men of science.

The commonest cases are those in which an accumulation of incomplete proofs is equivalent to a quasi-certainty with which, practically, we have to be satisfied. As a matter of fact, it is pretty nearly sufficient when the question is merely one of scientific curiosity. The

world is "traditus disputationibus nostris:" and we
have no right to ask that science shall always be without its enigmas, always in the sunshine of mathematical
certainty.

To be more scrupulous before we bow our heads in
conviction and respect to things of hallowed memory—
above all, before we call upon others to do so, is our
right and our duty. When religious veneration is in
question, we can scarcely be satisfied with hap-hazard
statements. If a thing is doubtful, say so. A cloud
of mystery or the absence of history is better than the
shadow of a deception, or a fancy rashly asserted. If
we are without Divine evidence, we feel the necessity
of the strongest scientific certainty.

But there is a perfect gulf between this conscientious jealousy, and the scepticism, or rather the un-
reasoning abhorrence of some minds on the subject
of religious traditions. Science ought to be modest.
How is it that men, who are so large-minded in
matters of ordinary demonstration, become so intractable when the question refers to sacred tradition ?
No accumulation of evidence outweighs, in their eyes,
the presumption that we are credulous. Clearly it
is prejudice which is influencing this judgment, not
science or logic.

We have a right to require of our adversaries that,
with regard to religious memories, they should be contented with evidence which they would accept in the
matter of Greek or Roman antiquities. Could any
one expect fresh evidence, year after year, that the

ancient Lutetia is identical with our Paris? I know
of no inscription, from the time of Julius Cæsar to that
of Julian, proving that the ruins of the Rue de la Harpe
are really those of the Palace of the Thermæ. Yet no
one has any doubt, either of the origin of Paris, or of
its antiquities.

The reason is that men do not consider moments, I
might say ages of silence and obscurity, as any real
signs that a chain of tradition is broken. When a
topographical tradition is connected with great events,
especially with national glories or sufferings, when its
river-like course has at first been among a simple
people, and, farther on, has spread far and wide among
different races, I am not obliged to concern myself with
certain difficulties of detail, nor to follow it at every
turn, so as to show what its course has been. It
must necessarily, in the lapse of ages, have passed
through some difficult phases, some periods of death
and devastation; but a barrier of sand or of rocks
does not prevent our tracing the course of a river,
neither does a passing cloud from knowing the
course of the sun. If, after an interruption, we come
again upon a tradition, which continues vigorous and
consistent with itself, with history, and with other
parallel documents, if we have every facility for ac-
counting for its eclipses and its re-appearances, then
we shall see in these accidents a proof of its strength
and regularity, not a reason for doubt and denial.

There are archæologists, who, seeing and desiring to
see nothing but their antiquities, exaggerate the im-

portance of monumental evidence at the expense of historical and traditional proofs. They want to amend everything by the aid of their science ;—history, philosophy, religion itself. And, under the pretext that nothing is so irresistible as a fact, they are inclined, on the one hand, to deny everything which is not carved in granite, and, on the other, they move heaven and earth to find an inscription, an orientation, by the help of which they may discredit received ideas or the evidence of the Sacred Scriptures. We should really have got into curious difficulties if the statements of certain scholars of the last century had been realised, instead of vanishing, as they have done, on closer inspection. God did not suffer His servants to be long perplexed by the famous zodiacs, and other similar enigmas.

We can look forward with calmness to any amount of development of the science of archæology, knowing beforehand that nothing can ever happen which will contradict our faith in any important point. On the contrary, experience has taught us that it always has been, and always will be confirmed.

Without going so far as the materialistic archæologists, certain Protestants are led by their tendencies to admit no evidence but that of stone and of the chisel, to rely on intuition alone, and to take no account of the oral tradition of ages and nations. Their instinct tells them that this evidence is fatally identical with that of the Church which they reject.

13

I can easily understand enthusiasm for a science which affords so wide a field of investigation as archæology. At the sight of a ruin we call up before our vision nations long extinct, and races that have passed away; we form conjectures as to their intellectual condition, and the force of their civilisation. We reconstruct their history and their physiognomy, as the geologist infers the species, the formation of a race of animals from merely examining a fossil.

But, in fact, while seemingly a science as exact and as independent as that of mathematics, archæology is one which has very little power of standing alone. It cannot dispense either with ancient languages, or chronology, or even with natural history and chemistry; it pre-supposes a knowledge of art at different periods, and in its relations with ethnology. Mistakes may be made in spite of the clearest inscriptions. We all know of ancient marbles and granites carried to distant sites merely to be employed as building materials as far back as the time of the Romans; and how, sometimes, inscriptions are found far away from the place for which they were intended. A slab, merely reversed, has been used for different buildings, at different epochs; other inscriptions have undergone alterations and changes of name, and present as many difficulties to amateurs as the most confused palimpsests.

. Well might, then, a Catholic assume, *à priori*, 1st. That the Holy Places venerated by the Church are the most authentic places in the world, because, most frequently, they have the witness both of Heaven and earth; the two kinds of authenticity uniting, and mutually confirming each other, and human tradition rising to the level of supernatural authority by mingling with that of the Church and the saints.

He has a right to believe, 2ndly, that true science never has been, and never will be in opposition to authenticity of a higher order. If there is apparent contradiction, it is—sometimes that men have misunderstood the Divine indications, and ascribe to the Church a conviction which she does not hold—and almost always that human science requires to be examined, and corrected in its calculations.

CHAPTER VII.

HOW TO SIMPLIFY THE QUESTION ?

WE have no intention of entering upon a regular discussion of every Christian antiquity. That would entail an examination to discriminate which are more or less approved by the Church, which she rejects, and which she leaves to the liberty of each individual. Of the traditions which she sanctions, it would be necessary to decide what forms their essence, and to discard what is merely accessory. Each individual fact having been once made clear, next would come the establishing of the cause, the discussion of authorities, the weighing of evidence for and against the

refutation of objections, and the final verdict. The
subject would fill volumes, and the general point of
view would be lost in a forest of detailed discussions.
We will, therefore, choose Palestine, and Jerusalem
especially, as one of the most important subjects of
our thesis, and as an instance of authenticity. If their
grand memories do not bear the stamp of truth to the
eyes of science, if they cannot be confidently accepted
by a person of good faith, what should we have left
to say for our other sanctuaries?

"The question is interesting," says the Rev. G.
Williams, the learned and impartial author of the
" Holy City ;" " if the Holy Places are dear to us for the
sake of the Man-God, we do not like to be told that
we are mistaken, and that we have been deceived."
There is a question of feeling involved, apart from that
of the Church's honour. An assertion which bids us
destroy our most cherished family recollections, requires proof. If it is a mere vague statement, desti-
tute of all foundation, it is our right and our duty to
reject it as an insult. We believe, and are prepared to
prove, that, with regard to most of the principal scenes
of our Lord's Life and Death, we have more consistent
and striking proofs of authenticity than those which
are usually considered sufficient in archæology ; and
that if our sacred memories cannot always boast of
the inscriptions or other ostentatious demonstrations
which we find on the monuments of the Pharaos or
the Cæsars, it is because they breathe of the humble
mysteries of the Faith, because they have been de-

fended from oblivion more by the unchangeable love of Christian nations than by the marvels of architecture and the other arts.

The question being thus confined to Palestine, we can also leave out any discussion of recent monuments, the origin of which is more or less known. There is no need to repeat what has been said about the consecration of churches. Generally speaking, no one thinks of discussing their authenticity. Even if no title-deeds, no instrument mentioning the consecration were in existence, the very fact of the use they are put to proves their dignity, even if their construction and other outward signs did not show the intention of the founders.

We will also pass over merely accessory legends. The Church does not sanction every invention or pious tale which may be due to the imagination of the people or to the pen of the chronicler. She is answerable for traditions only inasmuch and in the sense in which she accepts them.

Frequently she neither accepts nor rejects; she remains neutral. A legend may be innocent and pious, and yet may be founded on events of which there is no existing proof. If evidence is wanting, if all the links of the traditional chain are not visible, the Church will not feel bound to pronounce judgment; she will be silent, because she can neither condemn nor approve without right reasons. Does that justify any one in taxing her with ignorance, deception, or superstition ?

Before attacking an ecclesiastical legend, it is proper to examine what it is, whence it comes, who proposes it, and in what manner it is proposed.

We are bound to defend what is presented to us as founded on respectable and ancient evidence ; what is universal, and has always been received by the Catholic world—in short, the real traditions of the Church. Her rule is—unity in necessary things, liberty in doubtful ones, charity always. Therefore, we are at liberty to exercise our judgment in regard to isolated statements, mere conjectures, and opinions which are offered to us merely as such. We are in no way obliged to take up with every popular story—the fancies of the Greeks or the rabbis. There may be a doubtful tradition which we accept, so to speak, with a limited liability, without being bound to prove it, because, though it rests on facts more or less altered, it has a value of its own as an indication ; there may be a certain scientific theory which we may adopt in want of a better, till we are more fully informed on the subject.

This being granted, I will suppose that we have to decide on the tradition of the rock El-Sakkra, or on that of Adam's skull on Calvary, or on that of the centre* of the world in the church of the Holy Sepulchre.

We will put the last aside at once, as an invention of the Greeks, which is foreign to the real traditions of the place, and which has no firmer historical or

* The ὀμφαλός.

scientific basis than some eastern rhetorical expression taken too literally.

As to the singular rock under the dome of the mosque of Omar, and which, in all likelihood, occupied also some central position in Solomon's Temple, without believing, with the rabbis and the Turks, that this calcareous mass was the very first piece of solid matter created, or that God Himself placed it in the centre of the world, we are inclined to give it a real archæological value in ascertaining the site of the ancient Temple.

We neither vouch for nor reject the legend which connects the name of Calvary with the skull of our first father, because it is neither vouched for nor rejected by the Church; but we make use of it as an etymological indication, as the holy doctors did, and, like them, we see nothing in it but what is possible, venerable, and edifying. But we admit that it has never been offered by the Church to the faithful, as authoritatively as the traditions concerning the site of the principal events of the Life and Death of Christ.

Is it a reproach to the Pères de Terre Sainte, and the other guardians of the sanctuaries, that they have made mention of everything, even of what is evidently fabulous, and of made-up events? Surely not. Nay, it is, in some sort, their duty to bring forward every document they know of. What would be said of a judge, who, at the opening of a trial, were to leave out whatever opposed his own views? It would be said that he was pre-judging the question.

Among legends worthy of being regarded, there may be one, which, after having been rejected by the learned, is shown, by new discoveries and closer examination, to be worthy of notice; another, largely altered, may be freed from alloy; and even those which have no foundation, may, incidentally, subserve the cause of science and truth. All may be useful, as a kind of indication. Thus, whatever may be thought of the legend of the Sakkra, it would be enough, by its antiquity, to chastise the audacity of that hunter after novelties who would fain place the Holy Sepulchre there; and that of another doctor who takes pleasure in making the Temple of Jerusalem cross the valley of the Cedron, and boldly places it on the Mount of Offence. Anyhow, it is a help in deciding an important point with regard to the ancient sanctuary.

Can it be denied that there may be memories which are perfectly innocent, even edifying, and founded on truth, concerning which, nevertheless, the Church has a right to be silent, at the same time that she leaves her children full liberty to speak of them? The Church is not obliged to satisfy every curiosity; she neither approves nor condemns without legitimate reasons.

If evidence be insufficient—if the chain of tradition be defective—if there be some advantage, some delicacy, which leads her to reserve judgment—the Church will know, according to circumstances, how to say the right thing, to be silent, to overlook, to tolerate, or

even to smile; and no one has the right to treat this
liberty as ignorance or superstition.

There are certain critics in whose eyes everything is
false which cannot offer a material proof. On this
principle Horace would have been wrong in saying
that many a Hector and Achilles had been left in
oblivion for lack of an authority:

"... carent quia vate sacro."

He ought simply to have concluded that they had
never existed. We may contrast with these crude
judgments the candid remarks of a Protestant, the
Rev. Mr. Williams:—

"Granting it" (the identity of the sacred localities)
"to be a delusion, it is to him" (the devout pilgrim) "at
least a pleasing and profitable delusion, implicating
him in no guilt; and he might reasonably regard the
wisdom which would rob him of his gratification as
folly, and count his ignorance the greater bliss."

Still, there are places and traditions in regard to
which even an innocent illusion is made impossible;
and Mr. Williams feels this, for he adds, speaking of
the Holy Sepulchre, "When the moral character of one
important branch of the Church, if not of the whole
Church, is at stake, the question assumes a graver
aspect, and we are bound in charity, if not in gratitude, to weigh with the most suspicious jealousy the
evidence which would convict of deliberate fraud and
shameless hypocrisy, not only the bishops and clergy
at Jerusalem, but the brightest lights of the universal
Church at a period which we have been taught to

regard as 'uncorrupt,' when Christianity was 'most pure, and, indeed, golden.'*　For the plea of ignorance can hardly be admitted in their behalf, and would scarcely be an extenuation of their fault if it could. They were impostors, and not dupes, or they had sufficient evidence to believe that they really recovered the Sepulchre of our Lord."

These remarks are perfectly just; but we Catholics can go further. Not only is the honour of the churches of Palestine, and even those of Christendom, interested in the question, but the responsibility of a false system with regard to the Holy Places would lie on Him Who promised to be with His Church through all ages, Who guides her by His Spirit, and Whose working is manifested by the wonders of His grace and power.

Not that, up to the present time, the Church has made the Holy Places the subject of her absolute decisions.　But it cannot be supposed, without an heretical spirit, that in stirring up the devotion of nations to these local memories, both by her example, approbation, and solemn encouragement, the Church is favouring error and superstition.　In taking a position as the declared enemy of important traditions, notoriously recognised by the Church, a man might, perhaps, escape the brand of formal heresy, but would expose himself to the severest censures which are attached to blasphemous and scandalous temerity, savouring of heresy.

* Anglican Homilies.

St. Gregory Nazianzen teaches us that the rites, customs, and traditions of the Church owe their vigour, not so much to the wit of man as to the power of God and the strengthening hand of time; and Quaresimus, who quotes him, concludes from this that to rise up against what is proposed to us by the universal Church, and in its measure, by a particular church, as an object of faith, or simply of pious belief, seems to spring from a spirit obstinate, stubborn, and intractable.

CHAPTER VIII.

PROTESTANTS AND FREE-THINKERS AND THE QUESTION OF AUTHENTICITY IN THE HOLY LAND.

WE have already declared who are the enemies of the authenticity of the Holy Places. They are those of the Catholic Church, and, in general, of the supernatural. Protestants are in a false position with regard to sacred topography. They have rejected the principle of tradition, but they are forced back upon it by archæology, and the result is a manifold conflict: a conflict with themselves, to reconcile their principles and their antipathies; a conflict with Catholics on the subject of the traditions which they will not accept, and yet which they cannot do without; a conflict with infidelity, which they cannot resolve to follow into its lowest depths; and, lastly, a conflict with their coreligionists, who incline, some towards a return to the past, others towards progress, or infidelity, so that the task of refuting one another may safely be left to themselves.

The infidel, the materialist, deny the supernatural, and laugh to scorn the idea of certainty. They have never found sanctity either in their crucible or under their scalpel. Before discussing the question of consecrated places, they ought, as an indispensable preliminary, to be taught over again the first chapter of the catechism. But as they none the less argue and sneer, their objections must not be left unanswered. We are obliged to repel their attacks both for the honour of religion, and for the sake of the many weak souls who are always ready to take scandal, and to lower their flag before the slightest assault, while, at the same time, they keep alive a spark of faith.

Every shade of opinion is to be found among the European travellers who have explored and described Palestine for the last 200 years, from the Free-thinker, who goes to the last extreme of rebellion, to the Puseyite, who is separated from Rome only by a hair's breadth—from the *bel esprit* of the tavern to the learned metaphysician—from the frivolous woman, who chatters on every subject of which she is ignorant, up to what we call an austere puritan.

Infidelity, mocking scepticism, Voltairian sarcasm, predominate among the fractions of the Latin race who have turned against us; whilst Protestantism, in general, reigns among the Teutonic and Anglo-Saxon races, which contribute, and have always contributed, so many visitors to the Holy Land.

The German is outwardly, sometimes, thoroughly erudite. He is a Krupp canon, who, as he travels, is trampling down the road of science by sheer weight. Do not expect objective doctrine from him. There is something due to the "inner consciousness" even in his religious topography.

The Anglo-Saxon, the spoiled child of fortune, easily believes himself superior to all other races. In cutting himself off from Catholicism, he has adopted the Jewish ideas of temporal prosperity to a great extent. Even at home, he is accustomed to set himself up as an authority in some speciality of science or of daily life. What he knows, he knows well, and even when he is not thoroughly acquainted with it, he only succeeds the better in making the most of his knowledge, by dint of assurance. "When an Englishman knows anything," said a former governor of one of the American states, "he will keep himself modestly apart; but when he is as ignorant as a peacock, he will thrust himself in everywhere, and, one way or another, will make wonderful discoveries." Thanks to his energy and air of importance, such an individual, knowing, perhaps, just a little of history, or physical science, will be a member of four or five learned societies, will talk of progress, and lament the incurable inferiority of all races but his own. Certainly, it is a little dangerous when questions of a high religious bearing fall into the hands of people who so easily pass themselves off as oracles.

The American is an Anglo-Saxon more independent, more adventurous, more arrogant, than the Englishman. On certain points he is a perfect child, new to everything, and listening eagerly; but on others, he is persuaded that the future belongs to him—that he has only to go ahead and become the schoolmaster of the world. With his *aplomb*, his dollars, and his little stock of modern science, which he has a wonderful knack of making the most of, he comes, like a superior being, among us old Latins, and talks of us, on his return, as he would of Osages or Esquimaux, who required his assistance to show them the value of their own possessions.

Here is a book by a reverend gentleman from New York. Evidently the author is clever, and has a pretty fair stock of science. He is professor of natural history at the college of Salem, a member of the American Scientific Association, and of the Scientific Institute of Malta. He is at Bethlehem, at the midnight Mass. He is neither an unbeliever, nor fanatically hostile to all those persons who are crowding to the upper church, there to celebrate the great anniversary—he would even preach, if only he was asked to do so.

"This is," says his narrative, "the vicinity of the spot where the Saviour was born. This is near to the place where the angels sang the first heavenly song

that was ever recorded*—a song of the triumph of
God's mercy and of His justice too—and this the night
of the commemoration of such scenes and such holy
and glorious consequences. I could have given my
soul up to the rapture of such thoughts had there been
a correspondence in the form of worship and in the
music; but it was not possible to feel so. The scene
was so utterly at variance with all I had anticipated,
that for a time I was forced to forget even that I was
in a church, or at Bethlehem, or in Palestine at all."

And why so, reverend sir? You find the organ
tolerable, though small; the chanting of the Te Deum,
and other hymns, strikes you as devotional; the Nea-
politan organist is clever. . . . Yes, but the music becomes more animated. Let us see: is it not the over-
ture of Masaniello!! Then they light up—those eastern
faces beam with joy; they kneel, they sing. And
above all stand the priests at the altar with all their
"paraphernalia!" It is incomprehensible. Will his
reverence be carried away by indignation, and drive
out the profaners of the temple? At all events will
he leave it himself in the way of a solemn reproof?
No—he entrusts us with his little secrets, and explains
how it was that "he forgot." What could he do? On
his right was a group of those young girls of Bethlehem in whose veins, we are told, flows the blood of the

* Here the learned professor forgets the "Sanctus" of the
Cherubim which the prophet Ezechiel heard them sing in
heaven; but further on he confesses that his memory plays
him tricks.

fairest races in the world, including that of our Crusaders. They are, indeed, famed for their grace and
beauty. One of these, in a scarlet cap, is really remarkable. How can any one, who is something of an
artist, resist the temptation of making a sketch? The
album and pencil come out of the pocket, and the work
begins. The daughter of Eve is not long in perceiving
it; the first movement of the Christian maiden is to
draw her veil over her face, but coquetry gets the
upper hand; smiles are exchanged, the veil is put
back, the portrait is finished. The reverend gentleman
sees nothing but what is very natural in describing
this little scene minutely; and Haneefa's picture figures
as the frontispiece of his handsome octavo volume, by
way of introduction, so as to let us know what to expect of the nature of his book, which is full of interesting details of the geology and natural history of Palestine, and dedicated to his countryman, the Rev. E.
Robinson, the Christopher Columbus of the Holy Land
. . . in the eyes of people who are willing to take his
word for everything.

The next reverend author who meets us is English;
and at the first glance he appears to possess more
gravity of character; he spends a fortnight in Jerusalem, and comes upon some half-obliterated Hebrew
inscriptions on some tombs on the hill Haceldama;
the word Sion catches his eye. In a moment his
theory is formed, and in defiance of all tradition, he
fixes the site of the city of David, the ancient Jebus
to the south of the valley of the children of Hinnom,

right under the inscription. . . . As reasonably might
F. Faber, when he found the name of Driffield on a
tomb at Pera, have put that hamlet and the whole of
Gloucestershire instead of Constantinople on the Bos-
phorus. Protestants themselves have turned a deaf ear
to the suggestion.

Another writer is full of reverence for the memorials
of God's ancient people, especially if they are pointed
out by the Arabs. He would not acknowledge it, of
course, but he has less sympathy with the New Testament. It gives him a presentiment of monks! Naturally he is out of temper on reaching the Holy Sepulchre
with a religious as his cicerone. He is dissatisfied
with what he sees and does not see under the marble
coverings. At last the idea suggested to him by the
Anglo-Prussian Bishop Gobat, comes into his head:
"Surrexit—non est hic!" That is certain—they are
the words of the angel: "Christ is risen—He is not
here." It is an idle dream to seek Him here, even in
painting or in memory. We are free to adore Jehova
at the oak of Mambre, or where we please, but not at
the Sepulchre. To be sure—David foretold that that
Sepulchre should be glorious . . . but, after all, "non
est hic." There is not a place in the world of which
anything has been more distinctly said. So, our traveller takes his leave, doubtless, for fear of some mishap.
But his guide sticks to him, makes him pass through
the subterranean Church of the Invention of the Cross,
and tells him the nearly contemporary account of Sozomen. Every Catholic knows how the True Cross was

14

proved to be so by a sudden cure in the presence of the Empress St. Helena, of her suite, and of all Jerusalem. A miracle in the fourth century! Our traveller's patience is exhausted, and he makes a hasty exit, vowing never again to set foot in a building that has been thus profaned.

He is considerably more tolerant with regard to his co-religionists. A friend of his was moved to tears at the idea that he, too, had made his little Biblical discovery. He gives out, with *naïve* satisfaction, that he has discovered Agar's well in the desert to the south of Hebron, between Cades and Barad; he sees some likeness between the modern name Moi-lahi, and the scriptural one Bir-lahi-Rohi. Alas! the author of whom we have just spoken destroys his arguments by a simple calculation, but he does so with perfect courtesy. Woe to the reverend gentleman if he had worn the cowl instead of the white cravat!

We next make acquaintance with a member of the Bible Society; this gentleman is a kind of spiritual commercial traveller; he has only one idea, that a monk is superstitious, and that the reverse of whatever a Catholic says and thinks must be Gospel truth. Such a notion leads to rather strange consequences, for, after all, we do believe all fundamental truths. Fortunately, he does not stick to it too closely.

At Damascus, he refuses to believe that respectable Jews could have assassinated Father Thomas in 1840. Indeed, was there ever such a person as Father Thomas?

And, granting his existence, what was the great harm of killing a Franciscan friar ?

It is needless to say that he considers the eastern Catholics, the Maronites especially, as savages who are bound to disappear before the march of civilisation.

I may mention Dean Stanley, the author of "Sinai and Palestine," as a man of taste and learning; he draws the Biblical events for us in the natural framing of the scenes in which they took place. His work gives the idea of a topographical and picturesque Bible Concordance; it has the liveliness of a tourist's journal, while it spares us the account of the pipes that have been smoked, the halts that have been made, the horses that have been ridden. He enters thoroughly into the grand scenes he describes, on the very spot where they took place; and so he may be profitably consulted wherever anti-Catholic prejudice does not come into play; but he is all the more dangerous when he is in the opposition. In spite of a certain air of candour, he is all the while building up a system which puts our traditions on the footing of legends, whenever they have not the support of an inscription as plain as a certificate. "There are some countries," he says, "such as Greece, whose natural features—some cities, such as Rome, whose vast ruins—lend themselves with extraordinary facility to the growth of legends. . . . But in Jerusalem it is not so. The featureless rocks without the walls, the mere dust and ashes within, at once repel the attempt to amalgamate them with the fables which, by the very fact of their slight and almost imperceptible connection with the spots in question, betray their foreign parentage. A fragment of old sculpture lying at a house door is sufficient to mark the abode of Veronica; a broken column separated from its companions in a colonnade in the next street, is pointed out as that to which the decree of Pilate was affixed, or on which the cock crew; a faint line on the surface of a rock is the mark of the girdle which the Virgin dropped to convince Thomas. There is no attempt at fraud, or even at probability; nothing seems to have been too slight, too modern, for the tradition to lay hold of it. Criticism and belief are alike disarmed by the childlike, almost playful spirit in which the early pilgrims and Crusaders must have gone to and fro, seeking for places here and there in which to localise the dreams of their own imaginations."

It is true that Dean Stanley draws a distinction between great memories and traditions of matters of detail. But, really, he puts them on the same level in the end. At bottom, Dean Stanley is sophistical, like the rest, in supposing that there is no real tradition in matters of religion; that it has only an imaginary foundation, or that, in itself, it is valueless. It is sufficient to apply his system to things nearer home, in order to refute it. There is a place in London, near Hyde Park, formerly celebrated for the executions which took place outside the town. Every one has heard of Tyburn, where a gibbet stood constantly, and where the blood of the martyrs of Elizabeth's days mingled with that of the vilest criminals. Now, if I

were to ask Dean Stanley to show me the traditionary
site of this place, no doubt he would point it out unhesitatingly in the neighbourhood of the Marble Arch,
at the corner of Connaught Terrace, in the Edgware
Road. How would he receive an objection on my
part that I only saw modern buildings there, and that
there was nothing to indicate where the ancient gibbet
stood? Would he not be the first to answer that those
buildings are, all the same, the one true link of the
tradition, that the good sense of the public is satisfied
with it, although no monument attests it, and that the
greater the transformation, the more does it prove the
strength and tenacity of the tradition which has been
able to resist it, and to outlive such metamorphoses.

To how many monuments might not the same arguments be applied? But whenever systems supplant
true religion, reason is merely a compass disordered by
the storm.

In topography, as in other things, a little knowledge leads one away from religion and truth; deeper
knowledge brings one back to them.

We have already quoted the Rev. G. Williams, of
the University of Cambridge, and he may be instanced
as an example of candour and impartiality. With the
exception of some pages, or rather passages, his two
volumes on the "Holy City" might have been written
by the pen of a pious and learned Catholic. He takes
up his position as the skilful and conscientious champion
of tradition against the American audacity of Dr.
Robinson and the whole ultra-Protestant school; and

we cannot be very angry with him for not being able to understand the conduct of the Pères de Terre-Sainte in the incessant wrangling caused by the encroachments of the Greeks. It is very difficult for an outside observer to appreciate all the real merit of that obscure struggle between the self-devotion of poor and unarmed men on the one side, and on the other the constant pressure of an enemy always practised, and always ready to make use of Turkish fanaticism and the avarice of the pashas. The more petty and miserable this struggle of centuries appears, the more need has it of moral force and supernatural heroism. God alone knows all its merits, and He will reward it.

We shall meet Mr. Williams again more than once during our present discussions, and he will help and enlighten us in our researches. But we may now close this review, which is sufficient to enable us to judge of the hostile camp, and of the acquaintances we may meet there.

CHAPTER IX.

SUMMARY OF THE ATTACKS.

IF an attempt were made to sum up the attacks of Protestant travellers on the memorials of Palestine, it would amount to a general system, which might be expressed as follows :—

The Old Law was outward, and connected with places and recollections; but the New Law is a pure philosophy, which has no need to concern itself with external objects of this sort, except from a critical or scientific point of view. The first Christians were, before all things, a very exclusive literary party, which went by the Bible, and the Bible only. They were so spiritual, that they put from them the very memory of the places which were the scenes of our Lord's Life, Passion, and Resurrection; or, at any rate, they attached no importance to them. Moreover, they were so far from being stationary at Jerusalem, that they may be said merely to have passed through it, and to have been unable to hand down any memory or connected tradition. Again, the traditionary places have been so utterly altered, as to be unrecognisable—their very names must have been lost; and when peace was restored to the Church under Constantine, it was only by a notorious deception that St. Macarius pretended to find everything again. That patriarch invented an entire system of local devotions, which had no existence before his time. He took the first places at hand, and gave them the old names contrary to all rules of good sense. Others followed him in the same route; and this is why the whole Catholic system is nothing but a chaos of ignorance and superstition!

Superstition to believe that the Son of God was born in a certain place! Superstition to believe that He lived in a different manner from those moths which fly about without alighting anywhere! Superstition to believe that devotion may be kindled in those places, and may turn them into sanctuaries! Superstition to believe that those places of predilection are

places of grace and benediction! Superstition to consecrate one's life there to prayer and penance! Superstition to defend them from the profanation of the
wicked, the infidel, and the heretic! Superstition,
above all, to kneel and recite there the Lord's Prayer,
which, according to the Protestant Bibles themselves,
He taught us!

With regard to topography, the Latin, and especially
the Catholic monks, are not impartial witnesses, because they are interested in defending their system.
Infidels alone deserve absolute confidence, because they
have no interest in the matter. For the same reason,
Protestant and free-thinking travellers are in general
to be relied on. They all deserve the name and the
merit of learned men; but every scholar who wears
the dress of a monk, becomes ignorant at once; what
science he may have possessed before, becomes null
and valueless.

Every miracle or supernatural grace mentioned in
the canon of Scripture, is a proof of Divine intervention; but from the sixtieth year of the Christian era,
or very soon after, it is a sure proof of deception,
which it is unnecessary to investigate. Generally, the
continuance of names and memories is of some value
in archæology—it is a proof which is sufficient till
there is demonstration to the contrary; but when
Palestine, especially Calvary and the Holy Sepulchre,
are in question, the contrary principle must be admitted. St. Paul called the Church the pillar and
foundation of truth; but in matters of archæology

and history, she has only supported error and imposture, until, in our own time, thanks to the progress of rationalism, doubt and denial have come to the rescue, and offer a surer basis for our information.

To expose these ideas, is to refute them. We will, however, combat them, so far as our subject requires.

CHAPTER X.

THE MAIN POINT OF HISTORY WITH REGARD TO THE TOPOGRAPHY OF PALESTINE.

THE despisers of our religious memories are pretty well agreed that, from the time of the great Constantine, our traditions form a body so compact, so bound up with facts, with historical incidents, with titles and documents of every kind, so fully commented on by so many travellers, pilgrims, and writers of the most opposite belief, that it is unassailable on the score of continuity. But they say that it is vitiated in its origin, and, therefore, without value. Monks and pilgrims received it in blind confidence; they handed it down to monks and pilgrims of successive ages; but it is easy to see that they have all followed and still follow St. Jerome, whose works are well known. Quaresmius is only a huge commentary on the holy Doctor, who is himself only the new publisher of a more ancient author.

It was the semi-Arian courtier Eusebius of Cæsarea,

in whom Catholics themselves never placed unlimited confidence, who launched these traditions into the world, by his book of "Topics; or, the Biblical Scenes of Palestine." But Eusebius himself, in the eyes of our new men of learning, was only the tool of a clique of ambitious bishops, and of the Bishop of Jerusalem in particular.

This attack on the man whom Catholics have always called St. Macarius, simplifies the question wonderfully, and allows of our confining it to the first ages of Christianity.

Was Macarius, of Jerusalem, one of the champions of the Faith against the Arians at the Council of Nicæa, where his signature headed those of the bishops of Palestine, a saint or a juggler? He worked miracles, St. Epiphanius calls him one of the great prelates of his time, and the Church has raised him on her altars; but is not all this an additional proof of the depth of his hypocrisy?

We are to suppose him to have put the pen into the hand of Eusebius, in order to ensure to the see of Jerusalem its right of primogeniture and the favours of Constantine, by exhuming the buried memorials of the Old and New Testament. In proof of this plot of St. Macarius, we are presented with gratuitous assertions—assertion, that our Lord not having attached any importance to the places which He frequented, neither His apostles nor disciples had reason to trouble themselves about preserving their memory, and that thus the first and the essential link is wanting;

assertion, that there is no document to prove that
the Church concerned herself with the matter for her
300 model years ; and that, even had the Christians
wished to do so, they could not have succeeded, because they were not at Jerusalem during the siege,
and afterwards nothing was to be seen but unrecognisable ruins, heaps of rubbish, and buildings rebuilt by the Pagans, under which the objects of their
affections must have been deeply buried—last and
boldest assertion, the plot itself in all its details.

We have, then, to examine these different assertions
and afterwards to pronounce our verdict on the bishops
of Palestine ; to decide whether they drew the attention of the world to Holy Places by dishonest trickery ;
whether they were able and willing to deceive the
Christian world ; in a word, whether they were impostors.

CHAPTER XI.

WAS PRIMITIVE CHRISTIANITY HOSTILE TO THE LOCAL MEMORIES ?

WE have already seen that the theory of the Incarnation, far from being a formal relinquishment of the
idea of local sanctification, gave it a fresh impulse and
a new development ; and that this is the way in which
it appears to have been understood by the Evangelists.

The proofs of this are numerous. In the first place,

they thought, as the Jews did, that certain places were predestined by the Holy Spirit to be the venerated scenes of the chief events in the life of the Messias; they quote different passages from the prophets in support of this idea, and comment on them to convince the Jews; they set down in their writings, which are for all times and all people, these quotations, convincing to all who admit the inspiration of the sacred books.

Thus, in relating the birth of Christ, they mention the universal belief of the Jews and their doctors, who fixed that event at Bethlehem, and they rest on the words of Micheas, exalting that little city of Juda, because it was to witness the birth of the Messias, as it had done that of His ancestor David.

Another well-known prophecy regards the Temple. When it was rebuilt by Nehemias after the return from Babylon, the old Jews, who had seen in their childhood the glories of Solomon's Temple, wept on contrasting the second building with the first, but the prophet Aggeus consoles them by foretelling that the second Temple should be honoured by the presence of the "Desired of all Nations." If the Evangelists do not expressly quote the prophecy, we cannot doubt that it was in their minds when they give the account of Mary's purification, the presentation of her Child, Simeon's ecstasy, and Anna's prophecy, as well as the other occasions when Jesus appeared in the sacred building, beginning with the annual visits, during one of which, at the age of twelve, His conversation with the doctors took place, and ending with the great discourses, miracles, and authoritative acts of His public life.

We think, too, that the manner in which the evangelists relate our Lord's Resurrection, shows them to have been mindful of the prophecy that *the Sepulchre of the Messias shall be glorious.* At all events, how could the apostles, with this text before their eyes, possibly have turned the faithful aside from paying honour to the Sepulchre of Jesus? Could they have endured to see them direct their acts of veneration to another sepulchre which was not His? As we have explained elsewhere, the transient fact of the Resurrection was not enough for the adequate fulfilment of the prophecy. There is nothing to point to such a limitation. Would it be worth while to foretell the glory of a monument which was doomed to oblivion after three days? What! is it possible that the true Sepulchre should be forgotten by God, angels, and men for eighteen centuries —that another spot should have been actually venerated as the one pointed out by prophecy, and as the great memorial of regenerated humanity—that the apostles should have been the accomplices of this blunder and profanation? Impossible! According to the evangelists, our Lord Himself began to honour His Sepulchre as soon as He quitted it. He appointed angels to be its first heralds. His Mother and the holy women its first visitors; afterwards, Peter, John, and the rest. And yet we are to believe that the apostles neglected, forgot, and philosophised against the Holy Places!

Let those who say such things show us one line
which exalts the systematic contempt of local memorials to the dignity of a religious precept, or which so
much as forestalls the haughty indifference of our
modern days. On the contrary, does not a close examination of the Gospels show a tender and scrupulous
care to point out to us the various places which Jesus
has sanctified by His acts or prolonged stay, so accurately that posterity is able to recognise them ?

At all events it does not rest with us to prove that
the apostles did not set themselves the absurd task of
effacing from the hearts of the faithful the loving worship of sacred memories, in order to replace it by the
northern Puritanism of the seventeenth century. It
lies with our adversaries to prove that things have not
followed their natural course, and that a harsh discipline has checked the enthusiasm of the southern nations,
especially that of women, whose religion is, usually, all
heart and affection.

If piety towards the Places mentioned in the Bible
has always been crime, why do these gentlemen study
archæology ? How can that which was superstitious
and idolatrous in the Catholics of the first eighteen
centuries, become meritorious in the pedants of the
nineteenth ?

Even if neither Scriptures nor history had anything
to say on the subject, we should still have a right to
believe that the earliest foster-fathers of the Church
left her perfectly free in the holy tendernesses which

belonged to her state of infancy, and that veneration for the Holy Places is an apostolic practice. Persecutions have only revived it.

CHAPTER XII.

ORAL EVIDENCE OF THE FIRST CENTURIES.

BEFORE examining the traces left us by the tradition of reverence and love, let us begin by studying the course it must have taken—its channels—and the men from whom we have received it.

First Channel.—The Bishops and Clergy.

In the first place, we know (St. Paul and the Acts of the Apostles lead us to expect it) that, for a very long time, Jerusalem continued to be the grand centre and starting-point of every apostolic undertaking; and the Apostle of the Gentiles is no exception to this law. Even after the chair of Peter had been fixed, first at Antioch, and then at Rome, Jerusalem preserved her importance from what may be called family reasons. There was a jealous care to continue to her her pre-eminence, even after the flight of the Christians, the destruction of the city, and an almost exclusively pagan occupation, had sunk it, as to the numbers of the faithful, and its external importance, much below the level of Cæsarea, Antioch, and other neighbouring places. Even in the days when it was only known as Ælia Capitolina, it was defended by the majesty of its associations.

The first Council of Jerusalem had been an act of homage to the city of the Temple and the Cœnaculum. Its first patriarch was St. James, " the brother of the Lord." He certainly cannot be accused of being an enemy of sacred associations. We might, indeed, be tempted to suspect his judaizing tendencies to be in excess. Representative of a transition, and specially charged with the evangelising of the Jews, we see him living the life of the Nazarites, watching and praying in the Holy of Holies of the Temple, to which he is allowed an exceptional admission on account of the purity of his character. A terrace of the Temple was the scene of his last discourse and glorious martyrdom, shortly before the siege of the guilty city, whose punishment seemed deferred for his sake.

After a short interval, during which the Christians had retired to Pella, we find them returning to Jerusalem, and proceeding to a new election.

M. Poujoulat gives us the picture of the pious inhabitants re-entering that corpse-like city as follows :—

" C'est à peine s'ils pouvaient la reconnaitre, et sans doute, ils ne retenaient point leurs larmes à la vue d'un si grand désastre. Ils passèrent du deuil des ruines à la joie de prier auprès du sépulcre du Rédempteur, sur la montagne où son Sang avait coulé et d'adorer partout les traces divines."

It will be said, perhaps, that M. Poujoulat's vivid description is a somewhat startling exaggeration of the sober narrative of Hegesippus and Eusebius, but it is quite in conformity with nature. Besides, it appears, almost word for word, in the historian Josephus, who also tells us the impression made, not only on Jews, but on foreigners, by the sight of the desolated city even before its utter ruin.

"No one could see the wonderful suburbs of the great city changed into a heap of ruins without shedding tears. War had so entirely laid waste the chosen country of God that it did not even preserve the least trace of its former beauty, and any one in Jerusalem herself might have asked where stood formerly the city."

If such were the sentiments common at the time, we require something more than Mr. Robinson's assertion to make us believe that the Christians felt differently, and that they preserved a stoical indifference. The school we are combating would make of the successors of St. James so many bishops in residence at Pella, as if at that period there had been bishops *in partibus;* a purely gratuitous assertion, contradicted by all Eastern usages at that time, and by contemporary accounts, meagre though they be.

The interval which we find between the martyrdom of St. James and the election of his successor is explained by the fact that the Christians of Jerusalem were then in the diocese of another bishop. This interval was closed by their return from Pella, and St.

Epiphanius expressly states that it took place directly after the catastrophe. The short interval, far from being sufficient to detach them from cherished memories, must still more have endeared these memories to their broken hearts; and we do not wonder at finding the suffrages for a new bishop fall on St. Simeon, the son of Cleophas, and the "cousin of our Lord." After the apostles, there was no one so well able to hand down to the next generation the memory of what his eyes had seen. His martyrdom crowned a life of one hundred and twenty years, soon after the beginning of the second century.

After him we find a succession of fourteen bishops of the circumcision, within the short space of thirty-five years, which makes it probable that several of them were martyred. Those who came after the rebellion of Barcochebas and the second expulsion of the Jews seem to have made use of the opportunity to get rid of the remnants of legal observances, and to draw somewhat nearer to the Gentiles, with whom the struggle was always less violent when the Jews were not there to heap fuel on the fire. The third bishop was the illustrious St. Narcissus, whose long life of one hundred and sixteen years had enabled him to see the closing days of St. Simeon and the childhood of St. Macarius. During his episcopate, he was driven by calumny to retire into solitude; but God Himself avenged his good name, and he returned to his beloved Ælia, and was unanimously reinstated. As he was very old, he took for his coadjutor and future successor Bishop

Alexander. This was a twofold innovation, but a heavenly vision was sent to justify both the translation of a bishop to a see which was already occupied, and the practice of pilgrimages. For, as Eusebius tells us, "this prelate had come both to offer his prayers there, and to visit the Holy Places." For, according to the remark of the Rev. G. Williams, "pilgrimages date as far back, at least, as this time, and most of the eminent fathers of this century had visited the sacred localities."

The holy bishop became a confessor of the faith under Decius, and died in prison at Cæsarea. The Church at Jerusalem had a short time of peace under Mazabanes, and then we come to Bishop Hymenæus, whose memory, Eusebius says, was still fresh in his day.

With such predecessors, it may well be asked what need there was for St. Macarius to insert or sanction the invention of anything in the way of religious topography. In order to confirm the primacy of Jerusalem, he had only to question those around him, to gather up the memorials of his predecessors, and to walk in their footsteps. Why should he have needlessly invented impostures, the detection of which would have ruined his plans?

Second Channel.—The Faithful in Judæa and elsewhere: the neighbouring Christians.

The bishops and clergy were the natural guardians of the Holy Places and of religious traditions, and

everything tends to make us believe that they acted as
such. But they were not alone, and they had more
important interests to attend to; and this is a reason
for thinking that the laity of Jerusalem and Judæa, as
a rule, were even more active than the bishops in
guarding the traditions of the country. Up to the
reign of Hadrian, there were a certain number of Christians who were of the line of David, and with whom
the memory of Christ was literally a family question.
But may we not look upon all the faithful, in those
days of persecution, as one vast family, feeding on the
thoughts of the past, and finding their mutual consolation in dwelling on them? In the apostolic times
Jerusalem was the centre of a movement of charity,
and of an apostolate, which made her known far and
wide, and which drew other nations towards her. The
preaching of the gospel was a glory to Palestine, which
was still prosperous, fair and fruitful, and the new converts repaired thither for religious affairs, such as the
messages of the apostles, the succour of widows, various
consultations, and, above all, for the spectacle of that
multitude of the faithful, whose numbers went on increasing without their fervour being diminished.* It
was not as yet, perhaps, a pilgrimage; but who can
believe that the catechumens asking for every sort of
religious information, or the faithful from every quarter,
with both Testaments in their hands, came to Jerusalem,
and closed their eyes so as not to see the city whose
" foundations are in the holy mountains "—that much-

* *Vide* Acts of the Apostles, and the Epistles— passim.

loved Sion of which it is written, "The Lord loveth her gates more than the tabernacles of Jacob"—that Temple where so many wonders had been wrought; or, later on, the scene of its terrible destruction; the Calvary where Jesus suffered, and that "new monument" which He had quitted in His risen glory?

At the time of the siege of Jerusalem, the foreign visitors must have discontinued their journeys to the Holy City. Left to themselves, they might have lost the thread of the old memories—the inhabitants of Jerusalem were also partially dispersed, and had become strangers to their city. But there were in the mountains a sort of Bedouins, who were neither foreigners nor citizens, some of those pastoral, and more or less nomadic tribes, who are still to be found in the neighbourhood of the Dead Sea, and who attend the markets in the towns. They have but little tie to the soil, and they are very illiterate; but they are an intelligent race, so that their memory is all the more retentive of local memories, and of the fire-side tales of the encampments. They appear to be pilgrims by nature, and I am inclined to consider them as the especial guardians of traditions.

The good shepherds of Bethlehem form a portion of that chain, which has never since been interrupted, either by persecution, war, the fall of Jerusalem, or even Mussulman barbarity.

Third Channel.—The Jews.

For those who may be inclined to reject the testimony of the faithful, as being interested in the question, we can find other evidence. And, first of all, there are the Jews, "the stiff-necked people." Most of their sacred associations have become ours. The Temple, Sion, the Tower of David, the sacred pools, the passages of the Jordan, the waters of Siloe, and a thousand others, were ancient memorials of Israel before they spoke to us of Christ; and for a long, long time these memorials were intrusted to their jealous keeping. The Christians were not able to do more than glance furtively at them, till the day came when the pagans drove away Jews and Christians alike. They both came back again when they were able, but as John outran Peter to the sepulchre of Jesus after the Resurrection, so the younger people came first to the ruins of the buried city. Notwithstanding the severity of edicts, both Pagan and Mussulman, the Jews have never lost sight of their old objects of affection; they still have their quarter in Jerusalem, below the platform of the Temple, where they come to herd together, and to die near the sepulchres of their fathers. Every one knows the Jews' "Wailing-place," that remains of the gigantic wall, where they meet to bewail their exile below that Haram which they may not pass. Everywhere in the Holy Land, and especially in early times, their associations and ours have mutually checked each other, without leaving any serious discrepancy between two bodies more perseveringly hostile than any others have ever been.*

Fourth Channel.—Heretics.

The same may be said, up to a certain point, of heretical bodies. During the entire period of the bishops of the circumcision, which was one hundred and thirty-five years, the Church of Jerusalem boasted of a perfect freedom from heresy. But the accession of Bishop Marcus was signalised by the irruption of the sects of primitive times, who were in existence in the days of Eusebius, and so are our strongest voucher for the inviolability of the traditions of the period. If his topography is only an invention, how can their silence be explained ?

Fifth Channel.— The Pagans.

Even the pagans have done their part in guarding and handing down the traditions of sacred topography. Origen bears witness that they were not unacquainted with them, and that they were curious on the subject. But it was when their hatred was excited against religious memorials that their efforts contributed to transform the feelings of the faithful, which might otherwise have become weakened, into fresh and bleeding wounds. The attempts at consistent and systematic profanation, which will be spoken of farther on, prove the animosity which characterised the work. The

* The quotation from Origen in the next chapter furnishes an instance of the hostile attitude of the Jews.

pagans thought, reasonably enough, that all traditions, Jewish and Christian, would be utterly and for ever exterminated, but they never dreamed of the conversion of Constantine.

CHAPTER XIII.

WRITTEN TESTIMONIES.

EVEN if the first century had drawn up no *procès verbal* to prove which were the places dear to the faith, and the veneration paid to them, the omission would be capable of explanation, by saying that these memories were written in men's hearts, and that the reverence for them was so natural, that there was no need to record them. On the other hand, there are several reasons which might be given to explain why there was not, at first, a regular and public attestation of traditions.

To begin with': the first energies of Christianity were directed towards that which was without, to the great works of the Apostolate. The work of the first doctors of the Church was to teach fundamental doctrines, to compose the *credo*, to catechise, to draw the simple outlines of devotion, morals and discipline; to defend themselves against philosophers, pagans, and early heretics.

It was not till later that devotion was able to collect itself, and fell back upon its memories all the more tenderly that they seemed fading in the distance.

and in danger of being lost. When the banquet is at its height, no one thinks of "gathering up the fragments that remain, lest they should be lost." It is when it is ended that we begin to consider what remains for the morrow.

Official attestations at the very beginning would have been ill-timed, if not impossible. If we carry back our thoughts to the first ages of the Church, we find that the places, with which the holiest associations were connected, were in the hands of the Jews and Romans. Mothers pointed them out secretly to their children, as a treasure which might not even be coveted. Even public places, or those which were in the power of the faithful, could hardly be named openly, for fear of profanation. It was under cover of secrecy, and, as private property, protected by the common law, that the Cœnaculum, and other places of the sort, were at first employed as churches, and consecrated to purposes of devotion. After all, moreover, it is quite possible that there may have been descriptive books, title deeds, and other official documents, all trace of which has perished in successive devastations of the city.

1. *The Evangelists.*

But is it quite correct to say that we possess no writings on this subject ? As we have seen, our sacred books are an important item in the matter. It is true that the evangelists never professed to give us an "Onomasticon," or topographical dictionary. They do not come before us as archæologists; but their authority is none the less for that reason, for they tell us things "which they saw and heard." Their character is rather that of witnesses and historians than of exponents of a Divine philosophy; they tell us what Jesus did and what He taught, and they do not think it trivial to point out clearly the places where all this occurred. It may even be said that their descriptions are given with remarkable minuteness of detail. Whenever they mention the Mount of Olives, Gethsemani, the road to Bethania, &c., &c., they do so in terms which left no room for the possibility of a mistake in those days, when houses, walls, and even trees were still standing in the same places as when the events occurred. They give us the name of Calvary in Latin and Hebrew, and go on to say that close by there was a garden, and in that garden a new sepulchre. St. Luke tells us that many years after the treason of Judas, the piece of land bought of him by the Jews was still called "the field of blood;" they speak so as to be understood by future generations, and, at the least, so that their own generation might make comments for the instruction of succeeding ones.

2. *The historian Josephus.*

The evidence on sacred topography which, in order of time, immediately follows the apostles, is that of the historian Josephus, the author of the "Jewish Antiquities," and the faithful narrator of the last days of Jerusalem. It is true that he does not concern himself with Christian antiquities, as such, and that his tópographical descriptions have occasioned a multitude of difficulties among the learned; but these difficulties of detail are due to causes which ought not to invalidate his testimony; and the particulars which he gives us respecting the traditions common to Jews and Christians are of vast importance.

Mr. Williams says on this subject :—

"The exactness of his language" (namely, of Josephus in numerous passages) " is to me perfectly astonishing; and I do think that this author, to whom the Christian Church is perhaps more largely indebted than to any unbelieving historian, has not been appreciated as he deserves. I am convinced that in almost every case where he has been charged with misstatement, our ignorance rather than his knowledge is in fault. With fair allowance for Oriental hyperbole in his descriptive accounts (of works of art rather than nature), he is, as far as my experience goes, a most invaluable guide."

3. *Hegesippus and St. Justin.*

The Christians themselves were not long before they possessed other writings besides the sacred Scriptures. At the commencement of the eleventh century, St. Hegesippus, who was born a Jew, wrote his memoirs or commentaries, the style of which, says Eusebius, was very simple, "in order that he might imitate in that respect also those whom he imitated in his con-

duct." We only possess fragments of these writings;
but we know that the Bishop of Cæsarea used them
as guides in matters of history, and consequently of
topography, so far as they are connected with each
other. The fragments which he quotes justify his
praise; and one of these quotations describes the
devotions and the martyrdom of the holy Bishop
Simeon, solemn acts of homage paid by Christianity
to the old Temple on the eve of its destruction. We
only quote St. Justin out of respect for his memory:
he was born at Naplous; but the purpose of his
writings does not lead him into the region of antiquities. The only passage which could be quoted on
the subject of Bethlehem is much less striking than
the one we are about to mention.

4. *Origen.*

Origen is the author whom we have just referred
to; but his one passage on Bethlehem is enough to
show the spirit of the different parties with regard
to Christian memorials at the very period when people
might have begun to forget them, if ever they could
have been forgotten—the very period, in fact, when
some would fain persuade us that they were actually
lost sight of. His father, St. Leonidas, and his tutor,
Didymus the blind, might have had personal intercourse with St. Hegesippus and St. Justin. He is
usually taken up with his symbolical interpretations;
nevertheless, this is how, in his treatise against Celsus,

he speaks of the grotto of the Nativity, which the pagans were then endeavouring to profane by surrounding it with a sacred grove dedicated to the impure worship of Adonis :—

"As to the birth of Jesus Christ, if any desire proofs besides the prophecy of Micheas and the account given by the disciples of Jesus in the Gospels, we may tell them that, agreeably to the Scripture narrative, there are still shown at Bethlehem the grotto where He was born, and the manger where He lay wrapped in swaddling clothes. It is so commonly spoken of, that even unbelievers say to each other that the Jesus Whom the Christians venerate and adore was born in that cave. For my own part, I believe that before the coming of Christ, the chief priests and scribes, struck with the force and precision of the prophetic passage, taught that He was to be born at Bethlehem, and that this opinion was well known among the Jews ; accordingly, we read that the chief priests and scribes replied, in answer to Herod's question, that Christ was to be born in Bethlehem of Judæa, the city of David ; and St. John's Gospel says, more generally, that this was reported among the Jews. But after the coming of our Lord, those who made it their business to overthrow the belief that His Birth-place had ever been considered the subject of prophecy, opposed its being taught among the people."

We see, by these words of Origen, how lively Christian memories still were, after St. Alexander's episcopate, at the commencement of the third century. Then, as now, there was a hostile party.which strove to stifle them, but its efforts were regarded as a manœuvre and an innovation; and all the Robinsons in the world cannot disprove the fact that there was a considerable number of Christians in Palestine who had only one feeling on the subject, that of love and veneration. They united to the fervour of primitive days that spirit of devotion which loves to visit Palestine, Bible in hand. They made the one a commentary on the other, as both Catholics and Protestants do in our day, with this difference, indeed—that the latter are eager to find their brethren in fault, and to flatter themselves that they are making discoveries even where everything is known.

5. *Eusebius—The " Topikon."*

Origen died in 253, a little while after gloriously confessing his faith in the midst of tortures. Eusebius of Cæsarea, the author of the " Topikon," a work on Biblical places, was born at this time; for he speaks of St. Dionysius of Alexandria, who died eleven years later, as of a contemporary. This work, therefore, comprises, in the matter of local traditions, the period immediately succeeding that of Origen. It is a geographical dictionary, containing, in alphabetical order, nearly all the names of the towns, rivers, and mountains mentioned in the Scriptures, even those of villages and other places. The author has been careful to mark those which still retain the same names, and those which have changed or modified them.

The learned are agreed as to the utility and merit of this work, in which any want of precision arises from its having been written for contemporaries, and before it was the custom to fix the positions of places by observations of latitude and longitude. This writer does so by naming their distance from the principal towns, a mode sufficiently exact for his time, but which is so no longer, because several of the principal towns having disappeared, their own position has to be ascertained.

The following are a few examples of his method:—

" The Fuller's Field," mentioned by Isaias.—This is still shown in the suburbs of Jerusalem.

" Haceldama, the field of blood."—It is still shown at Ælia, to the south of Mount Sion.

" Golgotha, or Calvary," the place where Christ was crucified."—It is still shown at Ælia, to the north of Mount Sion.

Eusebius appeals to public notoriety as his authority, and it would be difficult to believe that he could venture to affirm it as he does, if there were the least possibility of his being contradicted.

This book is not a casual pamphlet, got up for the confirmation of an imposture. It is that of a learned historian who has written other works, and who is master of his subject.

I own that a scientific book is sometimes influenced by a foregone conclusion, or by motives of partiality; but it would be impossible to persuade a man of good sense that an entire geography has been distorted from beginning to end by a pure spirit of falsehood, and that the writer ventured to put it forward in his own country among a public capable of verifying its assertions.

Eusebius did not invent; he had no need to do so; he could not have wished to do so; it would have been the ruin of his credit. All that he, as a man of science, and an inhabitant of Palestine, had to do was to put into shape, and to fill up, what the very peasants could tell him of the places he was speaking of. Historical study had initiated him into his subject, and, being thoroughly master of it, he treats it with the care of an author who has a respect for his reputation. So far from being in the pay of the Bishop of Jerusalem, he was his vehement opponent at councils. More than this, he was his rival, for Cæsarea was then the civil metropolis of Palestine. Herod had erected it on the shores of the Mediterranean, in honour of Cæsar Augustus, and at that time it was at the height of its short period of splendour; whilst Ælia was but partly rebuilt. The courtier-prelate would naturally have been induced by the interests of his own see to neglect the great names connected with Jerusalem. If he does justice to them, it is that higher motives are at stake.

Other works of Eusebius—his " Ecclesiastical History," the " Life of Constantine," his eulogium—strengthen the testimony of his " Topikon." It is easy to see that it is a favourite subject, as well as a subject of the time, and if it be said that it was the bishop who made it a popular one, I may say, with equal right, that he selected it, and treated it successfully, because it was already popular.

No objection was raised by his contemporaries against the topography of Eusebius, and, as a proof of the general respect it met with, St. Jerome took the trouble to re-publish it in Latin, with the additions and alterations made necessary by time. For instance, Eusebius had described Gethsemani as "the place where our Lord prayed before His Passion," adding, "it is situated at the foot of the Mount of Olives, and the faithful are fond of going there also to pray." St. Jerome changes these last words thus: "There is a temple on its site at the foot of the Mount of Olives." These alterations in no way affect the authority of the work of Eusebius: on the contrary, they confirm it.

CHAPTER XIV.

TESTIMONY OF FACTS.

First Fact.—Pagan Profanations.

WE have said that the pagans themselves may be quoted in evidence of the continuity of the tradition of the Holy Places during the later persecutions, when the voices of both Jews and Christians were stifled by cries of suffering, exile, prison, slavery, and martyrdom.

And, in fact, history teaches us that persecution did

16

not spare even sacred memories. It sought to destroy them, to change their character, to profane them. Now, certainly, it is impossible to persecute what does not exist, and the very efforts of the pagans to make Christians forget the Holy Places did but, as it were, burn their memory indelibly into the hearts of their victims.

The Jews were forbidden to enter Jerusalem. The Holy City was partially rebuilt by Hadrian, under the name of Ælia Capitolina; and everything was done to make its former owners turn from it in disgust, by such devices as carving on its gates the figures of swine, which they held in abhorrence, and to give it the appearance of a thoroughly pagan city, full of theatres, public baths, and other similar buildings—above all, with idol-temples. A statue, and possibly a temple, of Jupiter Capitolinus, were erected on Mount Moria, the very spot where Solomon had exerted all his genius in honour of the true God. Such Christians as were not of Jewish origin were not formally included in the edict which forbade all circumcised persons to approach Jerusalem, but they were exposed to persecution; and it was out of hatred to associations especially cherished by them that Bethlehem was dedicated to the impure mysteries of Adonis! The debris of the ruins around Golgotha and the Holy Sepulchre were employed to make a broad platform, and there a temple of Venus was built on the very spot where the God of purity died upon the Cross.

Attempts have been made to deny this profanation.

It has been said that all the measures of Hadrian at Ælia Capitolina had reference to the Jews, and not in any way to the Christians, to whom, at times, he was favourably disposed. Dean Stanley considers that this objection of Mr. Robinson's has never been answered. But, in reality, does it deserve any answer? Does not everybody who has read a few pages of history know that most princes have had their good and their bad days? Are we to deny that the first Napoleon was the gaoler of Pius VII. because he restored religion in France? or that his nephew erected Voltaire's statue, because, two years before, he had built the Church of the Trinity? The character of Hadrian is well known; his reign is a tissue of contradictions. He respected the senate, and encouraged arts; yet in his jealous fits he slaughtered the most distinguished senators and artists. He killed his wife and his favourite, and afterwards caused divine honours to be paid to them! Is it surprising that he treated the Christians as capriciously? After a few impulsive acts of justice to them, he must have found them quite as much opposed as the Jews to his notions of compromise with regard to all forms of worship. He made many martyrs, and though from time to time he gave the Church leisure to breathe, still he is reckoned as the fourth great persecutor. Considering all this, how can Dean Stanley be surprised that popes and bishops have let Mr. Robinson and his arguments alone? At all events, the erection of the Temple of Venus is a fact, of which the learned Mr. Williams gives an unexpected proof by means of numismatics. "We are furnished," he says, "with a most gratifying and unlooked-for confirmation of the fact ... in the unsuspicious testimony of a coin of the reign of Antoninus Pius, in which the figure of Astarte, or Venus, is represented standing in a tetrastyle temple, with the legend C.A.C., which the most skilled in numismatics inform us can signify nothing else than 'Colonia Aelia Capitolina.' And whatever ambiguity there may be in this inscription ... the matter is placed beyond all doubt by the later coins of Aurelius and Severus, in which we have the same figure in the same temple, with the unequivocal legend, COL. AEL. CAP."

Second Fact.—Restoration under Constantine.

1. Preparation.

If other evidence were wanting, the fact of the occupation and systematic profanation of the Holy Places by the pagans could be proved by the corresponding fact of a general measure of restoration under Constantine. It had not this character of universality at first. At the outset of his reign, Constantine, engaged in the cares of his vast empire, was constrained to limit his efforts pretty nearly to protecting the Catholics from Jewish, heretical, or pagan persecutions in the provinces which had fallen to him. Very soon after his conversion, we find him issuing particular decrees with regard to certain places. As a rule, the pagans were in possession of the temples, revenues, and ancient privileges; and the Christians, just recovering from persecution, had enough to do to gain a social position suitable to their new mission of governing and reforming the world.

It was not till 326, ten years after the vision of the Labarum, that Constantine felt strong enough to throw the weight of his treasures and authority into the scale. The account of Eusebius, as we have remarked, is not a little pamphlet, *à propos* of the events of the day; it comes before us, closely connected with general facts, and is given due prominence in the three books mentioned above. The author relates the successive edicts and public acts of the sovereign, the conduct of empresses, bishops, and synods, as well as the public ceremonies, and the whole is borne out by the histories of Socrates and Sozomen, and by the evidence of several later writers. Certainly St. Macarius must have been a clever "Jesuit," to make the immense labours and the entire life of a famous historian, the writings of pagans and heretics, public documents, and well-known events, all subservient to his own ends! But let us come to facts.

In reality, never was an event more gradually and solemnly prepared than this pretended jugglery of St. Macarius: never was any more gloriously accomplished in the face of the world. During the first years of Constantine's reign, Palestine formed part of the dominions of the savage Maximin; after him it fell to Licinius, who with one hand signed the edicts of his colleague in favour of the Christians, and with the

other maintained the severity of former days, and
supplied fresh victims for the stake.

Rome and the Western empire saw splendid temples
rising to the honour of the true God, and gazed ex-
pectantly on the unhappy East, whose hopes and worship were still kept secret. The East, on her side,
hoped all things from the young liberator chosen by
Providence, and advancing with the Labarum at the
head of his armies, towards the scenes where the
sign of salvation and of his victories had first been
planted.

Immediately after the defeat of Licinius and the
Council of Nicæa, he turned his attention to those
devastated regions where, at last, it was possible to
dwell on the thought of the Man-God. Ælia might
be forgotten now; there was nothing to do but to
sweep away its impure traces. It was once again the
Jerusalem of David, and of the Israelites according to
the Gospel, the Jerusalem of Christ and of His apostles,
the city of the miracles of the Son of God, of His
glory and His adorable humiliations.

2. *Publicity of the enterprise.*

How popular the cause of Palestine was, may be
seen by the edicts of Constantine, who, in the midst
of his victories and journeys, does not cease turning
his attention thither, and enters into correspondence
with the three principal bishops—those of Jerusalem,
Tyre, and Cæsarea—sending them his edicts of re-

storation, and making them his helpers and advisers in the work. From the very first, we see the two most illustrious women of the court, the mother and mother-in-law of Constantine, hasten to Palestine. The latter was Eutropia, the widow of the persecutor Maximianus Hercules; she built a church near the oak of Mambre, after having destroyed the idols and altars which had been placed there. Constantine seems to have set apart the personal memorials of Jesus for his mother, the Empress St. Helena. She was eighty years old when she began her journey to Palestine; she urged on the works, and presided, in the emperor's name, at the dedication of the new buildings.

Before her arrival, an order from her son had removed the Temple of Venus; but it was in her presence that the rubbish was cleared away which hid both Calvary, the Holy Sepulchre, and the three crosses. The church of Bethlehem owed its existence to her especial care.

"The holy empress," says Eusebius, "desired to render thanks for her son, whose empire had become so glorious and powerful, and for her grandsons, the Cæsars blessed by God; and, notwithstanding the weight of years, finding in the counsels of her devotion and her royal mind, as it were, a second youth, she hastened to see with her eyes the land consecrated by God, and to visit the East and its numerous nations. After duly venerating the places marked by the Saviour's footsteps, and accomplishing, so far as she was concerned, the prophecy announcing that our worship should be offered 'where His Feet had trodden,' she was desirous of leaving behind her memorials useful to posterity, and she set herself in earnest to the work."

3. *Was this Restoration important?*

Eusebius speaks of the places visited by St. Helena as of well-known spots, not requiring to be particularly described; and it is because the monuments erected by her care were before the eyes of every one, that he does not trouble himself to enumerate them, and to give a detailed account of them, unless when he is led to speak of them by their historical importance. But we ought not to conclude from this, as the author of "Biblical Researches" insinuates, that she could only have built one or two at most. The historian's words would be inexplicable in their full sense, unless we admit, agreeably to tradition, that the Saint visited even Galilee, and built churches there.

It is the same with regard to the terms used by Eusebius, both in his "Ecclesiastical History," and in the "Life and Panegyric of Constantine," when speaking of the care and the arrangements of the emperor, which extended throughout Palestine.

The critic tries to discredit the whole of this history, because the author attributes certain churches sometimes to the mother and sometimes to the son; he sees in it contradiction, flattery, imposture, &c., &c. But, really, where can Mr. Robinson have lived? If I were to turn over the papers of the last fifteen years, I should be sure to find Napoleon mentioned as the author of the Paris improvements; the same praise would be given to M. Haussmann; then I should come upon the names of different architects who finished the Louvre, built the churches of the Trinity and of St. Augustine, the Grand Opera, the new thoroughfares, and the boulevards. Would that justify me in accusing all these journals of contradiction and falsehood, and in concluding either that these improvements never existed, or that they are the work of the Communists of 1871? At all events, whether they are the work of mother or son, or of both, there are five or six churches the building of which Eusebius describes—one at Bethlehem, two on the Mount of Olives, one on Calvary, that of Hebron, and that of Tyre. But he gives us clearly to understand that they were not the only ones, and this is enough to prove that no conclusion can be drawn denying the existence of the Basilicas built by Constantine at Nazareth, Tabor, and a dozen others mentioned by tradition.

It would have required a modesty truly heroic in the Bishop of Cæsarea not to have quoted the letter in which the Christian emperor calls him his " very dear brother," and enjoins him, as bishop of the capital, to consult with his brethren, so that "the parishes of his diocese, and those belonging to other bishops, priests, and deacons, may be provided with the necessary buildings, and that they may be repaired, enlarged, or built from the foundations, according to necessity." He adds that, with regard to the requisite funds, the prefects and magistrates of the provinces might be applied to, provided they had received instructions to that effect. Eusebius states, that things having been once put into legal form, the work was carried out *everywhere* with marvellous rapidity.

This letter seems to me sufficient reason for not taxing those authors with exaggeration who make the churches built by Constantine in Palestine amount to a very considerable number. At all events, we can tell these critics of at least one church built by Constantine which is not mentioned by Eusebius, that of Tiberias. We are told of it by St. Epiphanius, in the curious history of Count Joseph, as he heard it from the lips of that personage himself. In spite of the letters and favour of the emperor, this converted Jew had the greatest difficulty in overcoming the bigotry of his former co-religionists. In the end, however, he succeeded, and at last built a modest church on the site of a temple which had been begun by Hadrian, the foundations of which are still to be seen.

4. *What are we to think of the silence of Eusebius as to some Churches?*

This fact is sufficient to explain the silence of Eusebius concerning the building of several churches, at the same time that he seems inexhaustible in the details he gives of others. With regard to the churches of Calvary and the Holy Sepulchre, he dwells on everything: he recounts the mandates and letters of the emperor relating to the destruction of the temple and idols, the clearing of the ground, and the new buildings: he describes the progress of the works, and the beauties of the edifice, and, lastly, he makes us assist at the magnificent ceremonial of the consecration. All these events, in which the principal personages of the empire and the Church were either actors or witnesses, are related at length, with confirmatory notes, in three different works, and the account is confirmed by those of Sozomen, Socrates, and Theodoret.

We see that this first courtier-bishop is anxious to make it appear that he played his part in all this. He would willingly have it supposed that he did the whole; that he took occasion of the close of the Council of Nicæa to make the happy suggestion; that the idea of the letters written to St. Macarius emanated from him; that he followed all the proceedings with the zeal of a skilful minister; above all, that it was he who preached the dedication sermon, or, rather, the opening discourse, consisting of a wearisome panegyric of the emperor—an endless effusion which he has carefully preserved for us, and which, some time after, he recited to Constantine himself.

After all, it did not befit his character of historian, to give the journal of the architects, or the accounts of the contractors. When he does go into detail, it is, first, because he bears a part in the event, and then on account of the importance and solemnity of the edicts, of the grandeur of the associations, of the splendour of the buildings, of the crowds of nobles, bishops, and people, of the pomp of the ceremonies. Looking at it from this point of view, there is nothing to surprise us in his omitting to mention the "modest" church of Tiberias.

On the other hand, all these buildings were not the work of a day: the works may have been protracted at other places besides Tiberias, and in some instances may not only not have been finished, but actually not begun, till after the historian's death. We cannot, therefore, draw any conclusion from the silence of Eusebius; and if it is certain that Constantine remembered Tiberias, and did not neglect Galilee, why should he have forgotten Nazareth, Cana, and other places of equal interest?

Third Fact.—Does the finding of the Holy Cross injure the cause of the Holy Place?

But let us return to the Holy Sepulchre in particular. Amidst all the movements of which Eusebius speaks, St. Macarius only appears in the second rank, and is obscured by the bishop of the civil capital.

Will it be said that this modesty was only a trick, the better to ensure the final acknowledgment of his pre-eminence? But if this were so, to what purpose was it to risk a compromising imposture, when things were going on favourably, and he had nothing to do but to let them take their course?

Eusebius was writing, the emperor had sent letters

and edicts, the world was full of the subject of the Holy Places, the empress was on the spot, directing the work of recovery and restoration, when the miraculous Invention of the Holy Cross took place.

The whole world saw in this great event a mark of Divine approbation and sanction. And now we are to believe that it was a piece of legerdemain! Why? Because a miracle took place; and the author of " Biblical Researches," and persons who profess to swear by the Scriptures only, consider a miracle as a proof of deception! They should begin by destroying that very Bible, the book of miracles, past, present, and future.

If the finding of the Holy Cross were an imposture, the entire honour of the Church would be compromised by it. But I do not see how the question of the Holy Places would be affected from the archæological point of view. It is an outwork in the matter.

Here is the story of the miracle, as given by Tillemont, principally from the account of Sozomen, who professes, like Eusebius, to write from authentic documents :—

" The joy which was at first felt on the discovery of this treasure" (the three crosses, the title, and the nails), " was immediately damped by the difficulty of deciding which was the life-giving wood of the Saviour's cross, and which the two that had served for the punishment of the two thieves; so, as no man could throw light, on the subject, God must be appealed to; and the way of doing so was proposed by St. Macarius, the Bishop of Jerusalem. He was a prelate famed for his wisdom and piety, and had just overthrown the Arian heresy at the great Council of Nicæa. This holy bishop, learning that one of the most illustrious ladies of the city was grievously sick, told Helena that the three crosses must be brought to her house, and that they must implore God, on their knees, to cure her by the touch of the cross on which had been accomplished the redemption of the world. The empress, therefore, and all the people being present, the sick woman was touched with the two first crosses without any effect, but no sooner was the third applied than she rose immediately, perfectly cured, and stronger than she had ever been. It was insisted on, says Sozomen, that the same thing should be done to a dead body, which was instantly brought to life. S.S. Paulinus and Sulpicius Severus mention this last miracle only."

This resurrection is, no doubt, put in a subordinate place by Sozomen, because it happened later, and not before St. Helena and the assembled people. It is probable that the precious relic of the cross had, like others, its period of more striking prodigies. Eusebius makes a general mention of discoveries and miracles, but gives no details of an event which brings his rival prominently into the light, and in which he himself does not figure; but we must by no means infer from this that he was in ignorance of the circumstances. Miracles were commonly believed in those days; they always astonished, but they startled no one. Eusebius relates them when they come in his way, and have reference to general events, without attempting to fill his book with them.

On the other hand, with all his ingrain worldliness, and lack of sympathy for the modest holiness of his colleague, he does not fail to speak of him with due respect.

In a few words, then, the miracle which has been made the great difficulty in the whole question is this :—All the world is busied about the building of churches, and the restoration of the Holy Places. In the very centre of our sacred memories, when the work has begun in the presence of the most vener-able person of the empire, and of an assembled people, I see an aged pontiff, who, after fifteen centuries, is still invested with the glories of sanctity in the opinion of the whole Church. The three crosses are found. Before the eyes of that Christian throng, in their hands, is the very cross on which was wrought the world's redemption. All are filled with enthu-siasm and with the emotions of a grateful faith. There are no sceptics there : one and all, they are penetrated with that faith which spoke in the words of the woman with the issue of blood : "If I touch only the hem of His garment, I shall be healed." One and all, they press around the Saint, who, inspired by his faith, turns his steps towards the house of one of the prin-cipal ladies of the city, whose sickness was known to all. She touches that sacred wood—that wood fore-told by prophets as the salvation of the world—and, in the presence of· the multitude, she is perfectly

cured. Other miracles succeed this one. But now, lo
and behold! after fifteen hundred years, there are
clear-sighted geniuses who see the mind of the man
in all its blackness: he had three crosses buried
—he bribed a woman to feign sickness—and when
everything is ready for the comedy, the crosses are
discovered, and the woman pretends to be cured by
the touch of one of them.

But, this bribed woman was one of the first ladies
of Jerusalem. She must have feigned sickness for
months together. She, too, must have been obliged to
bribe her attendants, her servants, her physicians, to
be duped, or to pretend to be so. There were the workmen who buried the crosses, and those who dug them
up again, to be bribed. The neighbours, too, and the
passers-by must have been bribed to see nothing of all
the secret operations, and not to notice the newly-dug
earth. There was the silence of all the rude and
talkative agents concerned to be purchased. And all
these arrangements must have been planned so as to
fall in with the movements of the empress, of all the
clergy, and of a whole nation; and we are to believe
that this stupid, shallow, impossible plot was devised
by an old man of good sense, and artful enough to
have convinced the whole world of his sanctity! He
makes it, moreover, at a time when the universal
veneration which had been re-awakened for the Holy
Places had occasioned the conception, ordering, and
execution of important works—at a time when princes,
prefects, priests, and people were all on the *qui vive*

throughout Palestine, and especially at Jerusalem, on this subject, and when an imposture, without producing any advantage, might ruin everything. What can be conceived more clumsy than such a conspiracy, except, indeed, the supposition of its possibility ? I can more readily pardon the infidel, who comes to me with a jargon of cures, wrought by the imagination, ' nervous shocks, and the mysteries of magnetism.

CHAPTER XV.

ARCHÆOLOGICAL EVIDENCES.

First Evidence.—Character of the Ruins of Palestine, particularly at Jerusalem.

IT now remains for us to examine what archæological science, properly so called, tells us about the Holy Places in times of persecution. We must see whether it throws any light on our Christian traditions, or whether, on the contrary, it does not cast over them a fatal shadow.

What is said, by way of objection to our sacred traditions, amounts to this: everything has been destroyed and reduced to ashes. Destruction without a parallel has descended on Palestine, and, above all, on its capital; ruins have been heaped on ruins, and it would be vain to look for a decipherable inscription, or a recognisable monument. When the Christians returned timidly to the Holy City, they were not able

17

to find any clear indication of the spots they held so dear.

Well, I grant that we cannot expect to find at Jerusalem such scenes as we come upon in the desert —one of those cities overtaken by the sleep of death in all its prosperity, and the skeleton of which is preserved by the very fact of its lying forgotten under a shroud of sand. The archæology of Jerusalem must be unique, for there lie the dust and ashes of at least seven cities, each of which was built on the ruins of the last. But neither must we seek in Palestine for the marshy plains, the deltas of great rivers, in which whole cities may have been swallowed up, without leaving a trace behind.* Most of its cities are built on rock and mountain, and this is particularly the case with Jerusalem. Shut in on three sides by deep valleys, with the platform of Moria, and the terraces of the Temple on one side, Mount Sion's rocky ridges on the other, and the Tyropæon between the two, it has always retained certain landmarks which resist the influence of all destructive agencies.†

The historian Josephus compares it to a theatre, and Mr. Williams says, "Now, no comparison could possibly be more happy, as a glance at the plan will show. Let the form of an ancient theatre be remem-

---

* Corozain, Capharnaum, and Bethsaida may be exceptions.

† The adjoining plan is borrowed from Lieut. Conder's "Palest. Explor. Quarterly Statement, Oct. 1873," with some additions, partly from Capt. Warren's plan ("Recovery of Jerusalem," p. 298). The remarkable quadrangle marked 2462, at the north of the Temple area, is much too wide.

Pl. I.

APPROXIMATE PLAN

OF THE ROCK SITE OF JERUSALEM.

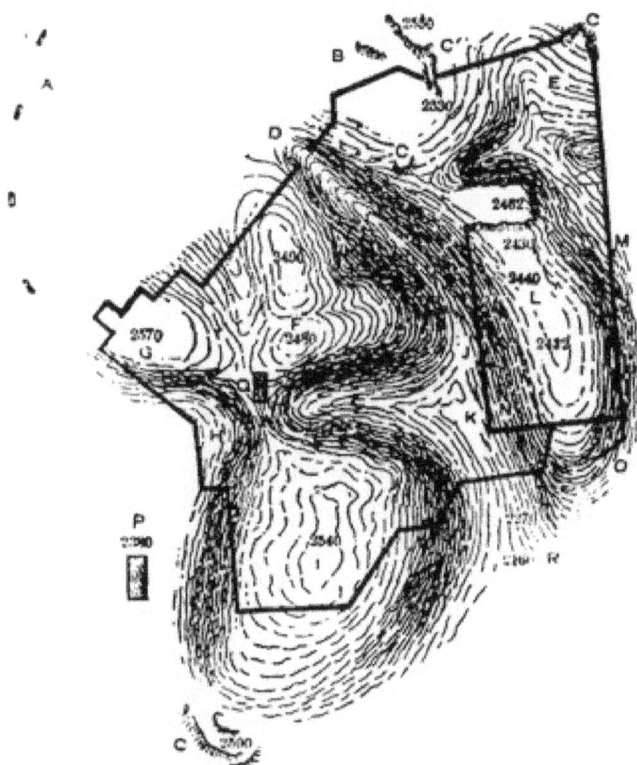

A Ancient Walls; drafted stones.	K Robinson's Arch.
B Grottoes.	L Moria, Dome of the Rock (Fer-
C Scarps.	gusson's H. Sepulchre).
D Damascus Gate.	M Golden Gate (Fergusson's Gol-
E Bezetha.	gotha and Basilica).
F Holy Sepulchre.	N Fergusson's Temple.
G Kalaat Jelud.	O Ophel's Wall.
H Tower of David.	P Birket el Sultan.
I Sion.	Q Pool.
J Wilson's Arch and Causeway.	R Valley of the Cedron.

bered—let the Temple-area be regarded as the scene—
the city surrounding it on three sides as the tiers of
seats for spectators, sloping down from all quarters
(except the south) in the direction of the Temple;
Bezetha in the north, Acra on the north-west, then the
eastern declivity, &c."

All that we have to do is to change the names. Let
us put the Dome of the rock and Haram-es-Scherif for
the Temple and its platform, Harat-Bab-Hytta for
Bezetha, the Mussulman quarter for Acra, the Jewish
and Armenian quarters for the slopes of the Tyropæon,
and the comparison of Josephus will be as true as it
was in the days of Herod.

A ravine may be filled up—a hundred of those little
narrow, irregular streets, where the poor are huddled
together, may be swept away—but all that does not
destroy the general aspect of the different quarters in
a site with a character so marked as that of Jerusalem.

No sooner have the storms of destruction passed
over—and we have seen that they have never been of
long duration—than the work of re-building begins,
and there is always some one to seek out and recognise
the old places and the old associtions. Hence, the
main streets, the great arteries, are not slow in re-
appearing under their old names, or under others
which are a guide to the old ones. During the Mussulman period, the destruction was, generally, superficial,
and only served to cover and protect the ancient ruins,
so that, long before there was a thought of clubbing

together to form a fund for the exploration of Palestine, the Rev. Mr. Stewart said that he had no doubt of the existence of innumerable relics of the former prosperity of Jerusalem; he thought that, if discovered, they would end the disputes of archæologists, but that they were all buried deep below the actual surface.

The excavations of late years have justified the traveller's conjectures. Such relics have, in fact, been found at an enormous depth. Hewn stones of gigantic dimensions, arches, subterranean passages, are heaped one upon another, till, at last, the rock itself is reached, cut in steps, chambers, aqueducts, cisterns and passages, in every possible way. As Tarquin's sewers are among the most ancient remains of Rome, so, perhaps, one of the remains of the ancient Jebus may be the sewer cut in the rock at the foot of the Tyropæon, the vaulted roof of which is still to be seen, pierced by a colossal voussoir, which has fallen from the ruins of a higher arch. The lords of the soil must have been men of a powerful and grand, but unartistic, civilisation. Whatever has been found in the way of carvings, pottery, or objects of art, properly speaking, even at a great depth, is seldom older than the Roman period. There are no ancient inscriptions, except, indeed, some quarry-marks on the first courses of stone of the great platform of the Temple.

It does not do to apply, unreservedly, to the old East our modern ideas of city improvements, of opening out streets, and of laying out boulevards. King Solomon, doubtless, had his Haussmann a thousand years before Christ, to build Mello by filling up the ravine between the Temple and his father's palace. But times of enormous activity are seldom very lasting in the East.

In periods of decay one must not look for original or artistic work. Men build with rubble, or bricks, on foundations of colossal blocks; earth, or plaster, takes the place of granite and marble; but streets, squares, &c., continue the same from age to age, except that a byeway is necessary to avoid the uncleared ruin, or to cross a ravine by the side of a fallen bridge.

In certain parts of the city, no doubt, when digging the foundations of a new building, remains are met with of walls crossing each other in all directions, at a great depth; but in others there are proofs of this fidelity of the Orientals to the old localities.

For instance, the modern church of St. John of the Greeks, is built over the ancient one of St. John of the Hospitallers, which is now the crypt of the new edifice, and twenty-five feet below the level of the court and street. The windows which lighted the church in the days of the Crusaders are still there, and to be seen from the inside. Excavations would show whether there is no other building beneath this crypt.

Second Evidence.—Natural Landmarks.

As we said before, Jerusalem has never so fallen into ruin as not to keep certain marks on the surface, if only the principal outlines of the site, and the remains of the chief buildings. And amongst these marks, which no destroying influence has been able entirely to obliterate or disfigure, I reckon nearly all the great memorials of our Lord.

1. *The Platform of the Temple.*

The Temple itself, the building where Jesus chose to be presented, and where He preached, has disappeared. We know that not a stone was to be left upon a stone. But one thing seems indestructible, its level area, the skeleton of its platform, and its perforated rock, the object of immemorial veneration, and of the superstitious tales of the rabbis. The Mussulmen have not failed to take possession of these stories, and they claim to inherit the blessings as well as the ownership of the spot. At all events, the sacred block occupied a remarkable position, and one more or less central, so that we can hardly choose a better starting-point for our measurements.

It is true that some would persuade us that the Temple was a furlong to the south of this rock; but it is impossible to place it, where Mr. Fergusson does, at the south-east corner of the Haram. The excavations and plans of Messrs. Warren and Conder prove to us that, in that case, the spot chosen by Areuna for his threshing-floor, and afterwards by Solomon for his great building, would have been a steep declivity, and almost the bottom of the Tyropæon. They would both, in turn, have had to undertake works such as are never entered upon except for the

enlargement of buildings worthy of expensive additions.

Why should they have done so? Was it revealed
to them that a learned F.R.A.S. would require the
adjacent platform to ground his theories upon? All
that a simple farmer, like Areuna, would think of, was
to choose a height exposed to the wind, for threshing
his sheaves. Solomon, guided, it may be, by the
remembrance of Abraham's sacrifice,* required a com-
manding site. Necessarily, his plan was on a grander
scale than that of the thresher, and, accordingly, we
learn from the historian Josephus, that the height had
to be enlarged. But there was nothing extraordinary
in the operation. Mount Moria presented a surface
of four hundred feet square, which could easily be
levelled for the main building, round which additions
on a lower level might then be grouped, thus forming
the esplanade without hiding any important part.

If, as Josephus asserts, the only portion of this
outer enclosure executed by the great king was the
eastern terrace with its double gallery, it is in vain
for inquirers to look for any work of Solomon's in
other directions; they will only be able to find that
of later kings, who first carried on the northern
esplanade and gallery, and then, finding the wall
of the adjacent quarter inconveniently near, moved
it to the requisite distance. It would be, then, that
the base of that remarkable rock, which is shown by

* "Offeres eum super unum *montium* quem monstravero
tibi."

Mr. Conder's plan to be twenty-two feet exceeding in height the block of the Sakkra, was scarped—a fitting pedestal for a tower, or, as it is at present, for a governor's palace. The western and southern galleries came in due time, to complete the work which the Assyrians, not long after, destroyed by fire and sword.

We are ignorant of the extent of this destruction; it is most likely that Zorobabel was able to make use of the old foundations in rebuilding the principal part, and that Herod did the same with regard to the surrounding buildings, which, however, he partially enlarged.* These successive operations can be followed pretty clearly, by studying the plans of Messrs. Warren and Conder, with the help of tradition, and an observation of the present state of the places; but this is not the case with Mr. Fergusson's theory, in which fresh difficulties meet us as we advance.

We know that during the siege of Titus, the Temple was both fortress and sanctuary; the centre alike of defence and of discord—both equally ferocious. We have, therefore, to find room in Herod's quadrangle—first, for the part strictly appropriated for worship, and then for a multitude of officers and soldiers, with their engines of war and provisions. I doubt the possibility of doing so in a space of 600 square feet at the south-western corner, or anywhere else. Even if the idea of a barrack of eight or ten storeys could have presented itself to the Jews of the first century, we know, as a fact, that the quarters of the priests had only two.

---

* Hecatœus, quoted by "J. F. Dict. of the Bible."

Doubtless the two inner courts for men and women were utilised, and also the outer square, the magazines, the porticoes, the basement, and even the entrance of the cisterns. But, even taking all this into account, the actual width is not more than would be requisite for all the stir of which the Temple was the scene at that time.

It is true that Mr. Fergusson has the authority of Josephus for his dimensions of a furlong; but whatever may be the value of that measurement in Palestine, why cannot the English author, who despises that authority when the height of the building is in question, allow that there may be an oversight of the writer, or an error of a copyist with regard to a calculation which appears to be at variance with Josephus himself, with the rabbis, or with common sense?

If the theory in question were sound, the centre of the plateau must have been crossed from north to south, and from east to west, by considerable walls. The great northern wall, with its galleries, which would have started close by Wilson's arch and causeway, then would have made an angle on the top, and formed the eastern wall; parallel with this latter wall would have been Justinian's church of St. Mary; higher still, the pretended Golgotha and the basilica of Constantine, forming a continuation of the Golden Gate; then, returning to the west, on the site of the Sakkra, the Tower of Antonia, and its communications with the Temple, there would have been the Eastern Gate, the Horse Gate, &c.

What is left of all this? What has been discovered of it by our explorers? I understand the disappearance of the great Temple from the plateau, whence the Hand of God and that of man have swept away its stones; and I see on the rock the space it must have occupied; but neither high nor low have Mr. Fergusson's walls and churches left an evident trace. Antonia, the Holy Sepulchre, the Sakkra, have superseded each other at the touch of his magic wand, without the trick having been seen by any one. How shall we explain the great tomb all but beneath the tower of Antonia, or the mistake of Constantine, or the forgetfulness of those who have shifted the traditions of the buildings of this emperor to those adjoining the Pool of Ezechias ?*

What the explorers really did see on the Haram, was a number of magnificent cisterns, for the most part cut in the rock. They prove that a large supply of water was required both for the legal purifications and for the necessities of life, and they extend far beyond the limits imagined by Mr. Fergusson. Again, what the patient and courageous investigations of our explorers have proved is the variety of masonry employed in the walls enclosing the Haram. On the

---

* On this point, Dr. Stanley is with us. He thinks that, after Constantine, traditions cannot have been lost, and that if the rock of the sepulchres of Joseph and Nicodemus is to be seen under the walls of the great church, there is no ground for denying the existence of that rock in the site of the central tomb. ("Sinai and Palestine," 466.)

rock hewn according to measure, they saw, 1st, blocks of colossal proportions in different layers, in which experts believe they make out three styles of ancient masonry, specially recognisable by what they call the Jewish marginal draft, some of these blocks even now bearing masons' marks, attributed by Mr. Deutsch to the Phœnician alphabet. They found, 2ndly, layers belonging to different phases of the Greco-Roman period, with the successive retouchings of different hands. 3rdly. That portion (easily recognisable) in which paltry Saracen rubble is mingled with some remains of the work of our Crusaders.

There is nothing to show us the dates of the ancient parts. We know that Solomon employed Sidonian workmen ; but we are ignorant as to the number of centuries during which the Sidonians were the stonemasons of Palestine ; and it is possible that they may have handed down their traditional marks to those who succeeded them. We are in similar uncertainty as to the Greek or Roman portions. There is no inscription retaining its original position, not excepting the very important "stele" of M. Clermont Ganneau.

Mr. Fergusson inserts his theory under cover of some of these enigmas. He sees them, and passes them by with the ease of an Alexandre Dumas. • Provided his theory is connected and well carried out, he gives himself no trouble about any difficulties at the outset. But are not these enigmas in reality more perplexing for him to solve than for us ? How would he prove that the great eastern, as well as the western wall of the

Haram is not anterior to Herod Agrippa, and that thousands of hands did not work at it ages before his time ?*

The statement of the historian Josephus, which cannot be a mistake, and still less an imposture in the face of contemporaries who had the ruins before their eyes, is that the enclosure of Herod was as broad as it was long. This statement is not in accordance with the measurement of the present one, which is longer by one-third from north to south than from east to west.

Nevertheless, there are marks of great antiquity from one end to the other of the two great walls. Mr. Warren found marks of Phoenician masons at the south-eastern corner, at a depth of nearly eighty feet, and the ruined arch remarked by Mr. Robinson is near the south-western corner. Even admitting these two corners to be the work of Solomon, it is possible to explain the circumstance by the tradition which represents that prince, great even in his errors, including even his *Stables* in the vast outlines of his plans. This may be the case. But Herod may have excluded that accessory part from his quadrangle, and seems to have done so.

The magnificent descriptions which Josephus gives

---

* All the remarks of the author in question are not to be despised. He says, following Josephus, that the Jews watched from the wall of the Temple the success of the struggles which were going on round the sepulchre of Alexander. It is all but certain that that spot lay to the north ; and consequently the Tower of Antonia could not occupy the whole breadth of the esplanade in that direction, as Mr. Lewin asserts.

us of the buildings of this king should not make us forget the works of other personages, who came long afterwards. These must still exist. The principal of them are those of Justinian in the sixth century. History says not a word of their destruction, and it requires nothing less than the mass of buildings to the south to justify the account of Procopius.

That contemporary author describes to us the architect Theodore, under the orders of the emperor, exerting all the resources of his genius, and all the mechanical knowledge of his time, for the transport of enormous blocks of stone destined for the substructures of a new temple. The architect has to contend with the steepness of the rocks, on which he had to secure the required space and level by means of arches and terraces. According to the best authorities, this church is still partially in existence. It was the church of St. Mary, or of the Presentation, in the days of the Crusaders, and is now the Mosque el Aksa.

It may be asked, why did not Justinian make use of the old platform, which seemed to present itself naturally for the building intended to commemorate the mysteries ? Mr. Williams suggests the reason. Our Lord had said that not a stone of the ancient building should be left upon a stone; and the Jews, who had tried to disprove the prophecy in the days of Julian the Apostate, by rebuilding it, had suffered for the attempt, a miraculous fire having consumed the directors, the workmen, and their works. It was natural, therefore, that Justinian should shrink from imitating the sacrilegious attempt, and so incurring a chastisement, the memory of which was still fresh in his time. Theodore made use of the old platform by making it, as it were, the magnificent avenue leading to a new temple; and that monument of obedience and of faith—a worthy symbol of the Christianity, which came to fulfil the ancient worship, and to extend it beyond its narrow limits—seems to survive all profanations, and to await better days. Including, at first, besides the church, a hospital, which afterwards passed into the hands of the Templars, and a palace for the emperor, it occupied, to the south, the whole width of the platform; and Theodore's efforts to harmonise the different parts have resulted in leaving our knowledge at fault. But Providence has left us a proof of the recent date of the outer walls to the south. A stone at the side of the lintel of the ancient gate which led under the church of St. Mary, bears the name of Hadrian.

The inscription is reversed, and consequently is of later date than the ruin, or the demolition of one of that emperor's buildings. We copy it, as quoted in Mr. Williams' second volume:

TITOAILHADRIANO
ANTONINOAVGPIO
PPPONTIFAVGVR.
DD PP

2. *Calvary.   The Holy Sepulchre.*

If there be another place in Jerusalem which the

PLAN OF JERUSALEM, WITH TRADITIONAL SITES.

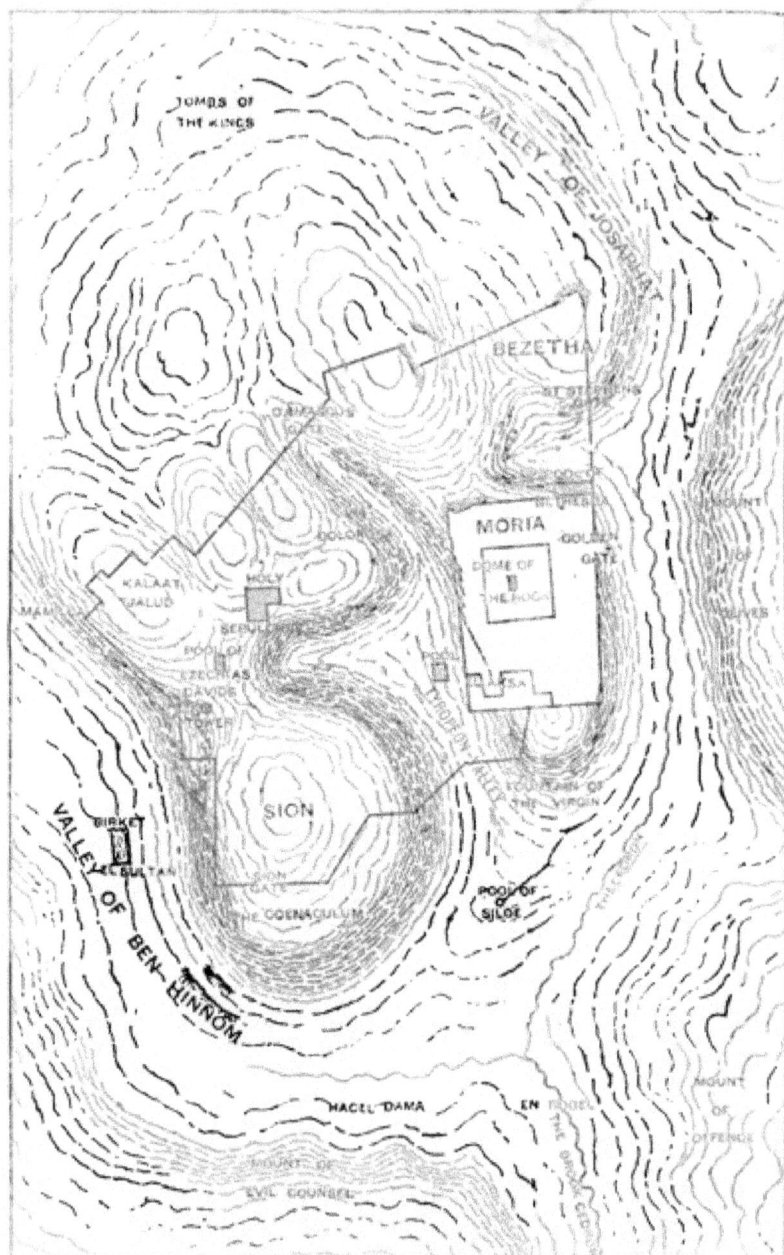

destruction under Titus can only have affected super-
ficially, it is the site of Calvary and of the Holy Sepulchre. Up to the time when Christianity claimed its
possession, it had been protected rather than injured
by a single and recent stratum of rubbish collected from
the neighbouring ruins. Under this stratum must
have been found, first, the rock of Calvary, not very
high, but still easily to be seen, in a rather confined
space, shut up within a re-entering angle, formed by
the meeting of the walls of the old city with those of
the enclosure enlarged by Nehemias. Two of the city
gates—the Judiciary Gate, and that of Gennath—
formed the entrance to this sort of theatre. The rock
must have been perfectly recognisable, not only by its
shape, and by the holes made in it for planting the
crosses, but, above all, by the deep and extraordinary
cleft, which could not escape the eyes of the workmen
employed in clearing the ground.

Less conspicuous, but in close proximity, was the
rock of the Sepulchre. This, too, it was impossible to
mistake. In the face of the native rock opened a
narrow corridor, in the side of which had been made
a cell for one corpse. Since the days of St. Helena,
the rock has been hewn outside, and isolated so as to
make it a detached monolith, like many that are to be
seen in the valley of Cedron.

But before that time, it is more than probable that
the block lay half embedded in its site, as nature had
left it. The other tombs in the neighbourhood, with
their one or more cells, were farther off, and well

known; they could only have made it easier to recognise the one which was being sought for. In the days of St. Macarius there must have been, if not the remains, at all events the distinct remembrance of the walls of David and Nehemias, as well as of the gates and other neighbouring objects, which would serve as a guide to the investigator.

Mr. J. Fergusson has taken it into his head to place the Holy Sepulchre under the Sakkra, and Calvary overlooking the Cedron; and his notions have been taken so seriously by Messrs. Smith and Grove, that they have not hesitated to mark Mount Sion in their beautiful atlas as forming a part of Moria, and Golgotha on the very brink of the valley of Josaphat.

He acknowledges that the Dome of the Rock is of Saracenic style, but he identifies the dimensions of the work of Abd el Melik with those of the building of Constantine described by Eusebius; and this is sufficient to make him assure us positively that the Khalif built upon the foundations of the Anastasis. The other reason he gives is, that only marble, not rock, is seen in the traditional Holy Sepulchre. At the Sakkra the rock can be seen and touched. Is Mr. J. Fergusson jesting? At the Holy Sepulchre I see the loculus, and every characteristic of a Jewish burial-place. The slab of marble shows me the rock, and cannot show anything else. It was placed there for reasons easy to understand, and at a time when there was not so much as a thought of the scepticism of our days.

Pl. III.

FERGUSSON'S TOPOGRAPHY OF THE BIBLE.

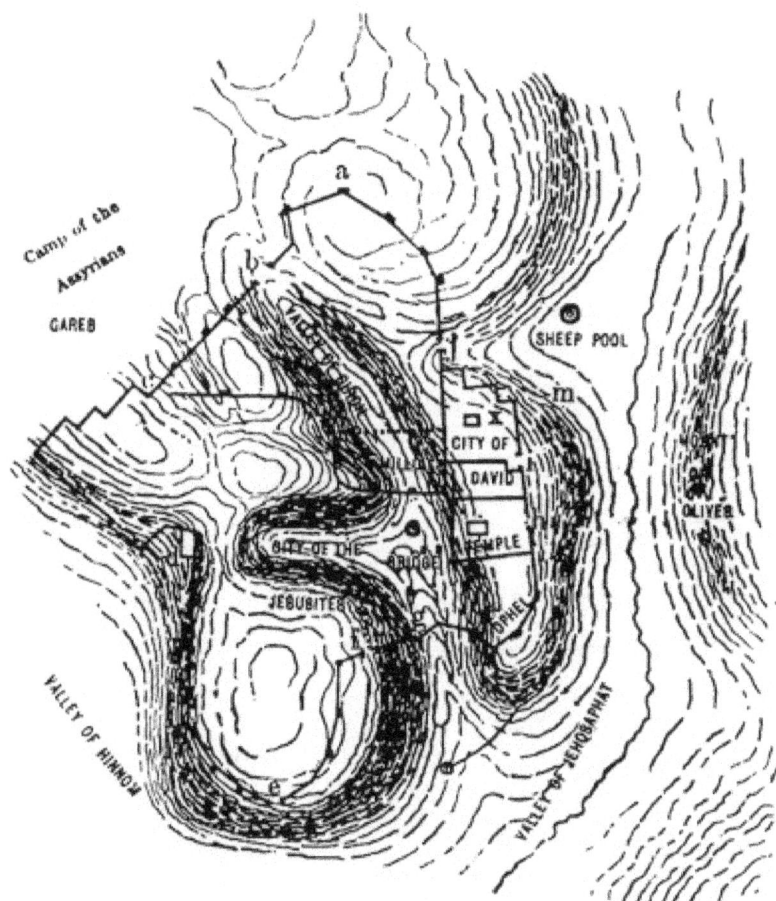

a Fish Gate.
b Old Gate.
c Gate of Ephraim.
d Tower of Furnaces.
e Valley Gate.
f Dung Gate.
g Fountain Gate.

h East Gate.
i Horse Gate.
j Sheep Gate.
m Golgotha, Golden Gate, Constantinian Basilica.
x Sepulchres of the Kings of Juda and Holy Sepulchre.

Certainly I should hardly recommend the guardians of the Holy Tomb to change its decorations for the satisfaction of every folly of the day. We might be asked to adopt a glass covering in the style of a museum, or, by way of greater security, some horrible iron grating, to keep the pilgrim at a distance and prevent his going in to see, with Magdalen "ubi posuerunt Eum." But for those useful marbles, which do not forbid any holy familiarity, the ground would now be hollowed two or three feet beneath the steps of the pilgrims, and the sides of the Tomb would be disfigured, if not destroyed, by pious or interested thefts, and by accidents, caprices, outrages, and impious fury.

It is true that at the Sakkra we see the native rock, and a remarkable excavation. But magnificent cisterns, also cut out of stone, are to be seen in the neighbourhood. Is there the slightest appearance of a sepulchre? I greatly doubt it.

We are told that the measurements given by Eusebius are irreconcilable with the dimensions of the traditionary spot, where everything has been destroyed. In the first place, if there are memories of a great destruction in the centre of the Nazarene quarter, it is because there was something to destroy. If there are no remains, how can there be any incompatibility? But, on the contrary, I find distinguished men who think that certain portions have resisted fires and other causes of destruction, men who have measured and examined them, and been able to reconcile everything.

We are told, further, that the Scriptural expression,

18

"Calvariæ locus," does not oblige us to translate it "Mount Calvary." But neither does it forbid it, and tradition authorises our doing so. The very idea of public executions, coming in support of that tradition, requires an elevated spot rather than the slope of a valley.

If we consult the designs of Mr. Conder on this point, we perceive that traditional Calvary, seen from the Porta Judiciaria, might have the appearance of a very insignificant rock ; but when seen from the heights of Sion, by spectators placed at different elevations—first on the terraces of Herod's palace, and of the Tower of David, then along the wall of Sion, and lastly at the foot of that wall before the gate of Gennath—the aspect it presented was entirely different, and might justify the name of "*Mount* Calvary."

3. *Sion.*

It is quite certain that at all periods, and particularly that of the Machabees, the name of Sion was extended to the whole of the city of Jerusalem and to the Holy Mountain. Our commentators agree on this point; but that does not prevent their considering Sion as having been originally a distinct mountain, or, more accurately, a portion of a distinct mountain. It was so understood by Eusebius, and by his translator, St. Jerome.* They have no doubt on the point, and till now their opinion was unchallenged.

* The following are the expressions of Eusebius, translated by St. Jerome :—

But our modern innovators have positively iden-
tified Sion and Moria. In the beautiful atlas annexed
by Messrs. Smith and Grove to the " Bible Dictionary,"
the names of Sion and Golgotha are marked on the
sides of the same mountain which would be, also, the
City of David, as if the matter were already decided
by science. However, we shall only confute this
theory indirectly, as we will now deal with Captain
Warren's view. In general he follows the great traditions, but he has not been able to resist the force of
example, and he, too, has a theory to give us as
a " mezzo-termine." The merits of this author, and his
Biblical erudition, which probably could not be equalled
among French engineers, does not allow us to keep
silence respecting his opinion.

Taking a review of the historical and poetical books
of the Old Testament, he proves satisfactorily that the
Holy City, in the Jewish period, consisted of three
perfectly distinct groups of buildings. First, the city
itself, the ancient Jebus, taken by storm after Josua's
death by the children of Juda and Benjamin ; secondly,
the citadel or castle of Sion, which resisted the attacks

Sion.—Mons urbis Jerusalem.

Acheldama.—Ager sanguinis qui hodieque monstratur in
Ælia ad australem plagam montis Sion.

Tapheth, legimus in Jeremia "aram Thapheth."—Est autem
in suburbanis Æliæ usque hodiè locus qui sic vocatur, juxta
piscinam Fullonis et agrum Acheldama.

Topheth.—In valle filiorum Ennom, ubi populus Israel gen-
tium simulacra venerabatur. Est autem locus in suburbanis
Jerusalem.

18—2

of the two tribes till the time when it became the "City of David," from the name of its conqueror; thirdly and lastly, Moria, the enclosure of the Temple and its dependencies.

The city, properly so called, occupied the heights at the top of the Tyropæon, stretching more or less to the north and south, according to different periods. It is in this direction, and not to the south-west, that Mr. Warren turns to find the City of David. He imagines that he has found it on the heights to the east of the gate of Damascus, which commands the quarter of Bezetha, and which is sometimes called Acra.*

Here, according to Captain Warren, and not to the south, we are to look for the City of David. The reason which he gives is this: the city must have been divided between the two tribes of Juda and Benjamin. The latter tribe being to the north, and Sion being in Benjamin's portion, it follows that the part of the city which fell to Juda can only be found by placing Sion as far off as the Acropolis, where stood the old palace of Helen.†

He quotes the very text of the Sacred Scriptures in proof of the city having been divided between the two tribes. Here, according to the Anglican version, is the description of the frontier of Juda: "The border

---

* Others place Acra elsewhere, even in hollows, in defiance of etymological, and all other reasons. Every one knows the situation of the Acra or Acropolis of Athens, Corinth, Syracuse, &c. In any case this controversy does not concern Catholic tradition.

† "Comparative Holiness," etc.—"Quart. Stat., July, 1869.

went up (from En-Rogel) by the valley of the son of
Hinnom, unto the south side of the Jebusite : the same
is Jerusalem : and the border went up to the top of
the mountain that lieth before the valley of Hinnom,
westward."

His reason for thinking that this line passed, not
only beneath the walls, but into the city itself, is, that
at the end of the chapter describing the portion of Juda,
the sacred historian adds that "the children of this
tribe could not drive the Jebusites out, but the Jebusites dwelt with the children of Juda at Jerusalem
unto this day."

The book of Judges also says that the children of
Juda, having taken Jerusalem (with the exception of
the citadel), set fire to it. . . . .But do these texts show
quite clearly that that part of the city was really occupied by the tribe of Juda ?

Juda is sometimes mentioned alone when the question is of enterprises undertaken together with Benjamin and Simeon, because of its preponderance in
numbers and authority over those two tribes. It is
true that the kingdom of Juda only dates from the
time of Roboam, but its ascendancy over the south
of Palestine had existed even in the time of the conquest.

In our own days the Crimean War was undertaken
in the interest of Turkey, but no one was surprised to
hear the success of the Anglo-French arms spoken of,
as if the Turks—the parties chiefly interested—had
nothing to do with the matter. In the same way, when

Juda is spoken of *à propos* of Jerusalem, without mentioning the particular proprietor, that circumstance has no bearing on the topographical question.

With regard to the text quoted, it seems that a boundary line, crossing Jerusalem, would have been differently described. It would have been said that it ascended from En-Rogel by the gorge of Mello, and passing through the city of the Jebusites, descended to the north at the top of the valley of Hinnom. This line, as the division of the two tribes, would certainly be very unnatural, whereas the one which runs along the valley of Hinnom is perfectly clear and intelligible, and capable of being reconciled with the words of the text. According to Sacy's translation, the line of demarcation, ascending by the valley in question, passes, not into the city, but to the southern side of the *"country"* of the Jebusites, where the city of Jerusalem stands. And there is nothing to prevent our adopting this interpretation. Even if we admit that it is the city, and not the country, which is spoken of, the Hebrew shows that the boundary is " at the shoulder," *i.e.*, at the side of, and not *in* Jerusalem.

The proof that this interpretation not only can but ought to be received, is that three chapters further on, when the boundaries of Benjamin are spoken of, we find the same expressions, in a reverse order, from east to west.

The frontier of Benjamin goes down from the mountain to the west, into the valley of Ennom, " to the southern side of the Jebusite," *i.e.*, Jerusalem, and goes on descending as far as En-Rogel. The expressions are identical, whence it follows that by admitting an encroachment of the boundary into Jerusalem, we make the same important land the property of the two different tribes at the same time. Besides, to make the boundary line cut through Jerusalem, would be an inexplicable exception to the Jewish rules of dividing a territory. It is evident that they had no notion of our modern way of dividing by ideal or geometrical lines. The lots were chosen by groups of populations: the towns with their villages. The formula is invariable: 10—20—30 towns with their villages. How could there have been an exception with regard to the suburbs, or any portion of the city? In the portion of Benjamin are mentioned, among other cities, "Jerusalem, Gabaath, Cariath, &c., fourteen towns in all, with their villages."

The reason for mentioning the Jebusites at the end of the chapter referring to Juda is, that they were not able to live in their citadel without some sort of territory. On the north and east there was the obstacle of the Benjamites, who were established in the city. On the side of Bethlehem, beyond Haceldama, they were more at liberty, and able to extend their labours, and even their depredations, as they pleased. They had then a constant subject of dispute with Juda. If the Jebusites had been in the Acra, they would have made their sortie to the north, and then they would not have come into immediate contact with Juda, unless Captain Warren will admit that the latter possessed all

the town, and that the Benjamites did not own an inch
of land there till the time of David; but it is especially
said in Judges (i. 21), that as the Benjamites were
not able completely to drive out the Jebusites, they
both lived in Jerusalem.

4. *The Pools and Aqueducts.*

The pools, in consequence of their usefulness—which
is so great in a city like Jerusalem, as to stir even
Mussulman apathy—have escaped the law by which the
lower parts have been levelled. Some springs certainly
existed in Jerusalem, but not sufficient for the requirements of the Temple and the priests, nor for the
religiou͛s and sanitary habits of the Jews, in their warm
climate. Immense works were set on foot at different
periods to supply this insufficiency. Solomon, Ezechias,
Nehemias, all turned their attention to the subject, and
the pools or ponds made by the wisest of kings near
Bethlehem, to serve as reservoirs, are still to be ad-
mired. This aqueduct is now dried up and ruined,
but the works of others still supply Jerusalem with a
fair amount of drinking water: they exist even on the
rock of Haram. Now, in days when our hydraulic
appliances were unknown, everything had to give way
to the cogency of the requisite slopes and levels.
Streets, palaces, every sort of building, must have
yielded the precedence to this necessity, and hence we
may conclude that these reservoirs of water have
helped to preserve the traditions of the quarters in

their immediate vicinity, in spite of other changes
which may in the end have occasioned the loss of their
names, and the very proofs of their identity.

Here we ought to remark that nearly all the
memorials of our Lord which are shown to pilgrims,
such as the arch of the Ecce Homo, the Via Dolorosa,
&c., are in the high parts of the city, which have
suffered least from the accumulation of ruins.

Under these circumstances, and with all these landmarks, is it wonderful that traditions have been kept
up even where everything has been overthrown and
altered ? They have always been able to retain sufficient hold to keep their ground, and to be preserved
from one generation to another ; any confusion that
has arisen is because the sectarian spirit has in-
terfered.

Third Evidence.—The Objects discovered in the Excavations.

If the objects of art and of industry left to us by
Jewish civilisation, valuable though they be, are compared with the Egyptian, Greek, Roman, Etruscan,
and other remains stored in our museums, their meagre-
ness will strike every one. The fact is capable of explanation, but to give it would carry us away from
our subject. It is enough to observe that the most
numerous discoveries are of that epoch of the Primitive Church which is so full of interest for us. No
doubt the excavations are going on, and we do not
know what they may reveal. But, meanwhile, this is

what the Rev. Chester Greville says about the Christian vases discovered in the excavations:—

"Of pottery which can unhesitatingly be assigned to the Christian period, the association possesses a large series of lamps. Some of these are distinguished by extremely curious inscriptions, and most of them possess a local character which is extremely interesting. Many lamp-types of more Western Christendom, from the Catacombs of Rome, Syracuse, and Carthage, such as the Good Shepherd, the Sacred Monogram ☧, the Dove, the Cock of St. Peter, and the Chalice, are entirely absent; and the same may be said of the disgusting and probably gnostic device of the toad associated with the Cross, so often found in the Catacombs of Alexandria and elsewhere in Egypt. The earthenware bottles with the effigy of St. Menas, an Egyptian saint who flourished in the fourth century, and whose name recalls the first Egyptian king, so commonly found with Christian lamps in Egypt, are also absent. The usual symbols of the Jerusalem lamps, which are all of a rude and cheap description, and which give an affecting indication of the poverty of the "saints" of the early Church of Jerusalem, are the Cross, the very Sign of their Salvation; the Seven-branched Candlestick, which reminded them, not only of the dimmed glories of Zion, but of Him who is the Light of the world; and the Palm Branch, which was dear to them, not merely for its own exquisite grace and beauty, but by its association with Psalm xcii., with the Gospel narrative John xii. 13, and with the Apocalyptic Vision,

wherein the glorified saints are described as 'clothed
with white robes, and palm branches in their hands'
(Rev. vii. 9). These emblems, which the Christians of
the 'Mother of Churches' used and rejoiced in, in common with their brethren in more westerly lands, are
more or less conventionalised in their treatment, and
are represented in a distinctive and different manner,
occurring in every instance, not, as is usual in the West
and even in Egypt, in the centre, but along the edge
and near the outer lips of the lamps, which are pear-
shaped, and in no instance round. *U*ninscribed round
lamps of a different description have, nevertheless,
been discovered, and probably belong to this period.

"The following inscriptions occur ; they are written
in barbarous Greek, the words being often mis-spelt :
. . . . *ΦΩΣ ΧΤ ΦΕΝΙ ΠΑΣΙΝ, A Cross*—'The Light
of Christ shines forth to all.'

" . . . . (Another) inscription appears to begin
with the letters *ΙΧΘ*, which may stand for *Ιησους
Χριστος Θεος*, or it may possibly allude to our Lord
under the well-known symbol of the Fish—*ΙΧΘΤΣ*
—the letters of which form the initials of the Greek
equivalent of 'Jesus Christ, the Son of God, the
Saviour.'

" . . . . The Christian lamps have been found, not
only in tombs, but in numerous excavations in and
about Jerusalem. It is remarkable that none of them
bear potters' marks on the under side."

This last observation of the Rev. G. Chester would
seem to point to a time of persecution, when the work-

man was desirous of avoiding whatever might draw attention to himself. The following are Captain Warren's remarks on one of these lamps, which he found in the Tyropæon, to the south-west of the Temple, in a bed of rubbish twenty feet in thickness, which covers an ancient pavement, and which is itself hidden by another twenty-three feet below the present surface. He says that it "has an inscription of Christian origin, similar to that on lamps which have been considered to be of the third or fourth centuries."

Archæologists will doubtless be able to fix the age of the intermediate pavement, which is nearly level with the threshold of the Gate of the Prophet, and which must have been anterior to the building of Wilson's Arch. But, at all events, according to the evidence of these two Protestants, we possess a collection of lamps manufactured by Christians of the date of the Catacombs: that is to say, the very period when Mr. Robinson would have us believe that the Christians were absent, scattered, disorganised, and absolutely without memorials.

We do not flatter ourselves with having solved every archæological difficulty in the preceding pages; it is enough for us if we have made our readers begin to perceive that, even after the researches of science, the most natural solutions are to be found in the ancient traditions. Progress has increased the darkness as well as the light. There is enough of the latter for good faith. Here, too, God seems to say to science, "Thou dost wish to be sufficient to thyself, and to dispense with

Me and My Church; but, when left to thyself, thou
wilt not gain more results in sacred archæology than
when thou seekest for the First Cause in thy crucible,
and biddest the scalpel reveal to thee the substance of
the soul."

CHAPTER XVI.

ARCHITECTURAL EVIDENCE.

1. *General Idea of Styles of Architecture in Palestine.*

WHAT has been said of the scarcity of the remains
of Jewish industry, applies equally to the remains of
their special architecture. It is easier to find the
works of the Troglodytes, who were their predecessors,
than those of God's own people. With the exception
of tombs, wells, and aqueducts, everything seems the
very ruin of ruins.

The interesting exploration of the Rev. Mr. Pal-
mer in the Badiat et Tih, or the desert of the wan-
derings of Israel, shows us vestiges of races which
have successively and gradually inhabited it, cut down
its timber, ruined and abandoned it, as clearly marked
as the most distinct geological strata. He thinks that
the wells which are found on the lowest slopes of Sinai,
and the round huts or Nawamis of unhewn stones
which crown the hills abutting on the Jebel Ejmeh,
may be ascribed to the Madianites; the tumuli enclosed by walls, or by upright stones, are most probably
remains of the Amalekites. The towns of the Horites

are still in existence, with their dwellings hollowed out
of the side of the rocks, their galleries of communication, and their terraces serving as an entrance court.
Then there are more modern towns and citadels possessing remarkable peculiarities. The Roman posts
are easily recognised, and the towns which saw the
beginning of the Christian era still have the remains
of churches and monasteries; but most of these curiously
preserved cities seem, by their simplicity of style, and
the absence of carvings and inscriptions, to denote the
austerity of Mosaic manners, though we could not
venture on assigning positive dates to them. The only
exceptions are the districts inhabited by Abraham,
Isaac, and Jacob. There we see the wells formed of
vast blocks of stone, just as they are described in the
sacred Scriptures, in places the names of which are not
materially changed, and in the valleys situated on the
road between Hebron and Egypt.

All this description helps us to understand the rest
of Palestine proper. We find there, too, the caves and
excavations of the Troglodytes in the sides of the limestone rocks which offered such admirable facilities for
the purpose. Those caves, which meet us at every
turn, are the same which so scandalised Mme. de Gas-
parin. She cannot reconcile herself to the idea of the
Philistines not having waited to ask her advice; but
we can imagine how well suited such dwellings, warm
in winter, cool in summer, and easy of defence, must
have been to the first inhabitants of Palestine.

However, it is rather a question of race than of

climate, for it does not appear that any of the succeeding races thought of excavating the rocks, except for quarries, cisterns, or tombs. Nevertheless, they made use of the ancient caves by joining on to them their houses to serve as a sort of outbuildings. I can easily believe that, among the Jews, public or private buildings, being built of simple and solid materials, very little decorated, and not much exposed to inclement weather, would last a long time, and be easily repaired without bearing traces of re-touching.

Architectural richness was reserved for the Temple, the synagogues, and the palaces. According to all probability, the details of the Ark of the Covenant, of the altars, and of the Tabernacle, gave tokens of recollections of Memphis. Later on, the workmen of David and Solomon must have introduced something of that Egyptian type into the building of the Temple, mingled with outlines borrowed from the monuments of Tyre and Sidon, the native places of many of their number. The same mixed type must have been easily recognised also in the second Temple, built by Zorobabel. The work of Solomon was recollected from childhood by those who directed the undertaking. Certainly, the copy was not exact. Assyrian types must have slipped into the new plans; and at the Feast of the Dedication of the new building, "the old men wept" at the sight of its inferiority.

We have no data to enable us to judge of Jewish art, properly so-called. The plans drawn by Vilalpand and others are certainly the fruit of labo-

rious study; they are valuable as an attempt to reconcile the measurements given by the sacred Scriptures, Josephus, and others. The architectural elevations give us, at most, a general idea of the whole;
but the details are purely imaginary, and certainly
convey no more notion of the reality than the columns
of Philæ would of a Corinthian portico. As to the
restoration under Herod, we have some further details.
He must have employed—he certainly did employ—
the Greek chisel for a number of accessories and new
additions, intended to harmonise with the old building.
And we are not without examples of this mixture; as
instances, we may mention the sepulchres of the valley
of Josaphat, where the cell was of an earlier period;
it was only later that it was detached from the mountain, and carved and decorated in the style then in
vogue.

On the other hand, there is some ground for supposing that the Temple of Jerusalem in its new form
had its effect in the inspiration which created the
marvels of Petra, Baalbec, Palmyra, and others; and
there are some remains of synagogues which are acknowledged to belong to this epoch, in which the
Greek chisel must have played its part under the same
influence.

But whatever may be the case with regard to these
derivative styles, the vast building was reduced to
ashes—there is not "a stone left upon a stone;" and
from the day of that great destruction, we find ourselves launched into the Roman period—a period of

activity altogether foreign and pagan : new cities, with idol-temples, theatres, baths, xysta, and other profane places which scandalised the old Jews.

Essentially, it is still the Greek style introduced by the race of Antiochus, but to which the Romans gave something of their rough, strong character. Later, the Greco-Roman becomes the Byzantine, and gives us the earliest Christian churches. But whatever may have been the Jewish style, there is no longer any trace of it. At the time of the Babylonish captivity, the exile of the Jews only lasted sixty years, but their dispersion under Titus continues still, and but for the Christians, the official population of the city restored by Hadrian would have forgotten its ancient name.

It is possible that there may be Christian churches in the East of an earlier date-than Constantine. The Rev. Mr. Girdlestone ascribes to the second century the church of Djerash, which is so remarkable for the inscription in Greek verse which ornaments the lintel of the entrance-door. Circumstances may have favoured the erection and preservation of monuments thus ostensibly dedicated to a proscribed worship. To whatever period a church may belong, its direction towards the east, and other particular signs, usually distinguish it from pagan temples, which, in their turn, generally possess a name, a history, emblems, and other special marks which make doubt or mistake all but impossible.

In short, the first period of Christian architecture

19

working boldly in the light of day only dates from
Constantine, and lasts only three centuries, including
the intervals caused by the persecutions of the Icono-
clasts and the Persian invasion. I grant that a period
of that length would be more than sufficient to obscure a multitude of questions, if their solution depended only upon the eye.

But, from the time of Constantine, history comes to
our aid. A certain number of churches are known to
have been built by Pulcheria, Eudoxia, and Theodosius.
Procopius has been careful to let us know the churches
erected by Justinian. After him, architecture becomes
greatly modified, both in consequence of the poverty
of the Christians, who were ruined, persecuted, and
reduced to slavery, and of the presence of a new, hasty,
and victorious race. From the Saracenic period to the
architecture of the Crusaders, there is but a step, and
then we have a vast difference from the architecture of
Constantine's days. It is impossible that there should
be any mistake.

All these circumstances taken together, narrow the
range of difficulties very much, and we may, without
incurring the charge of rashness, receive a tradition
which attributes a ruin to St. Helena or to her son,
when we find nothing in history or in the style of the
monument to contradict it.

Very often such contradictions exist only in appearance, and we must exercise a certain amount of prudence before we admit them. An Arabian author may
tell us that Abd el Melik built the Dome of the Rock,

without saying that it was on the site of Solomon's Temple; would any one infer from this that he contradicts the Book of Kings? In the same way, if an author tells us that the tomb of the Virgin was built by Pulcheria, this fact in no way disproves that Helena took a great part in the work; on the contrary, it proves the existence of a primitive monument, not only of the time of Helena, but even of the days before the Assumption. It does not do, therefore, to acknowledge without precaution every difficulty originating in differences of architectural style. We have seen in France more than one romanesque church, the semicircular windows of which were replaced by pointed ones in the thirteenth century; later on, the church has been restored by an intelligent hand, making it one again in style, and removing the pointed arches. A Byzantine church in Palestine may have suffered changes of this kind; in that case, a pointed window made by the Crusaders in a building of earlier date would in no way prove that its origin was not of the period of Constantine; it may present an enigma to science, and furnish the enemies of our traditions with a weapon, but in reality it proves nothing.

2. *Remains of Constantine's Basilicas.*

A minute discussion of every antiquity remaining to us of the religious monuments with which St. Helena and Constantine filled Palestine would carry us beyond the limits within which we must confine ourselves. But we cannot pass them by in absolute silence.

In the thirteenth century, the Greek Nicephorus gave a very detailed list of the churches and other monuments which public gratitude attributed to the mother and son. The following is an analysis of it :—

I. What was then called the New Jerusalem—that is to say, the entire collection of buildings of which the Holy Sepulchre was the centre, and which still forms the nucleus of the Christian quarter. He mentions particularly Calvary and the Anastasis.

II. Another splendid church at Bethlehem, containing the sacred cave and manger of the Nativity.

III. Another of equal splendour on the summit of the Mount of Olives, the scene of the Ascension.

IV. At Gethsemani, a beautiful church to the Mother of God, whose tomb was carefully enclosed within the sanctuary ; on account of the declivity, Helena had a marble staircase made on the eastern side.

V. On the spot where the angels told the good tidings to the shepherds, a church dedicated to the angels.

VI. Also at Bethlehem, another to the Mother of the Incarnate Word.

VII. Another to Joseph, the spouse of Mary.

VIII. Another very striking one at Bethania, in honour of Lazarus, 2000 paces from Jerusalem.

IX. At the spot where St. John the Baptist's cave is situated, not far from the sacred river Jordan, a magnificent church to the holy Precursor.

X. Another on the slope of the mountain, to the prophet Elias.

XI. The Church of the Twelve Thrones, in Galilee, where Jesus fed the 5000.

XII. Helena built churches in several places in honour of the apostles.

XIII. At Tiberias, she transformed the house of St. Peter's mother-in-law into a beautiful church, in honour of the apostle.

XIV. On Mount Tabor, where Melchisedech was said to have blessed Abraham.

XV. On the same mountain, a magnificent church in honour of the three witnesses of the Transfiguration.

XVI. At Nazareth, round the house where the angel saluted Mary, a very beautiful church to the Mother of God.

XVII. Another at Cana in Galilee, where the marriage of Simon the Canaanite was celebrated, at which the miraculous wine was drunk.

XVIII. At Sion an immense temple, containing the house in which the apostles met with closed doors, "for fear of the Jews," the room where the Last Supper was eaten, where the Washing of the Feet and the Descent of the Holy Ghost took place, and where St. James was elected first bishop of Jerusalem.

XIX. She also dedicated another church in the garden of Caiphas to the Prince of the apostles.

XX. At the instance of her son Constantine, she built, on the ruins of Greek idolatry, a large and beautiful church near the terebinth of Mambre. Lastly, this holy empress caused several other churches to be

built in these sacred places, so that their number
amounted to more than thirty. Constantine built one
also at Heliopolis, in Phœnicia, and many others in
different places. So far the analysis of Nicephorus.

In the building of these churches St. Helena, as
well as Constantine, could not take more than a general
interest. She only spent two years in Palestine, and
that at an advanced age. This did not, however, prevent her from visiting every part of it, as the author
whom we have just quoted affirms. She was able to
point out the principal places, to appove of plans, to get
her son's authority for their execution, and to encourage
the work of construction.

At all events, even if we have to make allowance
for popular exaggerations repeated by Nicephorus, his
account would still be a proof of the veneration in
which the memory of the saint was held in the thirteenth century, in Palestine, on account of the part
she had taken in the restoration of the Holy Places, and
that is sufficient to confirm the assertions of earlier
historians.

The authority of Nicephorus alone may not be
worth much, but his testimony ought to be put into
the scales when his words are the echo of preceding historians, or when they are corroborated by the archæological researches of our own day.

When the antiquarian discovers Christian remains,
or monuments of the Byzantine period, he is obliged
to place them in one of the four following classes :—

I. Those about which history and tradition say nothing explicit.

II. Those which are plainly attributed to some one of Constantine's successors.

III. Those which are attributed to that prince or his mother.

IV. Those which have undergone restorations attested by history.

I. Those in the first category, the trace of which is lost in the past, are sufficiently numerous to be appealed to as an exception in favour of the historians who have ascribed the building of a great number of churches to Helena and her son.

II. The churches of Justinian and others help to throw light on Christian traditions generally. We have no concern with them here, except so far as they are of assistance in clearing up the question of the buildings of Constantine.

III. Most of the edifices built in the reign of Constantine have disappeared; but there are some left, and these venerable relics are, in the opinion of competent judges, sufficiently recognisable to justify the accounts of Eusebius and of the historians who followed him. They are some portions of the Church of the Holy Sepulchre, and a large part of the Church of Bethlehem. We might, perhaps, add the ruins of the Church of Cana, and some others, but I wish only to enumerate those which are generally acknowledged by even Protestant authors.

IV. Reconstructions are far from being detrimental to tradition. If the adjusting of the new work is visible, or if the restoration is confirmed by history, then they are but so many links added to the chain of evidence.   Thus, what remains of the octagonal Church of the Ascension, rebuilt by the patriarch Modestus, helps us to go back to the church of the same form built by St. Helena. In the crypt which remains at the tomb of Mary we are unable to say what is the work of Constantine's mother; but the traces of the work of St. Pulcheria, and of the Crusaders, give us reason to believe that, at all events, she must have enlarged the excavation.

Will any one say that, after all, the sum total of the remains of Constantine's period is very meagre? I reply, that it is sufficient, and as much as we could expect after fifteen centuries, three-quarters of which have been under the *régime* of devastating Mussulmen.

The wonder is rather that so much remains, and we see a special providence in it, as well as the fruit of the perseverance of the children of St. Francis.

CHAPTER XVII.

NAZARETH AND LORETO.

In the foregoing chapters our main concern has been with Jerusalem, and we have given the reason for this; still, we must not conclude without a few words on the subject of one of our principal sanctuaries, belonging both to Italy and Palestine. It deserves mention on account of its dignity, and affords a striking instance of the application of our principles; and besides, though we have very little taste for the petty objections with which shallow wits like to fill their own heads, and those of others, when they can, still we wish to show that we do not shrink from them, and that, when necessary, we can answer them.

Our readers know that there is, on the coast of the Adriatic, half-way between Venice and Rome, a celebrated sanctuary known as Our Lady of Loreto. To this sanctuary the surrounding town owes its existence; a "holy city," complete in its hierarchy, bishop, chapter of canons, religious orders, educational and charitable institutions, temporal dependencies, and territory.

For six hundred years pilgrims from all parts of the Catholic world have flocked thither. A pilgrimage to Rome seems incomplete unless it is combined with a visit to Loreto. Kings and princes have gone there; others have sent splendid offerings; popes have en-

couraged the piety of all by rescripts, indulgences,
and every spiritual or temporal favour which it was
in their power to bestow. Finally, it is said that
Heaven itself has been pleased to reward the prayers
and the faith of nations and of individuals by floods
of graces and of supernatural wonders. Indeed, if
miracles are a proof of imposture, then Loreto especially must plead guilty. There are miracles in the
position and preservation of the fragile walls of the
Sta. Casa; miracles in the very nature of its materials,
which are not to be found in Italy; miracles of public
scourges that have been arrested, of sudden cures that
have been wrought, of tempests calmed, of deliverances
at critical moments, above all, a miracle of miracles in
the fact of its presence there.

According to Catholic tradition, the Sta. Casa is
nothing less than the Nazarene house of our Blessed
Lady, the scene of the angel's visit, and of the Incarnation of the Word of God—the chief sanctuary of the
Hidden Life of Him Who is the King of angels—the
lowly dwelling formerly built against the cliff with its
holy cave, which are still in existence. The Home
of the Holy Family has changed its place so as to
receive more veneration, to dispense more graces,
and to come nearer to bless our Western hemisphere.
This new Ark was carried by angels, first to Tersatz, in
Dalmatia, then to different places in the March of
Ancona, till, at last, it took up a fixed position on the
hill where it still stands. For six hundred years tradition has repeated this legend of miraculous journeys,

and of ceaseless benedictions; and I am ready to
admit, that, to a man who has not the faith, to a
stranger taken by surprise, it must seem an improbable
tale, worthy of the "Arabian Nights."

We are not, then, astonished at meeting with opponents. But were there no truth in the whole story,
then it would be a series of wholesale deceptions, of
inexplicable events, of superhuman trickery, impossible
to have been invented, executed, and maintained for a
period of centuries; a thing far more extraordinary
than all which we explain by angelic agency. However, let us see what both sides have to say.

The Cave of Nazareth and the Sta. Casa are perfectly well known, and the Catholic point of view has
become the popular one in France through the accounts of Dom Géramb, Louis Veuillot, Père Caillau,
and others. The work of the last is such that a missionary regarded it as sufficient to render untenable the
position of any Protestant who would study it in good
faith. Nevertheless, Mr. Ffoulkes challenges the Rev.
Father, accuses him of bad faith, and finds gaps in his
explanations and demonstrations. In proof of his
charge of bad faith, he mentions that Eusebius is
quoted among the authors who may be consulted on
the subject of the Holy House. And, indeed, if he
were quoted as speaking *explicitly* of the Sta. Casa, it
would be difficult to justify the historian of Our Lady
of Loreto, for Eusebius does not say, in so many
words, that the House of Nazareth was enshrined in a
basilica by St. Helena and her son, but, as we have

seen, he gives us clearly to understand that, besides the works executed by their orders at the Holy Sepulchre and at Bethlehem, they commanded that others should be undertaken to consecrate the places sanctified by the memory of Christ. If Nazareth is such a place, that is sufficient to make it reasonable and right to consult the author of the panegyric of Constantine, and to quote him as an authority. Had Père Caillau passed him over in silence, he would have been still more severely blamed.

Our Aristarchus, following the sacred building through the course of ages, stops us at every step to require from us extracts from its archives.

"Where was the Holy House during such a century? Where was it for those sixty years? Show us any one who mentions it."

All proofs go for nothing so long as Mr. Ffoulkes cannot see, year after year, the *procès verbaux* of the ediles of Nazareth, Tersatz, or Loreto, supported by the official plan, and have in his hand the baptismal register of all the Frangipani in the world. Protesting is a part of Mr. Ffoulkes's nature : he protested formerly even against Protestantism, and he did the same when passing through Catholicism. He does not belong to a materialistic school, but to one which accepts no evidence but that of the individual " ego." He would certainly quarrel with what we have said about the stream of tradition, the course of which is not really interrupted, because, for a certain period, it is lost to sight. Let us turn to a graver author.

As we before said, Dean Stanley is not one of those men who deal in coarse ridicule, and whose attacks can only be received with contempt. He has a respect for the Holy Places, and for Catholic traditions on scientific grounds, and because of certain sympathies which he has in common with us.

It is in a loving spirit that he describes Nazareth with its "fifteen gently rounded hills, (that) seem as if they had met to form an enclosure for its peaceful basin, and rise round it, like the edge of a shell, to guard it from intrusion." And quoting Quaresmius, he adds, poetically, "Nazareth is a rose, and, like a rose, has the same rounded form, enclosed by mountains, as the flower by its leaves."

But in spite of his emotion at sight of the lowly valley which witnessed the Incarnation, and the first steps of the Man-God, no sooner does the Reverend Dean set foot in the sanctuary,* than he is evidently out of his element; he cannot breathe freely among monks and pilgrims, and after a hasty general glance, he rushes to the church near the Fountain of Mary, which the Greeks, jealous of the Latins, assert to be the site of the Annunciation. As an impartial judge, he does not see why their claims—late as they were in urging them—should not be as well founded as ours. Everywhere he sees nothing but a tissue of uncertainty and contradiction; he sees three sanctuaries, each of which contradicts the other, and Loreto, in

* The same which was claimed by Louis XIII., and given to him by the Emir Farkh-Eddin.

particular, seems to him inadmissible, for these three reasons.

I. The dimensions are incompatible. The Sta. Casa of Loreto is considerably larger than the "Chapel of the Angel," shown at Nazareth as the site of the Holy House.

II. The materials are enough, of themselves, to refute the story of the translation. The House of Loreto is composed of polished stones of a reddish brown, of which there are no examples either at Nazareth, or throughout Palestine, whilst they are common in the neighbourhood of Ancona.

III. The Holy House might certainly have been built against a cave, like many others at Nazareth. But if the only ancient door of which there are traces at Loreto, was the one which communicated with the cave, then there was no mode of exit from either house or cave.

These assertions are new—at least, in part—and they are very positive. How are we to get out of the difficulty?

When Dean Stanley's book came out, there was in London a Cambridge convert, the friend and fellow-labourer of Father Faber, in the congregation of the Oratory. Being very devoted to our Blessed Lady and to the poor, he had founded in the centre of one of the most wretched and thickly-peopled parts of London, the Schools of Compassion, for boys and girls, the latter of whom were placed under the care of a community of French nuns from the diocese of Langres.

It was while labouring in this work that the seeds of a malady, which in the end took him away from his friends and from religion, were sown. He was advised to try a change of climate for the recovery of his health, and he took advantage of this necessity to go and study the questions raised by Dean Stanley, on the spot.

He returned from Italy and Palestine with valuable materials, which it was his intention to arrange and publish; but the course of the paralysis which was impending had only been checked by the change and the voyage, and all that he was able to accomplish was to write out the two opening conferences, which he without delay published under the title of "Loreto and Nazareth."

The plans which illustrate this little treatise are enough to dispose of the topographical objections. They show that the Cave of Nazareth had a double entrance, which the less careful Dean overlooked: they show, too, how the Holy House was built against the rock at the entrance of the cave, and what were, and what might have been, the different openings before the architects authorised by the Pope enclosed it in a second edifice of marble. These plans are in harmony with tradition. The learned and truthful Quaresmius, if read with attention, might teach Dean Stanley that about the year 1620 the work of restoration carried on in the sanctuary of Nazareth, laid bare the foundations of the original building, and that the measurements were found to coincide with those of the Sta. Casa of Loreto. The present sanctuary of the Annunciation at Nazareth is on the *site*, but has not dimensions scrupulously identical with those of the Sta. Casa, as is imagined by the Dean to be necessary. He has all this while been amusing himself in fighting with a shadow.

It would have been difficult for a simple priest, passing through Italy, to verify the nature of the materials of the Holy House. Pilgrims are prohibited, under pain of excommunication, from carrying away the smallest portion. But Cardinal Wiseman dealt with this difficulty. He had written on the subject to a Roman prelate, Mgr. Bartolini, who, when he too made a pilgrimage to the Holy Places, carefully collected the materials employed in the buildings at Nazareth, both ancient and modern. Furnished with the necessary authority, he also procured the different materials employed in the House of Loreto, and on his return he submitted his specimens, without saying whence they came, to be analysed by Dr. Ratti, Professor of Chemistry at the Sapienza in Rome. Examination proved that the stones thus analysed had no likeness to the volcanic stone found about Ancona; they consisted of limestone, more or less hard, and were of a gray colour, more or less tinged with red, and veined, according as magnesia, ferruginous clay, or silex predominated.

These different kinds of limestone are found in the quarries of Nazareth. The hardest variety, called Jabes, is regularly stratified, and comes away in blocks which have something of the appearance of bricks, and hence the first aspect of the Sta. Casa, which has struck some travellers. The other, and more friable sort, called Nahari, is also to be seen in the House of Loreto, but only in the filling up or interior details.

If, at Loreto, these stones are polished and nearly black, it is because, for eighteen centuries, they have received and lost various coatings, more or less coloured; it is because now they are exposed, night and day, to the smoke of lamps, to the vapour of the breaths, to the touch and the pious kisses of millions. Is it to be wondered at that they do not look as though they were fresh from the quarry ?

The examination of the cement was equally conclusive. It is not the excellent Italian pozzolana, but a mixture of pounded Nahari, plaster, and charcoal, just such as is found in the ancient and modern buildings of central Galilee.

Mgr. Bartolini published his " Osservazioni " in 1861 ; and Father Hutchison, feeling himself incapable of extending his own work as much as he could have desired, consoled himself with the thought that an extract from the Roman prelate's pamphlet would be sufficient on this point. A few hours before his death he corrected the proof sheets of " Loreto and Nazareth."· He strove with his last agony so as to leave behind him that act of homage to Mary, and to the traditions of the Church.

An unforeseen circumstance attracted public attention to this modest work, which may be said to have

20

blossomed on a tomb. A member of the late Father's family made an attack upon his will, laying claim even to sums which had for years been expended on various good works. In proof of the author's insanity he produced this book, in which was discussed "a flying house, transporting itself from one place to another, and crossing seas and mountains."

Upon this, the work was submitted to the judgment of a law-court. But the opponent of the will had counted too much on the anti-Catholic prejudices of his country. The judge observed, in summing up, that the possibility of miracles was a question which did not come within the province of the law, and that it could not be decided in the manner in which the opponent regarded it, without declaring the majority of Christians incapable of making a will. This point being set aside, it remained for the court to see whether there were any other signs of diseased brain in the late Father's book. Well—the arguments were clear and consistent, the conclusions well drawn, and, consequently, the volume, whatever might be its value as to the point it professed to prove, was evidence that the author had been, up to the last, in full possession of his mental powers. The verdict was given accordingly.

In 1866, Dean Stanley brought out a new edition of his great work on Palestine; and he had the good taste not to affect ignorance of the Oratorian Father's little book. He even adopts his plans, but takes care not to comment upon them. Alas! it is very difficult for a savant who is his own judge in the controversies he is engaged in, to put himself on the index, and to correct his own errors frankly. The Dean withdraws none of his objections; all he does is to own in an ambiguous note, that certain assertions of his have been questioned by the "candid" author, of "Loreto and Nazareth." He takes good care not to breathe a word of Mgr. Bartolini.

A weekly journal acted more boldly. In the opinion of the "Saturday Review," the manner of conducting the chemical examination was one example more of popish trickery. Why was not the opposite party invited? . . . English, German, French chemists? So long as only Monsignori and doctors of the Sapienza are concerned in the business, the limestone of the Sta. Casa is to be considered duly accused and convicted of being volcanic and fusible in character. The Pope must take warning—next time he must issue a summons to the chemists attached to the "Review," and it will be as well for him not to leave out the scientific staff of "Punch," and the "Charivari!"

Père Caillau did not feel the pressing need of the chemical analysis. He was satisfied with the evidence of his eyes in judging of stones, cement, stucco, and fragments of beams of various woods, cedar, pine, and olive, together with other remains, which agree perfectly with the origin ascribed to the building by Catholics.

Thanks to our adversaries, chemistry has now pronounced judgment, and it is proved to all who are not determined right or wrong to contradict and mock,

that the materials of the Sta. Casa came from beyond
seas, and that they are the same with those employed
at Nazareth.

For the moment, therefore, we may forget traditions,
historical documents, and the whole collection of moral
proofs which are to be found in Catholic authors, and
refer to this one material fact.

It can only be accounted for by four hypotheses: that
of an ill-explained pagan monument; of an imposture;
of an undertaking like that of the Campo Santo of Pisa;
or, lastly, of a miraculous translation.

Is the Sta. Casa a bit of pagan antiquity to which
a miraculous origin was erroneously ascribed by simple-
tons?

In the first place, this is not one of those all but
indestructible cyclopean buildings, which may be fairly
ascribed to races anterior to the period of Etruscan
civilisation. Neither can we suppose it to be one of
those Roman ruins which are to be found everywhere,
deep down, and half buried in a soil full of *débris*. On
the contrary, these slender walls hardly clear the dust
of the earth on which they stand.

Then—we know the history of Palestine and of
Italy. When we see an Egyptian obelisk at Rome, or
a Latin inscription in Syria, the explanation is perfectly
simple; but what historic data will explain why common stones, and other materials of no use to the Romans,
should have been brought from Nazareth to an unknown
hill near Ancona? And, lastly, by what extraordinary
coincidence did it happen, that peasants of the four-

teenth century, without a notion of physical science,
hit upon the exact truth in asserting that these remains,
which are supposed to have been forgotten for centuries, are a Nazarene house ? No, there is nothing
pagan about it. It is very certainly a recent monument, the presence of which on Italian soil is later than
the triumph of Constantine over the last of the great
persecutors.

Is the theory of a pious fraud (forgive the cant)
more admissible than that of a mistake ? Are we to
believe that impostors, wishing to play upon the credulity of the Middle Ages, went to the ends of Palestine
for materials, at a great expenditure of men, money,
and vessels ? No, the necessity of secrecy, no less than
avarice, would have suggested to them, that, in their
day, the materials which lay ready to their hand were
sufficient for the success of an imposture. Will any
one say that they foresaw the criticisms of the nineteenth century, and the experiments of Dr. Ratti, so
exactly, that not a thing was forgotten ? Perhaps the
angels gave them notice of our chemical and geological
discoveries !

Let us pass to the third hypothesis ? As the Pisans
brought over millions of solid feet of earth from Palestine to their famous cemetery, the Campo Santo, why
should not others have made use of their galleys to
wrest from the Mussulmans the smoking ruins of the
Holy House of Nazareth ?

I grant that this might have been done ; but who
did it ? As to the work of the Campo Santo, I see

employed in it a flourishing republic, an aristocracy powerful and rich through its trade with the Levant— the earth trodden by Divine Feet serves as ballast to its galleons when lightened of their freight. The Pisans glory in their pious exploit, and take good care not to conceal it from the world. At Loreto I see no one. Was it the Venetians ? But if they had rescued this treasure, they would not have left it on the way. They had only to choose a site in their splendid city, and to unload the materials on the spot. Was it an army of Crusaders, each carrying his stone from Nazareth, as was supposed in some book—I forget what—of the last century ? But the routes of their different bands are well known. They depended for their means of transport on maritime people more important than the fishermen of Recanati ; and would the latter have multiplied expense and difficulty in order to hoist up their precious charge to the top of a lonely hill at a distance from the sea and from their town. Lastly, was it one of the sovereign pontiffs ? But would he have selected, to the injury of Rome, an obscure spot on the borders of his States ?

In any case, no one, Venetians, Romans, or others would have concealed their performance of this enterprise ; least of all could the popes have kept it secret, or escaped the notice of the crowd of writers who, from interest or curiosity, hatred or love, are always watching them. They would have considered the bringing over of the Holy House as one of the glories of their pontificate ; and, as a matter of fact, when the news of

its presence became known in times of schism, persecution, and exile, no sooner were they at liberty than
they spared neither letters patent, nor marbles, nor
precious metals, to transmit to posterity the proof of
their devotion.

Whoever the men were who are supposed to have
brought over the materials of the Sta. Casa, they must
have left marks of reconstruction quite different from
those which do exist, and which are well known.
With the exception of the doors which have been
made to facilitate the entrance and exit of the pilgrims, there is no sign of re-building by blocks or
otherwise ; and the ancient descriptions tell us of remains of stucco and of antique paintings in the upper
portion, the least exposed to decay, which exclude all
idea of re-arrangement.

To say that the building could have been brought
over as a whole by human hands, would be to compli-
cate and multiply, without lessening the miracle.

After all, as a mere object of devotion, it matters
little to our piety whether it was brought over in the
mass or piecemeal by the Venetians, the Popes, or any
one else. Therefore, we should not care to attack that
hypothesis had it any solid foundation ; but far more
marvellous than the house moved by miracle, this supposition rests only on the air of which it is built—it
has neither traditions, credentials, nor probabilities.

We come, then, to the last hypothesis—that of the
miracle. And here we are borne along by the full
stream of tradition. Everything bears the mark of

simplicity and truth. Everything is consistent and capable of explanation : little obscurities of detail vanish in the light of the main fact—the supernatural preservation of a cottage in which the Eternal Word was pleased to dwell with a mortal mother, and where, it seems, it is His Will to bless, to the end of time, those who visit it in humility of heart.

No doubt it is just the miracle—as a miracle—which shocks the nerves of anti-Catholics; but what is to be done ? For myself—a philosopher of the school of Nazareth—I see, in the account of the angelic translation, a touching harmony with the customs of the Holy Family . . . the same mysterious brightness— the same defeat of human wisdom—the same simplicity—the same union of weakness and omnipotence. As at Bethlehem, shepherds are the first witnesses and preachers of the wonder which has come to pass. For a long time it is known only to that small number of whom Jesus thus spoke beforehand : " I confess to Thee, O Father, Lord of heaven and earth, because Thou hast hid these things from the wise and prudent, and hast revealed them to little ones."

The sincerity of their faith is rewarded, and God, to Whom it is impossible to sanction error or folly, multiplies His wonders on the favoured House. Priests and religious mount guard at its doors: people flock thither in pious pilgrimages : princes and kings pour out gold and jewels : and, lastly, the Sovereign Pontiff opens the treasury of indulgences, and heaps favours on those who "love the beauty of the House of God."

And, in spite of all this lustre, it continues to be "hidden from the wise and prudent, and revealed to little ones."

It is not a commandment of the Church to believe in the House of Loreto, under pain of losing the Faith. Never, since the writing of the Gospels, has she inserted into her credo a single miracle, not even that of Constantine's Labarum; but I know that she believes the promise of miraculous works made to her by her Divine Founder: I know that she believes in the time-honoured miracle of Loreto: I know that she loves and blesses, by every means in her power, the votaries of the Sta. Casa. I do not hesitate to kiss and to venerate, heart and soul, those walls on which the light of the Holy Ghost has fallen. I lie prostrate in thought before them, as though I saw on them the shadows of the Divine Infant and His Mother.

CONCLUSION.

AFTER the reasons which have been set forth in the preceding pages, it is evident that the tradition of the Holy Places is not the result of a piece of jugglery of St. Macarius. It dates from apostolic times: it descended to the Middle Ages by perfectly independent channels, as a piece of family property furnished with all the correct title-deeds and documents: we are in tolerable agreement with reason and science, with his-

tory and archæology. We trust that we have satisfactorily shown this, and that we have put inquirers
of well-disposed minds upon the road to fuller demonstrations. And what we have said of Jerusalem might
be said of Bethlehem, and Cana, and other places of
sacred memory. What we have said of Palestine
might be said of Naples and Rome, and all our privileged sanctuaries in Italy, Spain, France, Germany—
everywhere.

And now what remains, but to declare our love for
the places dear to our fathers, those sacred spots,
blessed by God and men, places of grace, benediction,
and holy presences? The more they are systematically
attacked and insulted by wicked men, the more will
we surround them with our veneration. They will no
longer allow truth a home of her own on earth. She
must no longer have strongholds enduring as a monument, handed down as an inheritance. They will not
grant the priesthood its dwellings, its towns, and its
capitals; they will not permit charity, innocence, and
misfortune to have their safe asylums, their places of
refuge, their fortresses; the Shepherd may not have
His fold, nor Eternal Justice Its throne: in a word,
they will not have God on earth—least of all, God
made man, and dwelling with us.

But we will have all these things, and we believe
that they ought to be: we believe that they are the
future of the world and the hope of coming generations. And this is why we resist those who forbid us,
in the name of their proud reason, to believe any

longer in the past, who bid us leave heaven to God—
if indeed there is a God—and to keep this present
world, with which He has no concern, for ourselves.
We, on the contrary, look for the signs of His benedictions in the midst of our fields, for the tracks of
His eternal love on our soil, for the traces of the passage of His Eternity among us, for the firm foundations of His Throne in the midst of our shifting sands.
We look for them, and we would surround them with
reverence and with the most lasting protection in our
power. He has no need of us; but we greatly need
that Christ's kingdom and the living Stone which He
has chosen should rest on the most solid and immova-
ble of earthly rights, and that the floods of hell should
break helplessly against its outward bulwarks and its
holy memories.

From this point of view we hail with confidence
every effort of true science : we are afraid of no progress, no modern discovery. Even when divorced
from the Faith, science does not always wear a cap
and bells, and very often questions, which were started
with a worldly or evil intention, are, in the end, of
use to true doctrine. We feel convinced that the impulse given to archæological science in particular will
issue in a more perfect knowledge of, and a deeper
love for, the Holy Places; and we shall rejoice to contribute as far as we are able to this two-fold object.

We love all our sanctuaries, and we will defend
them all against impious attacks ; but the holy hills
towards which we turn our looks of love and hope

most fondly, are Rome and Jerusalem. Rome, the
new Jerusalem, the city of the Church, the capital of
the regenerate world, the Eternal city of this fleeting
world, the throne of Jesus Christ in the persons of Peter
and of Pius. And, O Jerusalem, Land of Jesus and of
Mary, home of the exiles of this world—what shall
hinder us from turning our thoughts and desires towards thee, and from visiting, in heart at least, thy
soil which drank in the sweat, the tears, and the
Blood of Jesus, and of countless saints after Him?
Even curses make thee dearer, for have they not
changed into blessings for us? O land of ruins precious beyond words, how beautiful art thou still! Still
are there fountains hidden in thy arid valleys, and
olives on thy discrowned hills! Like some loving
mourner whose grief has dried up her tears, thou yet
bearest traces of an unearthly beauty. The wicked
can no more rob thee of the glories of age and of martyrdom, than the Mussulmans can dim thy southern
sun, and the grand outlines of thy horizon. Let sceptics
dig out thy ruins—they do but awaken and multiply their echoes and their memories. O Land of
Calvary, more and more shall the nations turn to thy
divine streams, saying more and more fervently, "Let
this Blood fall on us and on our children in showers
of mercy." Land of the glorious Sepulchre, they shall
fix their eyes on thee, to revive—in spite of all things,
and for ever—faith in the life that can never end,
and hope in the love that can never fail.

But we ought not to be satisfied with a barren

homage, nor content ourselves with a distant glance at our great sanctuaries. Let us learn, with the aged Jacob, to adore God everywhere in His dwellings, though the only signs of it be a few stones unworthy of His Majesty. On the other hand, let us learn, with Moses, to take delight in the beauty and order of the Sacred Tabernacles, and set store by the least details of their decoration.

Let us learn, too, with Samuel, to offer ourselves to the Sanctuary in the bloom of youth and innocence; there to feed our souls with holy joys, and to grow old without regret.

Let us learn, with David, to have but one desire— that the House of the Lord may be our home all the days of our life, and to understand that a day spent, even as "an abject," in His courts is better than thousands in the palaces of sinners.

Let us learn, with Solomon, to lavish our wealth, and all that we possess, to make dwellings worthy of the Divine Majesty, and then to wonder that the Most High should vouchsafe to annihilate Himself in them.

Let us learn, with Jeremias and the children of Israel, to weep over the ruins of the Sanctuary, and to "hang up our instruments" till the profanation is atoned for.

Let us learn, with Nehemias, to rebuild the ruins and to revive the feasts.

Let us learn, with the Machabees, to fight with the profaners, and to die in the struggle.

Let us learn, with the Magi, to leave our homes at

the heavenly sign, and to prepare gifts worthy of us
and of our worship; with the Shepherds, to hear the
angels' voices, to offer of our poverty, and to adore in
simplicity of heart.

Let us learn, with the blessed St. Anna, to take to
the Sanctuary the objects of our most legitimate affections, and to do everything to make the offering more
worthy of Him.

Let us learn, with the Virgin of virgins, to be the
living ornaments, more precious than all others in the
Temple, by modesty, humility, fervour, and all virtues.

Let us learn, with the Divine Saviour Himself, to
be consumed with zeal for the house of our Heavenly
Father, to make it the terror of the demons, the help of
the dead, the consolation of the living, and the place
of holocaust and perfect reparation for all the profanations of the world.

Let us learn, with the apostles, to bear everywhere
the spirit of consecration, and to multiply altars and
sacrifices.

Let us learn, with the early Christians, to go down,
when needed, into the catacombs, and to adorn them as
the gates of heaven.

Let us learn, with our fathers, to give Jesus His
place in the world, and to be lavish, in His honour, of
the inventions of our love.

Let us learn, with our Crusaders, to bear the Sacred
Oriflamme wherever there are barbarians to be re-
pulsed and Sanctuaries to be delivered.

Let us learn, with our Pères de Terre Sainte, to

spend ourselves wholly in obscure conflicts and thankless services.

Blessed are they who, like St. Thomas of Canterbury, combine knowledge with the gentleness of the lamb, and the boldness of the lion in defence of the altar!

Blessed, O Divine Lamb! are the souls whom the saints hear "crying under the altar that the blood they shed may be rewarded!"

Blessed are they who love the beauty of Thy house, and the dwelling-place of Thy glory!

Blessed are they whom Thou choosest and callest to dwell in Thy courts, and to be inebriated with the joys of Thy house, and the delights of Thy holy Temple!

Blessed are Thy guests, O Lord! They shall praise Thee through all eternity!

THE END.